Afghanistan, Pakistan & Iran Triangle

Afghanistan, Pakistan & Iran Triangle

Col. B.R. Khanna (Retd.)

GAURAV Book Centre Private Limited

Publisher
GAURAV BOOK CENTRE PVT LTD
4832/24,Prahlad Lane,S-207 Ansari
Road, Daryaganj, Delhi-110002
Ph.: 43570976, 23278261
Email: gauravbookcentre@gmail.com

Edition: 2017

ISBN: 978-93-83316-50-2

Laser Typesetting
JEE-VEE Graphics # 09911902109

Price: 1295/-

Printed
Neeta Press, Delhi

Contents

Preface

This book mainly focuses on Pak-Iran interests in Afghanistan. An attempt is made to explore the various turns and twists in Pak-Iran relations in Afghanistan. Bilateral relations between Pakistan and Iran were affected, derived and formed by their interest based policies in Afghanistan.

Iran possesses the world's second largest gas reserves. That alone makes it an attractive country to other states seeking to forge energy deals, one of which is Pakistan. By the year 2014, there will be a gas pipeline stretching over 2,000 kilometers from Iran to Pakistan to help the later resolve its acute energy problems. It is expected to have a capacity of 22 billion cubic meters and can be expanded to 55 billion cubic meters. The cost is expected to run at around 7.5 billion US dollars. Contrary to its name, plans for the so-called "Peace Pipeline" have been causing upset around the world for the past decade.

It is the most important current issue which establishes the brotherly relationship between the three traditional friends, and neighbouring Muslim Countries, Iran, Afghanistan and Pakistan, which are connected with each other by close geographical proximity, common heritage and deep socio-cultural and ethnolinguistic affinities. All these factors have made Iran and Pakistan an eternal and enduring friends since the emergence of Pakistan in 1947. The paper analyzes their common interests and similar policies on various regional and international issues. But Pakistan's relation with its North-Western neighbor, Afghanistan remained at lowest ebb since its inception.

This work is essentially useful for scholars researchers social activists academics government functionaries and the general reader alike.

—Author

1

Pakistan, Iran and Afghanistan Relations

Muhammad Nawaz Sharif, the new prime minister of Pakistan and leader of Pakistan Muslim League – Nawaz (PMLN) to the Islamic Republic of Iran earlier this month and his subsequent negotiations with various senior Iranian officials have drawn a lot of attention worldwide. Whether or not his visit could meet the expectations that had been already brought up by the Iranian press is quite a different issue. However, his trip to Iran can be considered very important from certain angles as it shows that these two important Muslim and neighbouring countries enjoy high potentials for the development of political, trade, cultural, military and security cooperation. During his trip to Iran, two expectations that Iran has from Sharif's government gained more prominence in the Iranian media:

1. Military and security cooperation along the common border; and
2. Making a final decision on the fate of Iran-Pakistan natural gas pipeline, which is also known as the Peace Pipeline.

As for the first topic, many issues should be discussed because many of those issues have not been understood correctly in Iran. As a result, certain expectations mentioned by the Iranian media in this regard are basically outside the power of Nawaz Sharif's party-based government of Pakistan. This means that he is not actually able to make and implement decisions with regard to this issue on his own. The presence of Abdul Malik Baloch, the chief minister of Pakistan's Balochistan Province, among the entourage of Nawaz Sharif during his trip to Tehran, was meant to convey a clear message to the Iranian side. In fact, the government of Nawaz Sharif intended to indirectly remind the Iranian counterpart that the main party to be dealt with in regard to what goes on in Balochistan Province is the local government, not the central government.

But is this all the truth? The realities on the ground prove otherwise. In reality, both the central government and the local government in Balochistan Province of Pakistan have limited power to influence the process of border developments along the common frontier between Iran and Pakistan. In practice, however, it is the Pakistani army which can act, or not act, firmly, and can control, or not control, the border. This reality should be taken in correctly and due attention should be also paid to limitations with which the provincial and central governments in Pakistan are currently faced. To put into force any decision or agreement which pertains to security along the borders will be conditional on the performance of the Pakistani army and secret services present in the country's Balochistan Province. As a result, the degree of accountability of the local government with regard to border security is similar to the accountability of the central government and even this amount of accountability is dubious at best. However, there are special reasons why the Pakistani army and the country's efficient border guards – who are present across Balochistan Province and are also known as the Frontier Corps (FC) – are not taking firm actions to control the border with Iran. Two most prominent of those reasons are:

1. Pakistan's border with Iran is not a security priority for the Pakistani army, because the army's foremost security concern is the country's border with India; and
2. Ideological radical forces present in Balochistan Province are supported by the Pakistani army because the army uses them to keep ethnic forces at bay.

It is generally believed that both the above issues are well known to the Iranian side, but the importance of maintaining security along the Iranian border has been mostly underestimated.

In reality, however, the Pakistani army and FC forces, which are stationed in Balochistan Province of Pakistan, are currently faced with unfulfilled demands of ethnic Baloch people in that province. As a result, lack of timely and proper response to demands of the Baloch people has fueled people's tendency to engage in armed struggle against the central government with the final goal of getting separated from Pakistan. Now, the Pakistani army considers itself duty-bound to control this separatist current through military means in order to protect the country's territorial integrity. On the other hand, however, the Pakistani army is employing radical Islamist and jihadist forces, especially in its ideological sense, in order to undermine ethnic elements in Balochistan Province and control the situation in that region while paying the lowest price in political and military terms. This policy is not very much different from the traditional jihadist policy of Pakistani army which has been so far applied to India, the main strategic rival of Pakistan, and Afghanistan. Therefore, we must not expect the Pakistani army to act differently. According to this policy, the ideological and radical elements are employed with ethnic motivations in order to protect the strategic interests of Pakistan and it doesn't make a difference to the Pakistani army where to implement this policy. This is the main reality which has not been understood correctly in Iran as a result of which this problem has been treated in a simplistic way.

Therefore, if the issue of security along the Iranian border is looked upon from the viewpoint of Pakistani army generals, it would be clear that it is not as important to Pakistani army as the Iranian side expects. The main concern of Pakistani army is to know what radical and ideological force is acting where, but as long as that force is at the service of the general jihadist strategy of Pakistani army, the consequences of its actions for other countries is not a main concern for the armed forces of Pakistan. Another important reality is that the "nationality," as an element to be reckoned with, is meaningless to the radical and ideological Islamic groups. The location of their fight is determined by environmental conditions as Islamist radicals enter the war for a bigger goal which transcends the limits of nations and nationalities. It is exactly for this reason that their potential for mobility and change of geographical location is high. Therefore, wherever conditions are deemed suitable, they start to act with no regard for the official borders of countries. Of course, radical Islamist groups usually choose a name in every country and every geographical region that they act, which is frequently chosen according to environmental conditions under which they act. However, it would be a total mistake to believe that ethnic motivations are the main thing which makes them tick.

The ethnic demands that are usually put forth by these mainly transnational and transregional groups, is just a tactic to facilitate their activities and pave the road for them to achieve their goals more easily. Within this framework, the security of regions located along the common border between Iran and Pakistan should be considered within the framework of a bigger strategy, which is actually of a jihadist quality and has the capacity to easily go beyond any internationally recognized border. This viewpoint is not basically different from the viewpoint that Pakistani army holds in this regard. Of course, the government of Pakistan, as an official power institution, cannot wish for insecurity along its border with Iran because insecurity would be basically not to Islamabad's benefit, nor it would strengthen the position of Pakistani government in the rivalry-based domestic power balance between the political and military sections of Pakistan's political system.

The issue regarding the construction of the Peace Pipeline is not much different from the issue of border security. Even with regard to this gas pipeline, the priority is not actually determined by the government of Nawaz Sharif. Therefore, his government cannot be expected to abide by all the obligations and the content of contracts that have been signed between previous presidents of the Islamic Republic and Pakistan. It is true that Pakistan is badly in need of suitable and economically viable fuel supply from the Islamic Republic of Iran and there is not the least speck of doubt about this reality. However, the country's urgent need to get fuel should not be necessarily taken to mean that Pakistan has no other options available to it. A Pakistan which in some seasons can even tolerate up to 18 hours of power cut in its main cities without breaking a sweat will be also able to put up with many other problems and difficulties. Whether this approach to the country's problems is correct or not, is quite a different issue. On the surface, the government of Prime Minister Nawaz Sharif is in charge of making a decision about implementing or not implementing the natural gas pipeline project, but in reality this is not the case. The foreign factor, especially pressure from the United States, which has a lot of leverage to pressure the government in Islamabad, should not be underestimated. The most commonly accepted assumption in this regard is that the hands of the Pakistani government are tied with regard to implementation of the Peace Pipeline and excuses offered by Islamabad such as the lack of necessary facilities to implement the project as well as limitations faced for funding the project, should not be taken seriously. Even if Iran accepted to fund the entire project, Pakistan would still be unable to go on with it under the present circumstances. It would be only able to continue with the project when all the existing conditions change and foreign pressure, as a determining factor, is reduced to a minimum, or at least to a level that would be tolerable for the government of Nawaz Sharif.

Despite the above facts and regardless of two major issues of border security and the Peace Pipeline, in reality, Iran and Pakistan enjoy enormous capacities for development of their political, economic and trade cooperation. The latest evidence to this fact was signing of nine memorandums of understanding during the recent trip of Nawaz Sharif to Tehran. Further cooperation between Iran and Pakistan will not only guarantee that common interests of two important and axial countries in the Islamic world will be met in the best possible way, but in a more general approach, it will be to the benefit of the entire Islamic world. All of this, however, is conditional on realism on the part of both countries and focusing on realistic expectations. This is especially true because it seems that the radical Islamic current, which has been so far supported by Pakistan in line with the jihadist strategy of Pakistani army, is now targeting the national security and foreign relations of Pakistan as well. If the new situation is combined with a suitable level of realism, it could be the beginning of a new process through which Pakistan would be able to reap the highest benefits, though other Islamic countries in the region would be also benefited by this process.

Last but not least, those who recently highlighted the possibility of mediation between Iran and Saudi Arabia by Nawaz Sharif have certainly ignored the great capacities that abound in Iran and, therefore, such moves should not be taken seriously. The Pakistani government does not have the key to the problem of border security in Balochistan region and a solution to this problem cannot be achieved through military means.

Sustainable development as well as fighting poverty and underdevelopment in Balochistan regions of both Pakistan and Iran is the ultimate solution. Therefore, cooperation between the two countries should be directed toward this goal. Otherwise, security agreements are frequently costly and finally of little or no effect.

PAKISTAN-IRAN BORDER STRESS

Pakistan and Iran are important neighbours on the rim of South Asia and the Middle East, with deep cultural, linguistic, religious and traditional ties. Recently, though, Iran has bolstered ties with India, engaging Indian military expertise in the development of a strategic road. The road connects Iran's Chabahar sea port and Afghanistan at the border town of Zaranj, running very close to Pakistan's border in the process. The presence of Indian element on its Balochistan border with Iran, unrest in its Balochistan province, and multiple claims of foreign interference in the internal security of that troubled province all add up to create a serious question mark over the future of security relations between Pakistan and Iran.

Since the revolution, Iran has been unafraid to explore multiple avenues to fulfil its perceived security needs, including proxy, guerilla and urban warfare. From using Hezbollah against Israeli forces to supporting the Assad regime in Syria, Iranian policy has had an outsized role in the Middle Eastern security environment. Although few Pakistani security experts believe that Iranian Shia exposure can dislodge Sunni dominance in Pakistan, the Pakistani public is very aware of the curse of sectarian violence and many believe it is a result of foreign interference.

Historically, Pakistan was among the first countries to recognize Iran's revolutionary regime. Amazingly, the Zia regime – itself often considered the cause of much sectarian violence – not only accepted Iran's revolution but also sent a high-level official delegation to endorse friendly relations with Iran. Pakistan banned many local anti-Shia militant organizations and was evenhanded in its approach to both Sunni and Shia militant organizations. Anti-Shia groups such as Sapah-e-Sahaba and Lashker-e-Jhangvi were banned and many of their operatives were detained in operations by Pakistani security forces. Anti-Sunni groups such as Sapah-e-Muhammad faced the same treatment. Both sides had been linked to assassinations and bombings. Neither Pakistan nor Iran ever allowed sectarian issues to disrupt their relations, even at the peak of sectarian Shia killings in Pakistan.

In the wake of the A. Q. Khan revelations, Iran decided to seek nuclear technology from other sources, and Pakistan's nuclear expertise lost its significance. Meanwhile, India began to develop closer relations with Iran. This led to a further cooling of ties between Iran and Pakistan.

The current tensions on the Pakistan-Iran border cannot be evaluated within the narrow context of the border area itself; broader strategic implications must also be considered. Pakistan has good relations with Iran's rival Saudi Arabia, which may be misinterpreted. However, few security analysts believe that Saudi Arabia can address its concerns about Iranian nuclear ambitions by buying nuclear weapons from Pakistan. Saudi Arabia cannot buy, create or import weapons of mass destruction as long as it remains within the NPT regime. Even if Saudi Arabia did elect to withdraw from the NPT regime and pursue nuclear weapons capability, it would surely have no shortage of willing suppliers. For its part, Pakistan is not well placed to meet the demands of any other country – it is hard pressed to maintain its own strategic deterrence posture against a much larger country. At any rate, if relations between India and Iran can flourish while New Delhi maintains military relations with Israel*, then surely Iran-Pakistan relations should not falter in the presence of Pakistan's dealings with the Sunni Arab world.

The second assumption in this regard is that Pakistan's nuclear weapons could fall into the wrong hands. This phrase "wrong hands" warrants some consideration. Chinese nuclear technology is in the hands of the Chinese, while Indian nuclear assets are under Indian control. The same goes for all other nuclear states. For an international relations realist, all of these weapons are in the "wrong hands," at least as far as the adversaries of these nuclear powers go.

Pakistan as a Muslim state has firm control over its nuclear assets. The IAEA has acknowledged the strengths of Pakistan's nuclear safeguards, achieved through a strong Personnel Reliability Program (PRP) and Human Reliability Program (HRP), which unlike those of Western powers also monitor religious issues. The A. Q. Khan episode is old and has been fully addressed by UNSCR 1540.

Iran is also a NPT member state and as such is (theoretically) prevented from developing nuclear weapons capabilities. Iran's concerns about Pakistan's rapidly growing nuclear arsenal are illogical for many reasons. First, Iran has never been a target of Pakistan's nuclear force – Islamabad views it as a friendly state. Pakistan's nuclear posture is designed to address the nuclear threat from its arch rival, India. Second, unlike Pakistan, Iran is a member of the NPT regime. As such it is bound to follow the IAEA's safeguards and protocols, which allow regular inspections of its nuclear installations, and cannot engage in a nuclear arms race. Third, Pakistan's security policy towards Iran is not based on hegemonic intentions; Pakistan respects the integrity and sovereignty of Iran and only seeks the same in return.

Pakistan has successfully established its writ on the border of Afghanistan, while the ongoing operation Zarb-e-Azb has dealt a major blow to the Pakistan Taliban. Armed operations in North and South Waziristan have implications for the border with Iran, given that the area of operation is quite nearby. Indian arms are being used against Pakistani forces in ongoing operations, demonstrating external interference in the region. While fighting externally funded terrorism on its soil, Pakistan is developing strict border controls. Recent border tensions between the two neighbours should not be interpreted as representing lasting conflict or reflecting ideological antipathy, as neither is supported by the facts on the ground.

AFGHANISTAN–PAKISTAN RELATIONS

Afghanistan–Pakistan relations began in 1949 after British India was partitioned into the Republic of India and the Islamic Republic of Pakistan. Afghanistan and Pakistan are usually described as inseparable states due to their historical, religious, cultural, linguistic, and ethnic ties, as well as their multiple trade and economic ties. Both neighbouring states are Islamic republics and part of the South Asian Association for Regional Cooperation. However, the relationship between the two has been affected by the Durand Line, the issues of Pashtunistan and Balochistan, the 1980s Soviet war, the rise of the Taliban, the 2001-present war in Afghanistan, and Afghanistan's relations with India and Shia Iran.

Southern and eastern Afghanistan is predominately a Pashto-speaking region, like the adjacent Khyber-Pakhtunkhwa, Federally Administered Tribal Areas, and northern Balochistan in Pakistan. This entire area is inhabited by the indigenous Pashtuns who belong to different Pashtun tribes. The Pashtuns have lived in this region for thousands of years, since at least the 1st millennium BC.

The Durand Line

The Afghan government does not recognize the Durand Line as the official border between the two states, claiming that the Durand Line Agreement has been void in the past due to violations by Pakistan as well as other reasons. Pakistan, on the other side, issued a warning to Afghanistan that it would not "tolerate any violations of its borders". Relations have continued to be strained, as several top Afghan officials stated that they are weary of Pakistan's negative influence in the country. The Afghan government usually accuses Pakistan of using its intelligence agency, the Inter-Services Intelligence (ISI), in aiding the Taliban militants. Pakistan has denied the allegations but has said it does not have full control of the actions of the ISI. Relations became even more strained as the United States supports an Afghan invasion of rogue tribal regions.

Other Contemporary Issues

Following the Soviet invasion of Afghanistan in 1979, the Pakistani government played a vital role in supporting the Mujahideen and assisting Afghan refugees. Pakistan absorbed an estimated 3 million refugees and provided shelter, education, and places to work. After the Soviet withdrawal in February 1989, Pakistan, with cooperation from the world community, continued to provide extensive support for displaced Afghans. In 1999, the United States provided approximately $70 million in humanitarian assistance to Afghanistan and Afghan refugees in Pakistan, mainly through multilateral organizations and Non-governmental organizations (NGOs).

Pakistani strategists view Afghanistan as providing "strategic depth" in the event of a war with neighbouring India. In the event that the Indian Army crosses into Pakistan, the Pakistan Army would temporary locate supplies in Afghanistan and prepare for a counter-offensive. Furthermore, many Pakistanis see in Afghanistan and Afghans a common bond based on religion, history, culture, language and ethnic ties. At various times, Pakistan backed the mujahideen against the Soviets, mujahideen against each other and the Taliban against the Iranian-backed Northern Alliance. The overthrow of the Taliban regime in November 2001 has seen somewhat strained relations between Afghanistan and Pakistan. The present Karzai administration in Kabul feels that the remnants of the former Taliban government are being supported by factions within Pakistan for the same above reasons. However, Pakistan has said the government cannot control all elements of its intelligence agency, the ISI, which several countries accuse of contributing to instability in Afghanistan. In 2006 Afghan President Hamid Karzai warned that "Iran and Pakistan and others are not fooling anyone" when it come to interfering in his country.

"If they don't stop, the consequences will be ... that the region will suffer with us equally. In the past we have suffered alone; this time everybody will suffer with us.... Any effort to divide Afghanistan ethnically or weaken it will create the same thing in the neighbouring

countries. All the countries in the neighborhood have the same ethnic groups that we have, so they should know that it is a different ball game this time." —Hamid Karzai, *February 17, 2006*

Afghan-Pak Transit Trade Agreement

In October 2010, Afghanistan and Pakistan finally inked together the long-awaited Afghan-Pak Transit Trade Agreement (APTTA) between the two states. The landmark agreement was signed by Pakistani Commerce Minister Makhdoom Amin Fahim and Anwar ul-Haq Ahady, Afghan Ministry of Commerce. The ceremony was attended by Richard Holbrooke, U.S. Special Representative for Afghanistan and Pakistan, and a number of foreign ambassadors, Afghan parliamentarians and senior officials. In July 2010, a Memorandum of understanding (MoU) was reached between the two states, which was observed by U.S. Secretary of State Hillary Clinton. It would allow each nation's shipping trucks into the others; Afghan container trucks will be allowed to drive through Pakistan to the Wagah border with India, including to the port cities of Karachi and Gwadar. Also in July 2010, the two states signed a Memorandum of Understanding agreeing the construction of rail tracks in Afghanistan to connect with Pakistan Railways (PR). Work on the proposed project is set to start in the next four months, which has been in the making since at least 2005. In November 2010, the two states formed a joint chamber of commerce to expande trade relations and solve the problems traders face. The APTTA agreement is to take affect in February 2011.

Relationship between Pakistan and Afghanistan

A poll showed that Afghans rated India as the most favourable country, while Pakistan was the least favoured country with only 2% popularity.

2

Golden Crescent: Afghanistan, Iran, and Pakistan

The Golden Crescent is the name given to one of Asia's two principal areas of illicit opium production (with the other being the Golden Triangle), located at the crossroads of Central, South, and Western Asia. This space overlaps three nations, Afghanistan, Iran, and Pakistan, whose mountainous peripheries define the crescent, though only Afghanistan and Pakistan produce opium, with Iran being a consumer and trans-shipment route for the smuggled opiates.

The United Nations Office on Drugs and Crime (UNODC) heroin production estimates for the past 10 years show significant changes in the primary source areas. Heroin production in Southeast Asia declined dramatically, while heroin production in Southwest Asia expanded. In 1991, Afghanistan became the world's primary opium producer, with a yield of 1,782 metric tons (U.S. State Department estimates), surpassing Myanmar, formerly the world leader in opium production. The decrease in heroin production from Myanmar is the result of several years of unfavorable growing conditions and new government policies of forced eradication. Afghan heroin production increased during the same time frame, with a notable decrease in 2001 allegedly as a result of the Taliban's fatwa against heroin production. Afghanistan now produces over 90% of the world's *non-pharmaceutical-grade* opium. In addition to opiates, Afghanistan is also the world's largest producer of hashish.

HISTORY

The Golden Crescent has a much longer history of opium production than does Southeast Asia's Golden Triangle. The Golden Triangle emerged as a modern-day opium-producing entity only in the 1980s, after the Golden Crescent did so in the 1950s. The Golden Triangle began making an impact on the opium and morphine market in the 1980s and has steadily increased its output since then in order to match the increasing demand. During the invasion of Afghanistan in 2001, a retaliation to the September 11th terrorist attacks, the Golden Crescent's opium production took a huge hit, producing almost 90% less opium than in 2000.

At the peak of its opium production in 2007, the Golden Crescent produced more than 8,000 of the world's almost 9,000 total tons of opium, a near monopoly. The Golden Crescent also dominates the cannabis resin market due to the high resin yields of the region (145 kg/ha), four times more than Morocco (36 kg/ha). The Golden Crescent also caters to a much larger market, about 64% more than the Golden Triangle. It produces and distributes over 2,500 megatons of opiates to Africa, Europe, the Americas and Central Asia and supplies almost 9.5 million opiate users worldwide.

Despite worldwide efforts to capture and seize as much opium product as possible, total opiate seizures only brought in 23.5% of the total estimated product distributed worldwide. Of these seizures around 97% of opium and morphine seizures are made in the Middle East and heroin seizures are made mostly in the Middle East or Europe. In Afghanistan only one percent of the heroin that is exported illegally is intercepted and destroyed by the national governments. Although Afghanistan is the major producer of opiates in the Golden Crescent, most of the seizures are made in Iran, their neighbor to the west. This is because traffickers are arrested while crossing the border from Afghanistan to Iran so that they can distribute the product to Europe and Africa where there is a high demand for opiates. The majority of these traffickers who transport the drugs produced in the Golden Crescent that are arrested at customs in the Middle East are Russian, Uzbek and Tajik. In Pakistan the majority of traffickers arrested are 38 percent Nigerians and 32 percent Pakistanis. These traffickers, essential to the transportation of the drugs from the source to end-user markets, make large profits because of how risky the job is. A rough estimate of how many people are currently involved in drug trafficking is likely above one million. The majority of opium produced in Afghanistan comes from the Kandahar and Helmand provinces, Helmand being the major producer. Of the 5,300 tons of opium produced in Afghanistan, 2,700 tons is transformed into heroin. In 2008, almost half of the heroin produced was used in Iran. Although Afghanistan is the leading producer, only 7% was used there.

Markets

Although the Golden Triangle heroin dominates the Asian illegal drug markets, the Golden Crescent is increasingly becoming a source of illicit drugs trafficked into western China, particularly the nearby Xinjiang Province.

OPIUM PRODUCTION IN AFGHANISTAN

Afghanistan has been the greatest illicit opium producer in the entire world, ahead of Burma (Myanmar), the "Golden Triangle", and Latin America since 1992, excluding the year 2001. Afghanistan is the main producer of opium in the "Golden Crescent". Opium production in Afghanistan has been on the rise since U.S. occupation started in 2001. Based on UNODC data, there has been more opium poppy cultivation in each of the past four growing seasons (2004–2007) than in any one year during Taliban rule. Also, more land is now used for opium in Afghanistan than for coca cultivation in Latin America. In 2007, 92% of the *non-pharmaceutical-grade* opiates on the world market originated in Afghanistan. This amounts to an export value of about $4 billion, with a quarter being earned by opium farmers and the rest going to district officials, insurgents, warlords, and drug traffickers. In the seven years (1994–2000) prior to a Taliban opium ban, the Afghan farmers' share of gross income from opium was divided among 200,000 families. In addition to opiates, Afghanistan is also the largest producer of cannabis (mostly as hashish) in the world. In 2004, a fatwa was issued by Muslim clerics claiming that opium production is contrary to the sharia law and any opium producers would face punishments in accordance with the sharia.

BACKGROUND (1979–PRESENT)

Soviet period (1979–1989)

As the Afghan government began to lose control of provinces during the Soviet invasion of 1979–80, warlords flourished and with it opium production as regional commanders searched for ways to generate money to purchase weapons, according to the UN. (At this time the US was pursuing an "arms-length" supporting strategy of the Afghan freedom-fighters or Mujahideen, the main purpose being to cripple the USSR slowly into withdrawal through attrition rather than effect a quick and decisive overthrow.)

As explained by Zbigniew Brzezinski

The secret operation was an excellent idea. It drew the Russians into the Afghan trap and you want me to regret it? On the day that the Soviets officially crossed the border, I wrote to President Carter, saying, in essence: 'We now have the opportunity of giving to the USSR its Vietnam War.' It was alleged by the Soviets on multiple occasions that American CIA agents were helping smuggle opium out of Afghanistan, either into the West, in order to raise money for the Afghan resistance or into the Soviet Union in order to weaken it through drug addiction. According to Alfred McCoy, the CIA supported various Afghan drug lords, for instance Gulbuddin Hekmatyar and others such as Haji Ayub Afridi.

Another factor was the eradication efforts inside Pakistan (whose Inter-Services Intelligence was coincidentally huge supporters of the Mujahideen). The Pakistani government, USAID and other groups were involved in attempting to eliminate poppy cultivation from certain areas of the Northwest Frontier Province (now Khyber Pakhtunkhwa) bordering Afghanistan. The opium industry shifted from Pakistan into Afghanistan during the decade of the 1980s.

Warlord period (1989–1994)

When the Soviet Army was forced to withdraw in 1989, a power vacuum was created. Various Mujahideen factions started fighting against each other for power. With the discontinuation of Western support, they resorted ever more to poppy cultivation to finance their military existence.

Rise of the Taliban (1994–2001)

During the Taliban rule, Afghanistan saw a bumper opium crop of 4,500 metric tons in 1999,. In July 2000, Taliban leader Mullah Mohammed Omar, collaborating with the United Nations to eradicate heroin production in Afghanistan, declared that growing poppies was un-Islamic, resulting in one of the world's most successful anti-drug campaigns. The Taliban enforced a ban on poppy farming via threats, forced eradication, and public punishment of transgressors. The result was a 99% reduction in the area of opium poppy farming in Taliban-controlled areas, roughly three quarters of the world's supply of heroin at the time. The ban was effective only briefly due to the deposition of the Taliban in 2002.

However, some people, believe that certain parties benefited from the price increase during the ban. Some, even believe it was a form of Market manipulation on the part of certain drug lords. Dried opium, unlike most agricultural products, can easily be stored for long periods without refrigeration or other expensive equipment. With huge stashes of opium stored in secret hideaways. Taliban, and other groups became involved in the drug trade were in theory able to make huge personal profits during the price spikes after the 2000 ban and the chaos following 9/11.

Since 2008 the Taliban insurgency has been supporting farmers growing poppy as a source of income for insurgent operations.

PRESENT WAR IN AFGHANISTAN

By November 2001, the collapse of the economy and the scarcity of other sources of revenue forced many of the country's farmers to resort back to growing opium for export.(1,300 km^2 in 2004 according to the United Nations Office on Drugs and Crime.)

In December 2001, a number of prominent Afghans met in Bonn, Germany, under United Nations (UN) auspices to develop a plan to reestablish the State of Afghanistan, including provisions for a new constitution and national elections. As part of that agreement, the United Kingdom (UK) was designated the lead country in addressing counter-narcotics issues in Afghanistan. Afghanistan subsequently implemented its new constitution and held national elections. On December 7, 2004, Hamid Karzai was formally sworn in as president of a democratic Afghanistan."

Two of the following three growing seasons saw record levels of opium poppy cultivation. Corrupt officials may have undermined the government's enforcement efforts. Afghan farmers claimed that "government officials take bribes for turning a blind eye to the drug trade while punishing poor opium growers".

Another obstacle to getting rid of poppy cultivation in Afghanistan is the reluctant collaboration between US forces and Afghan warlords in hunting drug traffickers. In the absence of Taliban, the warlords largely control the opium trade but are also highly useful to the US forces in scouting, providing local intelligence, keeping their own territories clean from Al-Qaeda and Taliban insurgents, and even taking part in military operations.

While U.S. and allied efforts to combat the drug trade have been stepped up, the effort is hampered by the fact that many suspected drug traffickers are now top officials in the Karzai government. Estimates made in 2006 by the United Nations Office on Drugs and Crime (UNODC) estimate that 52% of the nation's GDP, amounting to $2.7 billion annually, is generated by the drug trade. The rise in production has been linked to the deteriorating security situation, as production is markedly lower in areas with stable security. By some, the extermination of the poppy crops is not seen as a viable option because the sale of poppies constitutes the livelihood of Afghanistan's rural farmers. Some 3.3 million Afghans are involved in producing opium. Opium is more profitable than wheat and destroying opium fields could possibly lead to discontent or unrest among the indigent population. Some poppy eradication programs have, however, proven effective, especially in the north of Afghanistan. The opium poppy eradication program of Balkh Governor Ustad Atta Mohammad Noor between 2005 and 2007 successfully reduced poppy cultivation in Balkh Province from 7,200 hectares in 2005 to zero by 2007.

Former U.S. State Department Principal Deputy Assistant Secretary for the Bureau of International Narcotics and Law Enforcement Affairs Thomas Schweich, in a New York Times article dated July 27, 2007, asserts that opium production is protected by the government of Hamid Karzai as well as by the Taliban, as all parties to political conflict in Afghanistan as well as criminals benefit from opium production, and, in Schweich's opinion, the U.S. military turns a blind eye to opium production as not being central to its anti-terrorism mission. In March 2010, NATO rejected Russian proposals for Afghan poppy spraying, citing concerns over income of Afghan people. There have also been allegations of American and European involvement in Afghanistan's drug trafficking with links to Taliban.

On October 28, 2010 agents of Russia's Federal Service for the Control of Narcotics joined Afghan and American antidrug forces in an operation to destroy a major drug production site near Jalalabad. In the operation 932 kg (2,055 lb) of high quality heroin and 156 kg (344 lb) of opium, with a street value of US$250 million, and a large amount of technical equipment was destroyed. This was the first anti-drug operation to include Russian agents. According to Viktor Ivanov, Director of Russia's Federal Service for the Control of Narcotics, this marks an advance in relations between Moscow and Washington. Afghan President Hamid Karzai called the operation a violation of Afghan sovereignty and international law.

As had been the case in Indochina during the Vietnam War the US invasion has in fact been causal in a massive increase in opium production, the aforementioned eradication efforts being largely window dressing. A SIGAR report showed a threefold increase in area under cultivation between 2002 and 2014 An December 2014 UNAIDS study showed an increase of 7% in one year alone.

Foreign involvement

Approximately 40,000 foreign troops attempted to manage "security" in Afghanistan, principally of 32,000 regular soldiers from 37 North Atlantic Treaty Organization (NATO) forces: the International Security Assistance Force. 8,000 US and other special operations forces, mainly privately contracted soldier of fortune, make up the balance. There is significant resistance, both from the ideological/theocratic Taliban, especially in southern Afghanistan, and also independent local warlords and drug organizations. Antonio Maria Costa, Executive Director of the United Nations Office on Drugs and Crime (UNODC), described the situation this way: "There is no rule of law in most of the southern parts of Afghanistan—the bullets rule."

PRODUCTION AND DISTRIBUTION REGIONS

Drug Trafficking

The following areas of Afghanistan play a role in the drug traffic:

- Production
  - "Southern region" of Helmand and Kandahar provinces, on the border with Pakistan, which are the highest-volume areas for drug transactions. There is a traditional route from Helmand, through Pakistan, to Iran
- Smuggling
  - Herat, in Herat Province, the Northern Alliance stronghold, which borders Iran
  - Faizabad, in Badakhshan province, which has borders with Tajikstan, Pakistan, and China.

Labor Practices

According to the U.S. Department of Labor's 2014 *List of Goods Produced by Child Labor or Forced Labor*, opium production is one of the sectors that rely on child labor in Afghanistan. Poppies being the source of the crude drug, children are still recruited to harvest these flowers in the country's farming fields.

DRUG TRAFFICKING AND IMPACT AROUND THE WORLD

According to EU agencies, Afghanistan has been Europe's main heroin supplier for more than 10 years. Heroin enters Europe primarily by two major land routes: the long-standing 'Balkan route' through Turkey; and, since the mid-1990s, the 'northern route', which leaves northern Afghanistan through Central Asia and on to Russia (and is sometimes colloquially referred to as the 'silk route'). Estimated number of problem opioids users in EU: 1.5 million (1.3–1.7 million), average prevalence between 4 and 5 cases per 1,000 adult population (aged 15–64). In 2005 there were around 7,000 acute drug deaths, with opioids being found in around 70% of them. There was a minimum of 49,000 seizures resulting in the interception of an estimated 19.4 tonnes of heroin. Countries reporting the largest number of seizures (descending order): UK (2005), Spain, Germany, Greece, France. Countries reporting the largest quantities of heroin seized in 2005 (descending order): Turkey, UK, Italy, France, the Netherlands.

Presently with the resurgence of high output production of opium and heroin in post-Taliban Afghanistan, there is an ongoing heroin addiction epidemic in Russia which is claiming 30,000 lives each year, mostly among young people. There were two and half million heroin addicts in Russia by 2009.

MEDICAL PRODUCTION

The International Council on Security and Development (ICOS) has proposed legalizing opium production for medical purposes. Opium can be manufactured into codeine and morphine, both legal pain-killers. The reason for their proposal is that it will not only solve the problem of illicit opium production in Afghanistan, but will also lower the price of prescription drugs worldwide, thus making healthcare more affordable for those requiring those drugs.

Others have argued that legalizing opium production would neither solve the problem nor would it be workable in practice. They argue that illegal diversion of the crop could only be minimized if the Afghans had the necessary resources, institutional capacity and control mechanisms in place to ensure that they were the sole purchaser of opiate raw materials. For them, there is currently no infrastructure in place to set up and administer such a scheme. They reason that in the absence of an effective control system, traffickers would be free to continue to exploit the market and there would be a high risk that licit cultivation would be used for illegal purposes and that the Afghan government would be in direct competition with the traffickers, thereby driving up the price of opium, and attracting more farmers to cultivate. The Afghan government has ruled out licit cultivation as a means of tackling the illegal drug trade: however in Turkey in the 1970s, legalizing opium production, with US support brought illicit trafficking under control within four years. Afghan villages have strong local control systems based around the village shura, which with the support of the Afghan government and its international allies, could provide the basis for an effective control system. This idea is developed in the recent Senlis Council report "Poppy for Medicine" which proposes a technical model for the implementation of poppy licensing and the legal control of cultivation and production of Afghan morphine.

Some believe that there is also little evidence to show that Afghan opium would be economically competitive in a global market place. Australia, France, India, Spain, and Turkey currently dominate the export market for licit opiates. Due to the high cost of production in countries where cultivation is undertaken on small landholdings, such as India and Turkey, licit production requires market support (the production costs for the equivalent of 1 kg of morphine in 1999 was US$56 in Australia, US$159.77 in India and US$250 in Turkey). The current cost of production of one kilogram of morphine equivalent in Afghanistan is approximately US$450. However, a poppy for medicine project in Afghanistan could provide a cheap pain relief option for pain sufferers who find morphine prices extremely elevated.

The price of illicit opium far exceeds that of licit, (in India, in 2000, the price for licit opium was US$13–29 per kilo, but for illicit US$155–206). Although there are many complex reasons behind the decision to grow poppy, one of them is the current economic dependence of poppy farmers on the illicit trade. Whilst traffickers continue to be free to exploit the illicit market, legalization would not change this. Demand for illicit opiates would not disappear even if Afghan opium were used for licit purposes and a vacuum would open that traffickers could exploit. However, currently 100% of Afghan opium is diverted to the illegal opium trade and funds in some cases terrorist activities. Despite eradication efforts since the international intervention in 2001, poppy cultivation and illicit opium production has increased, as UNODC figures show. A licensing system would bring farmers and villages into a supportive relationship with the Afghan government, instead of alienating the population by destroying their livelihood, and provide the economic diversification that could help cultivators break ties with the illicit opium trade.

The International Narcotics Control Board states that an over production in licit opiates since 2000 has led to stockpiles in producing countries 'that could cover demand for two years'. Thus, some say Afghan opium would contribute to an already oversupplied market and would potentially cause the supply and demand imbalance that the UN control system was designed. However, the World Health Organisation points out that there is an acute global shortage of poppy-based medicines such as morphine and codeine. This is largely due to chronic underprescription (especially in countries where morphine is extremely highly priced). The International Narcotics Control Board which regulates opium supply throughout the world enforces the 1961 Single Convention on Narcotic Drugs: this law provides that countries can only demand the raw poppy materials corresponding to the use of opium-based medicines over the last two years and thus limits countries who have low levels of prescription in terms of the amounts they can demand. As such, 77% of the world's opium supplies are being used by only six countries, leaving the rest of the world lacking in essential medicines such as morphine and codeine. A second-tier supply system, that complements the current UN control system by supplying opium-based medicines to countries currently not receiving the poppy-based pain relief medicines needed, would maintain the balance established by the UN system and provide a market to Afghan-made poppy-based medicines.

OPIUM ADDICTION WITHIN AFGHAN SOCIETY

Afghanistan has seen a high rate of opium addiction among refugees returning from Iran and Pakistan. Zalmai Afzali, spokesman for the Ministry of Counter-Narcotics in Afghanistan reports an increase in the total number of drug users by over half a million, to 1.5 million, between 2005 and 2010.

The Afghan economy and opium

The 2004 United Nations Development Programme ranked Afghanistan number 173 of 177 countries, using a human development index, with Afghanistan near or at the bottom of virtually every development indicator including nutrition, infant mortality, life expectancy, and literacy. Several factors encourage opium production, the greatest being economic: the high rate of return on investment from opium poppy cultivation has driven an agricultural shift in Afghanistan from growing traditional crops to growing opium poppy.

Opium cultivation on this scale is not traditional, and in the area controlled by the Helmand Valley Authority in the 1950s the crop was largely suppressed.

"Despite the fact that only 12 percent of its land is arable, agriculture is a way of life for 70 percent of Afghans and is the country's primary source of income. During good years, Afghanistan produced enough food to feed its people as well as supply a surplus for export. Its traditional agricultural products include wheat, corn, barley, rice, cotton, fruit, nuts, and grapes. However, its agricultural economy has suffered considerably [...] Afghanistan's largest and fastest cash crop is opium."

Poppy Cultivation and the Opium Trade have been said to have had a more significant impact on the civilians in Afghanistan than the impact of wheat farming and livestock trading. As farmers in Afghanistan were once heavily reliant on wheat farming to make sufficient income, the development of poppy cultivation has given many of these farmers a boost in capital, even though the Opium Trade may be a more dangerous product to distribute. In addition, as the demand for Opium has elevated, women have more opportunity to work in the same setting as their male counterpart.

Afghanistan's rugged terrain encourages local autonomy, which, in some cases, means local leadership committed to an opium economy. The terrain makes surveillance and enforcement difficult.

Afghanistan's economy has thus evolved to the point where it is now highly dependent on opium. Although less than 4 percent of arable land in Afghanistan was used for opium poppy cultivation in 2006, revenue from the harvest brought in over $3 billion—more than 35 percent of the country's total gross national product (GNP). According to Antonio Costa, "Opium poppy cultivation, processing, and transport have become Afghanistan's top employers, its main source of capital, and the principal base of its economy." Today, a record 2.9 million Afghanis from 28 of 34 provinces are involved in opium cultivation in some way, which represents nearly 10 percent of the population. Although Afghanistan's overall economy is being boosted by opium profits, less than 20 percent of the $3 billion in opium profits actually goes to impoverished farmers, while more than 80 percent goes into the pockets of Afghan's opium traffickers and kingpins and their political connections. Even heftier profits are generated outside of Afghanistan by international drug traffickers and dealers.

Traditionally, processing of Afghan's opium into heroin has taken place outside of Afghanistan; however, in an effort to reap more profits internally, Afghan drug kingpins have stepped up heroin processing within their borders. Heroin processing labs have proliferated in Afghanistan since the late 1990s, particularly in the unstable southern region, further complicating stabilization efforts. With the reemergence of the Taliban and the virtual absence of the rule of law in the countryside, opium production and heroin processing have dramatically increased, especially in the southern province of Helmand.

According to the United Nations Office on Drugs and Crime (UNODC) *2007 Afghanistan Opium Survey*, Afghanistan produced approximately 8,200 metric tonnes of opium – nearly double the estimate of global annual consumption. In an April 25, 2007 op-ed in the *Washington Post*, Antonio Maria Costa, Executive Director of UNODC, asked "Does opium defy the laws of economics? Historically, no. In 2001, prices surged tenfold from 2000, to a record high, after the Taliban all but eliminated opium poppy cultivation across the Afghan territory under its control. So why, with last year's bumper crop, is the opposite not occurring? Early estimates suggest that opium cultivation is likely to increase again this year. That should be an added incentive to sell.

He speculated, "So where is it? I fear there may be a more sinister explanation for why the bottom has not fallen out of the opium market: major traffickers are withholding significant amounts.

"Drug traffickers have a symbiotic relationship with insurgents and terrorist groups such as the Taliban and al-Qaeda. Instability makes opium cultivation possible; opium buys protection and pays for weapons and foot soldiers, and these in turn create an environment in which drug lords, insurgents and terrorists can operate with impunity.

"Opium is the glue that holds this murky relationship together. If profits fall, these sinister forces have the most to lose. I suspect that the big traffickers are hoarding surplus opium as a hedge against future price shocks and as a source of funding for future terrorist attacks, in Afghanistan or elsewhere."

Opium economy has influenced villagers options for generating income

Due to globalization and the development of trade, traditional ways of sustaining life for villagers has been forced to change. Before, people relied on wheat farming and livestock, whereas today, poppy cultivation is the most prominent economic activity. This can be attributed to higher profits from poppy cultivation and lack of opportunity for other farming practices due to land scarcity and more accessible loans from money providers for this activity.

War, economic instability, and poverty caused changes in the way villagers maintained their villages. Competition for scarce land and resources resulted in unsustainable practices, causing soil erosion and therefore making the land less productive. The cultivation of poppy, however, generated greater profits than wheat farming for the farming villagers due to the higher yielding possibilities with less land (poppies require less irrigation than wheat), and greater demand for the profitable drug trade of the highly valued opium, prepared from poppies. Many emigrants to places such as Pakistan and Iran witnessed the profitability of poppy cultivation in land development, through association with local landowners and businessmen, and were inspired to bring about the same economic improvement in their own lives and villages. Also, opium trade proved to be more cost-efficient than livestock trade, since large amounts of opium are easier to transport than livestock. Local shopkeepers used capital, which was acquired from buying opium resins from farmers and selling them to dealers at the Tajikistan-Afghanistan border, to invest in their own small shops, generating more income. Poor villagers saw this as a good investment opportunity, as it meant more efficient farming of one product with the possibility of creating economic stability in their villages.

Impacts of opium production within Afghan villages

Aside from the obvious threat of addiction, opium production is changing the dynamic of many Afghan villages. Wealth distribution, for example, has changed significantly as the opium economy has created a "new rich" in which young men have control. This newfound wealth for the young men of Afghanistan is troubling to many of the village leaders as before they were revered for their wisdom, and now are given little if any respect. It has also been noted that relationships among fathers and sons, neighbours, and family in general, are drastically changing as leadership roles in the economy continue to shift. As the young men have increased contact with the outer world, they have become aware of different methods of performing traditional tasks, which have created tensions between the young men and the white beards. Also, there has been a shift from the level of co-operation, trust, and reciprocity within villages to a move of self-interest, all of which have been adversely affected by the war.

PRODUCTION AND AFGHAN GOVERNANCE

While the Taliban were considered a threat both to the human rights of Afghans, and to other areas of the world by providing a sanctuary for transnational terrorists, they also demonstrated an ability to strictly enforce a moratorium on opium production. Since their overthrow in 2001, stopping their enforcement with methods including beheading, opium poppy cultivation has been steadily increasing for over the past two decades. There is evidence that the Taliban ban carried the seeds of its own lack of sustainability, due to a many-fold increase in the burden of opium-related debt (locking many households into dependence on future opium poppy cultivation), forcing asset sales to make ends meet, etc. It also appears that the opium ban weakened the Taliban politically. Thus the sustainability of the ban beyond the first year was highly doubtful, even if the Taliban had not been overthrown in late 2001.

"Even though the Karzai government made opium poppy cultivation and trafficking illegal in 2002, many farmers, driven by poverty, continue to cultivate opium poppy to provide for their families. Indeed, poverty is the primary reason given by Afghan farmers for choosing to cultivate opium poppy." With a farm gate price of approximately $125 per kilogram for dry opium, an Afghan farmer can make 17 times more profit growing opium poppy ($4,622 per hectare), than by growing wheat ($266 per hectare). "Opium poppy is also drought resistant, easy to transport and store, and, unlike many crops, requires no refrigeration and does not spoil." With Afghanistan's limited irrigation, in which qanats (karez) still play a big role, transportation and other agricultural infrastructure, growing alternative crops is not only less profitable, but more difficult.

In 2006, opium production in the province increased over 162 percent and now accounts for 42 percent of Afghan's total opium output. According to the UNODC, the opium situation in the southern provinces is "out of control."

Corruption and the erosion of the rule of law

Corruption associated with the opium economy has spread to all levels of the Afghan government from the police to the parliament, and is eroding the rule of law. Farmers routinely bribe police and counternarcotics eradication personnel to turn a blind eye. Law enforcement personnel are also paid off by drug traffickers to ignore or, in some cases, protect their movements. Afghan government officials are now believed to be involved in at least 70 percent of opium trafficking, and experts estimate that at least 13 former or present provincial governors are directly involved in the drug trade...In some cases...[local leaders] are the same individuals who cooperated with the United States in ousting the Taliban in 2001.

Working with the UK and the Afghan government, the United States developed its own strategy to counter the opium problem in Afghanistan, which has the following five pillars:

1. alternative livelihoods
2. elimination and eradication
3. interdiction
4. law enforcement and justice reform
5. public information

The Department of State (DoS), the U.S. Agency for International Development (USAID), the Department of Defense (DoD), and the Department of Justice (DoJ) are the primary organizations involved in carrying out this counternarcotics strategy for the US. The role of the CIA has not been mentioned. UNODC's executive director believes these measures are insufficient: "What can be done? Since NATO forces are wary of making enemies out of opium farmers by being associated with eradication, and since the Afghan government is opposed to spraying poppy fields, rounding up the major traffickers may be the best available option for disrupting Afghanistan's lucrative opium market."

Both demand and supply reduction are important. "the consuming countries need to get serious about curbing drug addiction. If there was less demand for heroin, the bottom really would fall out of the opium market." Farmers economically dependent on opium must have viable alternatives that give sustainable income. On the supply side, identifying the most-wanted traffickers and subjecting them to international arrest warrants with extradition, asset seizure, and travel bans could help. While it is not easy to destroy opium storage and heroin production laboratories, it is far easier to destroy drugs at the source than in transit.

Afghanistan's neighbours are either accomplices or victims in the opium trade, so they need to be part of the solution. They could, for example, improve intelligence-sharing and border security to ensure that more opium is seized. At the moment, less than a quarter of the world's opium is intercepted, compared with around half of global cocaine output.

This complicates, of course, the complex US relations with Pakistan and Iran.

Nexus between the drug industry and Hawala

There is an important nexus between drugs and hawala (informal money transfer system) in Afghanistan. The UN analysis is based on interviews with a sample of 54 hawala dealers in the main centers of hawala activity of Afghanistan as well as during a visit to Peshawar, Pakistan. In addition, interviews were conducted with users of the hawala system (drug dealers, businessmen, traders, international aid workers), regulators (government officials, central bank personnel), and formal service providers (bankers, accountants). In addition to hawala, they found protection payments and connections, by which the drug industry has major linkages with local administration as well as high levels of the national government.

Different localities studied by the UNODC give different views of the laundering of drug funds. It is difficult to get a solid sense of the overall economy. In Faizabad, for example, indicated that during certain times of the year close to 100% of the liquidity of the hawala system in the province is derived from drugs, whereas in Herat, the Northern Alliance stronghold, it was estimated that only 30% of the hawala market's overall transaction volume is directly linked to drugs. Analysis of data gathered in places like Herat was complicated by confirmed links between drug money and legitimate imports. The southern region (Helmand and Kandahar provinces) is also a key centre for money laundering in Afghanistan (about 60% of the funds are drug related and 80–90% of the hawala dealers in Kandahar [the former Taliban stronghold] and Helmand are involved in money transfers related to narcotics).

Helmand has emerged as a key facilitator of the opium trade, both between provinces and exports, while overall estimates of the local hawala markets' drug-related component are of a similar order of magnitude to those in Kandahar. This finding adds weight to the notion that the major trading centers in these two neighbouring provinces should be treated as essentially one market. Bearing this in mind, the study calculated that Helmand could account for roughly US$800 million of Afghanistan's drug-related hawala business and that Herat is the second largest contributor, with in the range of US$ 300–500 million of drug money laundered annually.

Furthermore, Dubai appears to be a central clearing house for international hawala activities. In addition, various cities in Pakistan, notably Peshawar, Quetta, and Karachi, are major transaction centers. It appears that even in the case of drug shipments to Iran, payments for them come into Afghanistan from Pakistan...the hawala system has been key to the deepening and widening of the "informal economy" in Afghanistan, where there is anonymity and the opportunity to launder money.

Hawala, however, also contributes positively to the regional economy. It has been central to the survival of Afghanistan's financial system through war. According to Maimbo (2003), "integral to processes of early developmentand vital for the continued delivery of funds to the provinces." "The hawala system also plays an important role in currency exchange. It participates in the Central Bank's regular foreign currency auctions, and was instrumental in the successful introduction of a new currency for Afghanistan in 2002–2003."

OPIUM SMUGGLING INTO IRAN

While Herat is not the highest-volume area of opium trade, Herat, and the other Iranian border areas of Farah, and Nimroz, have some of the highest prices, presumably due to demand from the Iranian market. "Opium prices are especially high in Iran, where law enforcement is strict and where a large share of the opiate consumption market is still for opium rather than heroin. Not surprisingly, it appears that very significant profits can be made by crossing the Iranian border or by entering Central Asian countries like Tajikistan." According to UNODC estimates bulk of Afghanistan's opium production goes to Iran either for consumption or for on-ward export to other countries in the region and Europe. Iran currently has the largest prevalence of opiate consumption in its population globally. Iran also accounts for 84% of total opiate seizures by law enforcement agencies in the world, interdicting tens of thousands of tons of opiates annually. The Iranian government has gone through several phases in dealing with its drug problem.

First, during the 1980s, its approach was supply-sided: "Law-and-order policies with zero tolerance led to the arrest of tens of thousands of addicts and the execution of thousands of narcotics traffickers." "There are an estimated 68,000 Iranians imprisoned for drug trafficking and another 32,000 for drug addiction (out of a total prison population of 170,000, based on 2001 statistics)"

Beehner said "Tehran also has spent millions of dollars and deployed thousands of troops to secure its porous 1,000-mile border with Afghanistan and Pakistan... a few hundred Iranian drug police die each year in battles with smugglers. Referring to the head of the UNODC office in Iran, Roberto Arbitrio, Beehner quoted Arbitrio in an interview with *The Times*. "You have drug groups like guerrilla forces, [who]... shoot with rocket launchers, heavy machine guns, and Kalashnikovs."

A second-phase strategy came under then-President Mohammad Khatami, focused more on prevention and treatment. Drug traffic is considered a security problem, and much of it is associated with Baluchi tribesmen, who recognize traditional tribal rather than national borders. Current (2007) reports cite Iranian concern with ethnic guerillas on the borders, possibly supported by the CIA.

Iranian drug strategy changed again under President Mahmoud Ahmadinejad, who took office in 2005. Iran's drug policy has been reconsidered and shifted back toward supply interdiction and boosting border security. It is unclear if this is connected to more wide-ranging concerns with border security, perhaps in relation to Baluchi guerillas in Iran.

Iran has alleged that certain drugs are manufactured in Afghanistan under guidance of western powers and solely sent to Iran for consumption such as certain compounds of heroin, Crack cocaine and CNS stimulants. Iran has also alleged that large quantities of Acetic anhydride and Hydrochloric acid are brought to Afghanistan from Europe to be used in manufacturing of drugs as Afghanistan does not have the chemical industry to produce the compounds locally.

Samii's 2003 paper described Iran's "primary approach to the narcotics threat [as] interdiction. Iran shares a 936 kilometer border with Afghanistan and a 909 kilometer border with Pakistan, and the terrain in the two eastern provinces—Sistan va Baluchistan and Khorasan—is very rough. The Iranian government has set up static defenses along this border. This includes concrete dams, berms, trenches, and minefields...

As per UN drug report of 2011, Iran accounts for highest rate of opium and heroin seizure rates in the world, intercepting 89% of all seized opium in the world. Within a span of thirty years, 3700 Iranian police officers have been killed and tens of thousands more injured in counter narcotics operations mostly on Afghan and Pakistan borders.

COUNTER-NARCOTICS POLICY

Given the fact that a third of the combined legal and illegal Afghan economy is based on the illegal opium industry, counter-narcotics policy is currently one of the most important elements of domestic politics. Despite law enforcement measures with a dominant focus on crop eradication programs, Afghan opium production has doubled in just two years. This has shown that currently there is no correlation between poppy crop eradication and the level of poppy cultivation or opium production. The reason for this is the underlying economic nature of the opium problem. Poverty and structural unemployment are the main reason for 3.3 million Afghans' full dependence on poppies.

Poppy crop eradication could even have damaging side-effects for Afghanistan's process of stabilization and reconstruction. Director of policy research for the Senlis Council, Jorrit Kamminga, says: the poppy eradication campaign has been ineffective, counterproductive and could well give the Taliban the decisive advantage in their struggle for the hearts and minds of the Afghan people. He is referring to US-inspired aerial fumigation campaigns, planned for spring 2008 but never initiated. So far, crop eradication is done manually or mechanically from the ground. Chemical spraying could further destabilize rural areas and risk losing support for NATO's stabilization mission.

Alternative crops

Since the Taliban allegedly makes Afghanistan's opium business easy, offering credit, seeds and fertilizer to farmers to grow the drugs that fuel the Taliban insurgency, the US authorities are determined to change that momentum by offering similar incentives to steer farmers away from the drug trade and toward alternative, legitimate crops, like grapes, wheat and saffron.

THE NEXT POWER TRIANGLE

Two Muslim nations in the Middle East have a long history of struggle for democracy. One, of course, is Turkey. Now the world's most democratic Muslim country, it offers vivid proof that Islam and freedom can thrive side by side. It has for decades been a member of the North Atlantic Treaty Organization and closely tied to the United States. Today, even while loosening its traditional enforcement of militant secularism, it is embarking on the most ambitious diplomatic project in its history, seeking to project power by resolving regional conflicts through dialogue and compromise.

President Barack Obama chose Turkey to be the first Muslim country he visited while in office, telling the Grand National Assembly, "Turkey's greatness lies in your ability to be at the center of things. This is not where East and West divide. This is where they come together."

There is only one other Muslim country in the Middle East where the democratic heart beats as passionately as it does in Turkey. It is also the only country that might suddenly emerge to rival or even surpass Turkey's level of political freedom. That country is Iran. The explosion of protest after Iran's disputed 2009 presidential election brought down fierce repression, but it was also thrilling confirmation that the ideals of democracy have taken deep root in that country. Beneath the heavy veneer of theocratic rule, a vibrant civil society thrives. No generation in the world understands democracy better or wishes for it more fervently than do young Iranians.

In the future, it is not Turkey alone where "they come together." Improbable as it may seem right now, given the current regime in Iran, a partnership that unites Turkey, Iran, and the United States is the future and makes sense for two reasons: The three countries share strategic interests, and their people share values. Our evolving relationship with a changing Turkey offers a model for the kind of relationship we might one day—not necessarily tomorrow—have with a changing Iran. This is the tantalizing possibility of a new way for the U.S. to engage with the Middle East in the 21st century.

Today we work in the region primarily through two bilateral relationships—with Israel and with Saudi Arabia. These pairings served Washington well during the Cold War. They have not, however, produced a stable Middle East. On the contrary, the region is torn by violence, hatred, terror, and war. The dilemma can be simply stated: America wants to stabilize the Middle East, but its policies are having the opposite effect.

Nowhere in the world is an overarching strategy more glaringly absent or more desperately needed than in the Middle East. For years, outside powers—especially the United States—have staggered through the region's forbidding deserts, steppes, and oil fields with policies that are manifest failures. During this period, threats emerging from the Middle East have become steadily more urgent and terrifying.

A new triangular relationship involving the United States, Turkey, and Iran cannot emerge overnight. In order to become a reliable American partner, Iran would have to change dramatically. Turkey would also have to change, although not nearly as much. So would the United States. Our world, how-ever, advances only as a result of strategic vision. First must come a grand concept, a destination; once the destination is clear, all parties can concentrate on finding the way to reach it.

Turkey has been a political and military ally of the United States for more than half a century, an alliance that peaked during the Cold War when Turkey was a reliable frontline state in the confrontation with Soviet power. In every other way, though, Turkey was a country on the periphery. It was near the Middle

East, the Balkans, the Caucasus, North Africa, and the Slavic world but not part of any of them. Turkey was a Cold War outlier, a strategic afterthought with no distinct role in the world or even its own region.

After giving itself what one scholar has called a "historical lobotomy" in the 1920s, the Republic of Turkey spent three-quarters of a century denying and hiding from its Ottoman past, when the Turks ruled a vast empire that spread from Algiers to Mecca to Budapest. That may have made sense; the fragile new country of Turkey had urgent challenges at home, did not want to be seen as neo-imperialist, and embraced Western security goals as its own.

For most of Turkey's modern history, the Muslim world has seen it as an apostate. Atatuerk's secularizing reforms pulled it so far from Islam that it seemed to have no religious legitimacy. It was perceived as Washington's lackey, stigmatized by its embrace of American policies that many Muslims found abhorrent.

Neither of those objections applies to Turkey today. It is governed by pious Muslims and has its own foreign policy. Its leaders are warmly welcomed in many places where, in the past, they would not even have cared to visit.

And since the end of the Cold War, few countries have so completely redesigned their approach to the world. On the new world map, Turkey is no longer on the edge of anything. It is once again the epicenter of the immense Eurasian landmass. The combination of Turkey's location, its Ottoman heritage, and its successful blend of Islam and democracy gives it enormous strategic potential. It is seizing that potential in ways that benefit not only itself but also the United States and the West.

When Israel wished to begin secret talks with Syria, it asked Turkey to arrange them. After Sunnis in Iraq decided to boycott national elections, Turkey persuaded them to change their minds and participate. Whenever Turkish officials land in a bitterly divided country like Lebanon or Pakistan or Afghanistan, every faction is eager to talk to them. Turkey is working to calm tensions between Iran and the United States, between Syria and Iraq, between Armenia and Azerbaijan. No country's diplomats are as welcome in both Tehran and Washington; both Moscow and Tbilisi; both Damascus and Cairo. No other nation is respected by Hamas, Hezbollah, and the Taliban while also maintaining good ties with the Israeli, Lebanese, and Afghan governments.

Foreign Minister Ahmet Davutoglu's grand concept, which he calls "strategic depth," envisions Turkey as a hyperactive peacemaker. His first project was to resolve all of Turkey's disputes with its neighbours; in this he has been largely successful. His next ambition is grander, not just "zero problems with neighbours" but "zero problems between neighbours." Every dispute in Turkey's extended neighborhood, he argues, threatens peace and limits chances for regional development; all are therefore of urgent concern to Turkey.

Turkey has found remarkably little resistance to its new ambition. By intervening only when asked and maintaining good relations with such a wide range of governments and factions, it plays a role no other country can. It has unique credentials. Turkey is big—more than 70 million people with the largest economy in the Middle East. Its Ottoman past gives it enormous historical weight. It is also a highly alluring model, not just because of its relative prosperity but also because its society is relatively free, notably in the freedoms accorded women.

The Lebanese scholar Fares Braizat spoke for many Middle East intellectuals when he called Turkey "a role model that has successfully balanced tradition and modernization." Mahmoud Abbas, the Palestinian leader, admires Turkey as "a model on the way to democracy." Sedat Laciner, an influential adviser to the Turkish foreign ministry who runs a think tank in Ankara, goes even further. "There is no country like Turkey. It is Muslim, a NATO member, and an EU candidate... It is an antidote to al-Qaeda extremism [and] the best place to make a call to the Muslim world for cooperation with the U.S."

Although Turkey is on its way to becoming one of the world's indispensable powers, it still has one important hurdle to leap. Having resolved nearly all of its international disputes, it must now finish putting its domestic affairs in order. Turkish law still limits freedom of speech. The military still plays a role in politics that is unacceptable in a democratic country. Minorities are still less than fully protected—it is not just Kurds, whose culture was brutalized by years of official repression, who face discrimination but also Christians, non-mainstream Muslims, and unbelievers. A streak of chauvinistic nationalism still runs through Turkey's political culture. The press is weak and corrupted. Political parties are closed autocracies. The education system is rigid and discourages free thinking. Until Turkish democracy is made whole, its ability to serve as a beacon of freedom will be limited.

Henry Kissinger crystallized the conventional view of Iran when asked how the United States should deal with its Muslim enemies.

"They want to humiliate us," he said. "We need to humiliate them." Many Americans see Iran the way their grandparents saw Germany, as a bad actor that causes nothing but trouble. For a time in the mid-1940s, Allied leaders considered the option of punishing Germany by cutting it into pieces, demolishing its factories, and forcing it to earn its living from agriculture alone. That plan was based on emotion: anger at the horror Germany had inflicted on the world and determination to make its people suffer. Cooler heads prevailed, though, and a different plan emerged. Germany was divided by the Cold War, but West Germany was brought into the European family. Four decades later, Germany was peacefully reunited. It has become a normal country, a promoter of peace instead of a maker of war.

The parallel to today's Iran is not exact, since Germany was defeated in war, while Iran is intact and self-confident. Nonetheless, the underlying dilemma is the same. Is it better to sanction and punish a troublemaker or entice it toward normality?

Beneath that question lies a deeper one: Does the United States shape its foreign policy according to emotion or by cool calculation of self-interest?

This is the essence of the conundrum that has turned relations between Washington and Tehran into one of the world's longest-lasting confrontations. Some powerful Americans are still trapped by their anger at Iran, stemming from the deeply traumatic hostage crisis of 1979-1981 and Iran's largely successful efforts over the next 30 years to make trouble for the United States wherever possible. These Americans have spent decades trying to punish Iran. Negotiating, reconciling, and perhaps even building a partnership with Iran seemed to them a form of surrender.

But the goal of diplomacy—or of avoiding diplomacy—should not be to punish, inflict pain, extract tribute, or redeem festering emotions. Nor should it be seen as a way to make friends. Its essential purpose is to advance interests. The tragedy of America's long estrangement from Iran is that it has undermined America's own interests.

There are a host of abstract reasons to negotiate with Iran, and just as many others not to do so. None are truly important. What matters is that none of the chief American goals in the Middle East—pacifying Iraq, stabilizing Lebanon, ending the Israel-Palestine stalemate, weakening Islamic fundamentalism, crushing al-Qaeda, moderating nuclear competition, reducing the threat of future wars—can be achieved without Iran's cooperation. As the last 30 years of history amply prove, an isolated Iran is a spoiler. A calm and prosperous Iran can be to the Middle East what a calm and prosperous Germany has been to Europe: a stabilizing power, a provider of security, and a motor of economic development.

During the first years of the 21st century, Iran's power in the Middle East dramatically increased. This happened largely because of spectacularly ill-conceived actions taken by the country that has posited itself as Iran's greatest enemy: the United States. Crippling American sanctions turned out to be not so crippling after all; they impoverished ordinary Iranians, enriched a class of smugglers tied to the regime, and led Iran to develop a web of new economic ties to more pragmatic countries, including Russia and China. Then, during the presidency of George W. Bush, the United States deposed the two regimes in neighbouring countries that were Iran's most bitter enemies: Saddam Hussein's in Iraq and the Taliban's in Afghanistan.

America's strategic miscalculations were based in part on ignorance. Bruce Riedel, a former CIA analyst who advised three presidents on the Middle East and South Asia, has asserted that "for 30 years, the United States has tried to deal with Iran and its revolutionary ideology without a well-grounded understanding of what motivates and inspires Iranians." American policies aimed at isolating Iran have had precisely the opposite effect, isolating Americans from the information and contacts they need in order to deal effectively with Iran. "I was the point person on Iran from 2005 to 2008, and I never once met an Iranian official," former Undersecretary of State Nicholas Burns has recalled.

Blinded by emotion, the United States sank into willful ignorance. Secretary of State Condoleezza Rice seemed almost proud of it. "We don't really have people who know Iran inside our own system," she admitted in 2007 when asked by *The Wall Street Journal*'s editorial board about the prospects for a changed relationship. "We don't really have very good veracity or a feel for the place."

As a new president seeks to reshape American foreign policy, and as new concerns about Iran emerge, especially about its nuclear program, the United States is reconsidering its approach. The emotions that prevented a rapprochement in the past have not evaporated, as was made clear when the administration petulantly rejected an effort by Brazil and Turkey to find a peaceful way out of the escalating crisis over Iran's nuclear program. For the first time, however, there are signs that Washington is considering the advantages that might emerge from a new understanding between the United States and Iran:

- Iran can do more than any other country, including the United States, to assure long-term peace in Iraq.
- Iran can also help stabilize Afghanistan, where it has been engaged for centuries.
- A stable and secure Iran, no longer in need of a scapegoat, might stop threatening Israel.
- Iran can tame militant groups like Hamas and Hezbollah, which would contribute to Israeli security, help stabilize Lebanon, and dramatically improve the prospects for peace between Israel and its Arab neighbours.
- Reconciliation between Iran and the United States would decisively improve relations between the United States and the Muslim world.

- Iran will have less incentive to invite Russian power into the Middle East, something the United States is rightly eager to avoid.
- Iran is an enemy of al-Qaeda and would cooperate in a transnational effort to crush it.
- Iran has 10 percent of the world's oil reserves and 16 percent of its natural gas; if the United States does not exploit and buy it, Russia and China will, thereby increasing their strategic leverage in the region.
- An Iran that no longer feels threatened by the United States might be more willing to compromise on nuclear issues.

What would the United States have to do in order to secure these results? Above all, it would have to recognize Iran as an important power with legitimate security interests. Successive American presidents have rejected the idea of compromise for exactly this reason. They wished to punish and contain Iran, not reward it with a promotion to regional-power status. That ignored the reality that Iran needs no promotion. It is already a regional power. The United States may wish that this were not the case, but self-delusion is an unsound basis for foreign policy.

No aspect of Iran's behaviour during the first decade of the new century has been more troubling to outsiders than its pursuit of a nuclear program. It is not unreasonable for Iran to want the capacity to generate nuclear energy. Its nuclear program, in fact, was first begun with American encouragement, during Mohammad Reza Shah's regime.

What troubles the outside world, though, is that Iran's drive for nuclear power is shrouded in secrecy and subterfuge, leading to the eminently reasonable suspicion that its true goal is not nuclear power but nuclear weaponry. Just as worrisome is the fact that as Iran presses ahead with its nuclear program, it is broadening its regional ambitions, testing ballistic missiles, and recklessly threatening Israel. Even Israeli leaders may not truly fear that Iran would attack their country with nuclear weapons; that would bring instant retaliation and lead to Iran's death as a nation. The Israelis and others realize, however, that a nuclear-armed Iran would be able to intimidate its neighbours in ways that would ultimately endanger Israel's security. A nuclear-armed Iran might well set off an arms race in the region, with Egypt, Saudi Arabia, Turkey, and perhaps other countries pressing for nuclear weapons of their own—a race that could set off a regional conflagration. Seeking to curb Iran's nuclear program, or at least force it into the open as Iran's treaty obligations require, is a legitimate and urgent task for the outside world.

The intensifying danger that Iran's nuclear program poses to regional and global security is not a reason to continue isolating Iran but a reason to do the opposite: Engage urgently with its government in the hope of avoiding its emergence as a full-fledged nuclear power. Threats and sanctions will not achieve this, nor will military attack. Negotiation may also fail, but the stakes are so high that refusing to try is folly.

The shocking violence that Iranian leaders used to suffocate protests after the 2009 presidential election likewise does not change the strategic logic of reconciliation between Washington and Tehran. It must, however, remind Americans that they cannot fall into the trap that has soured their relationships with some other countries: making deals between ruling elites that exclude the citizenry. As the United States pursues its strategic interest by seeking an accommodation with Iran, it must do nothing to undermine Iran's brave democratic movement.

Iran is the only Muslim country in the world where most people are reliably pro-American. This pro-American sentiment in Iran is a priceless strategic asset for the United States. For practical as well as moral reasons, American negotiators should make no concessions to Iran's regime that weaken Iranians who are persecuted for defending democratic values.

Opposition figures in Iran find themselves in a difficult situation in which there are no good options. The best of the bad options is for the regime to become integrated with the outside world, to be lured out of its fear, to build bridges to countries where debate, dissent, and protest are considered healthy signs of stability. If Iranian democrats change their minds about that—if they begin asking other countries to cut off their contacts with the regime—the United States will have to reconsider the logic of engagement. Until then, it should press ahead.

The months of protest in Iran reflect the legacy of Iran's hundred—year march toward democracy. There are seldom post-election protests in Egypt, because Egyptians expect elections to be rigged, and none in Saudi Arabia because there are no national elections at all. Today's Iranians believe they are entitled to their vote and voice. They are the heirs to five generations of freedom fighters, including those of the 1906 Constitutional Revolution and those who defended the nationalist Prime Minister Mohammad Mossadegh nearly half a century later. Their sacrifice shows how brightly the flame of freedom still burns in Iran—although, unlike in Turkey, it is not allowed to burn in public.

The political evolution of Iran has not ended. The regime now in power will not be in power forever. When it changes, evolves, or falls, the Iranian people will demand the democracy for which so many of them yearn. This cannot be said for other countries in the region, because they do not have long democratic traditions.

Under the right circumstances, Iran might even emerge from its half-century of dictatorship as more democratic than Turkey. When and if it does, its people should know that the United States has always stood by them.

Direct, bilateral, comprehensive, and unconditional negotiations hold the only hope for a diplomatic breakthrough between Iran and the United States. Iran has incentives to make a deal. It craves legitimacy. It has security needs that only the United States can meet. Its government is unpopular, its economy is reeling from a combination of high inflation and low oil prices, its society is groaning under a host of social ills, its young generation is deeply alienated, and many of its most talented sons and daughters have either emigrated or hope to do so.

It may prove impossible for the United States to make Iran a partner as long as the current regime is in power, but Americans should do nothing that will make that partnership more difficult to achieve when conditions are right. Instead they should ask, as the 13th-century Persian poet Rumi did, "Why do you stay in prison when the door is so wide open?"

THE NEW GOLDEN TRIANGLE OF AFGHAN OPIUM

Afghanistan's notorious reputation of being the world's largest opium producer is only getting stronger in an atmosphere of corruption and state patronage. The new menacing triangle in the west, producing 70% of opium and 90% of the country's heroin, has surpassed the 1980s Golden Crescent in area.

Nature achieved this year what six years of United States-led anti-narcotics enforcement could not do in Afghanistan. Bad weather effected a decline in the country's opium production by ruining a sizable chunk of the crop.

For Afghanistan, narcotics and insurgency are intertwined and inseparable problems. Illicit cultivation of opium was used by the US to finance the insurrection against the Najibullah government.

Many members of the Mujahideen, who were the Central Intelligence Agency's paws, are now holding powerful posts in the US-propped Hamid Karzai government. These collaborations have ensured the Karzai government's failure to contain opium production.

Many members of the Mujahideen, who were the Central Intelligence Agency's paws, are now holding powerful posts in the US-propped Hamid Karzai government.

In December 2005, the US Drug Enforcement Administration (DEA) seized nine tonnes of opium from the house of the then Governor of Helmand, Sher Muhammad Akhundzada – the DEA is the only US organisation that seems sincere about reducing narcotics trafficking.

Patronising environment

But, American and British military intelligence forces ensured that he was made a Member of Parliament. Similar is the case of Izzatullah Wasifi, the Director of the General Independent Administration of Anti-Corruption (GIAAC). He was arrested in July 1987 with 600 grammes of heroin in Caesar's Palace Hotel, Las Vegas.

President Karzai's step-brother Ahmed Wali Karzai is reported to be the ablest protector of all drug traffickers. With such patronage given by US forces and some people in the Afghan government, it is no surprise that opium production does not decrease.

President Karzai's step-brother Ahmed Wali Karzai is reported to be the ablest protector of all drug traffickers. With such patronage given by US forces and some people in the Afghan government, it is no surprise that opium production does not decrease.

The latest United Nations Rapid Survey for 2008 has projected that Afghanistan produced 8,200 tonnes of opium in 2007. During the days of the much-maligned Najibullah government in the 1980s, the average opium production was only around 300 tonnes annually.

That narcotics money supports the Taliban has been well known, but the Americans have begun to accept it only now. One billion dollars a year is spent to control narcotics trafficking in Afghanistan, yet opium seizures decrease. As the fields gain in area, so does the power of the Taliban.

IRAN EXAMPLE

Iran, which loses about 300 soldiers a year in its efforts to prevent narcotics trafficking, spends less than one-tenth this amount but is eight times as successful in seizing drugs. The Taliban pays its soldiers $300 each a month, whereas the Afghan soldier earns only $40 a month.

This is because the Taliban soldiers' salaries are met by the opium contractor of an area. The muster rolls of the Afghan police and Army show more soldiers than are actually present.

The salaries of the ghost soldiers are pocketed by the officers. The war against drugs and the Taliban is bound to fail in such an atmosphere of corruption and collusion.

In 2007, Iran seized 2,31,352 kg of Afghan opium while Afghanistan could seize only 90,990 kg. Afghanistan seized 9,079 kg of heroin while Pakistan seized 24,341 kg, Iran 12,493 kg and China 9,085 kg.

In 2007, Iran seized 2,31,352 kg of Afghan opium while Afghanistan could seize only 90,990 kg. Afghanistan seized 9,079 kg of heroin while Pakistan seized 24,341 kg, Iran 12,493 kg and China 9,085 kg.

Thus Afghanistan, which produces 90% of the world's opium and heroin, seizes only 27% of the opium and 10% of the heroin. The North Atlantic Treaty Organisation (NATO) forces have actually made Afghanistan a safe place to grow opium.

DANGEROUS TRIANGLE

With such ineffectiveness, a new and more dangerous triangle has emerged in western Afghanistan. It encloses contiguous areas of Afghanistan's borders with Iran and Pakistan. Within this triangle comes 70% of the opium and 90% of the country's heroin cultivation; the majority of the 110 narcotics-trafficking routes in the country are also here.

Opium cultivation, heroin refining and the trafficking in these are protected activities here. It surpasses the Golden Crescent of the 1980s in area and is more menacing.

Afghanistan has a 920-km-long border with Iran. Most of it is easy-to-cross deserts. The Iranians have set up forts on their side of the border and have also made 28 forts for Afghanistan. The most troublesome province is Nimruz.

India is building a 300-km-long road from Zaranj to Delaram, where most of this province's opium is cultivated. Nimruz, which is in the southwest corner of the triangle, is a Baluch speaking area, as are adjacent territories in Pakistan and Iran.

A huge refining facility run by the Baluch community flourishes in Baramcha in southwest Nimruz and close to Helmand. The Baluch facility has the protection of the largely Pashtun Taliban forces, and is not disturbed by the enforcement agencies in its production of high-quality heroin.

NATO support

The rampant venality of the Afghans has the tacit support of the US-led NATO forces. Multi-million dollar contracts and expensive consultancies are given, mainly to American and British companies, to find ways to contain narcotics trafficking; but no one asks for results.

Afghanistan has received $14 billion as aid in the last six years but there is nothing to show that it has been utilised honestly. As for dishonest utilisation, one can see huge, ugly and gaudy buildings, each worth millions of dollars, in the Sherpur and Wazir Akbar Khan suburbs of Kabul.

Afghanistan has received $14 billion as aid in the last six years but there is nothing to show that it has been utilised honestly. As for dishonest utilisation, one can see huge, ugly and gaudy buildings, each worth millions of dollars, in the Sherpur and Wazir Akbar Khan suburbs of Kabul.

These are owned by Afghans and sub-let to foreigners. Narco kleptocracy, narco terrorism and narco politics rule Afghanistan. Except for 3,00,000 or so citizens, who earn thousands of dollars, about 28 million people in the country earn an average of $35 a month. There is complete failure in every sphere of civil society.

Opium is supposed to be destroyed by US contractors, who courageously hit only the fields of the poorest farmers. Some of these farmers have to repay huge loans taken before sowing opium poppy seeds by selling their daughters or sisters to the traffickers who advanced them the money.

DEPENDENCE ON OPIUM

The lives of 14 million people in the country are dependent on opium. Many poor farmers have a better-than-average life because of opium. Hence mere eradication will not solve the problem as six years of enforcement failure has lamentably proved.

It is not merely an enforcement headache but a political one. In an impoverished country where establishing a Coca-Cola plant is touted as industrialisation, there is not much hope for increasing prosperity.

The cement factories and the textile mills of the 1980s have not yet been revived. A more respectable, humane and practical alternative to opium cultivation will have to be found.

In Herat and Farah to the north, smuggling is more audacious. Here, in post after lonely sand-swept post, I heard the familiar refrain of drugs being moved in cavalcades that are protected by anti-tank rockets and heavy machine guns.

These too come in through the open border, and are paid for from the drug money. So organised is the entire operation.

Seizures on the Afghan side are actually offerings the border villagers have to make to buy peace with the troops. Development projects are only meant for official reports so that more money can be siphoned off in their name.

After travelling miles on a dusty road to Kohasan, a town east of Islam Qala near the Iran border, I was surprised by a 600-metre-long tarred road. At the end of it was a huge signboard proclaiming that it had been built by the United States Agency for International Development (USAID).

Contempt for the US

I stopped at a tailor's shop nearby and asked a few people what they thought of the improvement in their lives since the US occupation.

The response was abusive contempt. They had praise for Iran which gave them electricity and the excellent three-lane tarred road from Meshed to Herat, and for India which is building a dam on the Hirai rud (river).

But what surprised me was the affection and regard they still had for the Najibullah regime, which they consider the golden period in Afghanistan's history. In those days, they could save $5 from a monthly income of $35 but today it is impossible to save anything though they make $150 a month on an average.

Legalisng poppy cultivation

Legalising opium cultivation is now a serious alternative for the country. Turkey in the 1970s had done so with its illicit opium poppy cultivation.

Legalising opium cultivation is now a serious alternative for the country. Turkey in the 1970s had done so with its illicit opium poppy cultivation.

A London-based organisation, the Senlis Council, has, after considerable field research, made a Poppy for Medicine (P4M) proposal, which has received overwhelming support from the European Parliament.

P4M suggests that the crop should be legalised, since enforcement and eradication have failed miserably in Afghanistan.

As per this plan, the village council (shura) will supervise the cultivation. It will have the power to delicense and penalise any farmer within its fold if he diverts his opium crop.

The farmer is the "least corrupt" of the entire Afghan society. It is deprivation that has forced him to cultivate opium. With poverty and creditors banging at his door, the farmer pays the Taliban to protect his opium.

ADVANTAGE OF P4M

The biggest advantage of the P4M scheme is that the Taliban will eventually be starved of funds that sustain it now.

All the opium produced in Afghanistan at present is illegal. With the P4M proposal, the quantity of legal opium garnered would be much more than the 180 tonnes that is seized annually.

This simple and practical plan has many advantages: it can make farmers happy, most of the opium produced will no longer go for illicit purposes, there will be more funds for development at the village level, and as each year passes there will be fewer farmers cultivating opium.

The Afghanistan government opposes this plan because the US and British authorities are against it. Also, it does not suit the traffickers. Most Afghans support this idea, but they do not have a say.

The other motivation to go for this scheme is that there is not enough cheap morphine – a derivative of opium and the most efficacious painkiller – to go around. Eighty per cent of all the morphine produced in the world is consumed by just eight countries.

Even among them (in the US 55.5 mg per head is consumed annually) only 40% can afford morphine.

In India, morphine is produced by the government and a 10 mg tablet costs about three cents (Rs.1.26), whereas the same tablet is sold for $60 by American and British multinational companies.

At least 140 tonnes of extra morphine is required to meet the current shortage. Once the system improves, the diversion could be restricted to around 30%, which is what it is in India.

Afghan opium has much higher morphine content than opium produced elsewhere.

If it is true that morphine consumption has reached saturation, as the International Narcotics Control Board says, why are the United Kingdom and the US growing opium in thousands of hectares surreptitiously?

They are buying less and less from India and Turkey on the specious excuse that there is no demand for morphine.

Meanwhile, with enforcement failing and with the Taliban getting richer, security in many countries far away from the region is being threatened.

AFGHAN TRIANGLE: OPIUM, OIL AND TALIBAN

After humiliating the Red Army in Afghanistan and making Uncle Sam the sole world power – The Mujahideen Islamist leaders fell from the favour of America and its proxy governments in Saudi Arabia and Pakistan – in the fear that they might establish an Iran-friendly Islamic regime in Kabul. Therefore, a new group based on Saudi-version of Islamic state was given birth by CIA, ISI and Riyadh, which with the active help from Pakistan Air Force – forced two prominent Mujahideed leaders, Afghan President Rabbani and Afghan Prime Minister Gulbedin, to seek refuge in Iran in 1996. These two leaders were treated like foreign dignatories till the Taliban were ousted from power by their former midwife, the US.

The 9/11 was used as an excuse to make devil out of Taliban and their guest Osama Bin Laden. Both were blamed for 9/11 – though Taliban in their six-year-rule, did not had a single commercial or military plane or modern telecommunication network – but they were able to pull-out the greatest terror attack on American soil.

And how evil Taliban were – a Zionist Jew writer, Eben Kaplan, wrote in the journal of the most powerful Zionist think tank, 'Council on Foreign Relations' (it's reported that 400 of its members including its Jew president Richard Haass, Hilary Clinton and Dennis Ross are part of Obama's administration) under the title *The Taliban in Afghanistan*, on July 2, 2008:

"Public reaction to Taliban's rule was not wholly negative. While the rigid social standards (Wahhabism) fostered resentment, the Taliban cracked down on corruption that had run rampant through the government for years. The new leaders also brought stability to Afghanistan, greatly reducing the infighting between warlords that had devastated the civilian population. Seven year after their ouster, the Taliban continue to provide a semblance of stability in regions where coalition and government officials have been unable to restore order and provide basic services......"

Richard Haass, president CFR, who is also a senior adviser to Obama on foreign policy – has never criticized Zionist-regime's "thugocracy" against all its Arab neighbours – has in his June 26 interview with Bernard Gwertzman said: "The Iranian theocracy has become a "thugocracy" (having defeated the "Zion Revolution" in the aftermath of Ahmadinejad's huge victory) – but the Iranian regime will likely prevail because of its use of force against the population. This makes the urgency of negotiating an end to country's nuclear program more pronounced, and possibly more difficult. Iranian challenge (to Israel) still exists, and may actually be somewhat worse....."

So the question comes to mind is: why occupy Afghanistan when the leaders of both Afghan Mujahideen and Taliban were pro-America? The answer lies in the planning of the pro-Israel high-ranking officials in Clinton and Bush administrations – long before September 11, 2001 tragedy. The planned occupation of Afghanistan was based on two factors of greed – the Caspian Sea oil reserves and Taliban's ban on Poppy cultivation – the source of US$600 billion opium business in 2007 (second to oil and arms trade).

Taliban, on several occasions, offered to turn over Osama Bin Laden to a third country for trail, once Washington and Jewish media blamed him for masterminding the 9/11 – However, both Clinton and Bush administrations rejected those offers.

American puppet regimes were neded both in Afghanistan and Pakistan to built the cheapest oil pipeline from Caspian Sea to Gwader port in Balochistan via Afghanistan.Furthermore, both these countries are itself rich in oil/gas and other natural resources:

"Massive untapped gas reserves are believed to be lying beneath Pakistan's remotest deserts, but they're being held hostage by armed tribal groups demanding a better deal from the central government," – AFP, September 1, 2001.

Taliban's eradication program led to a 94% decline in opium cultivation by 2000. According to UN's 2001 figures, opium cultivation had fallen to 185 tons. Immediately, following US occupation in December 2001 – production increased dramatically, regaining its historical levels – 6,100 tons in 2006 (a 3200% increase in five years).

And who are the greatest beneficiaries of opium cultivated in Afghanistan, India and the rest of Far East countries – David Sassoon (1792-1864) and his family of course. Historically, Rothschild-controlled Britain won Hong Kong by launching the Opium Wars to give the Sassoons exclusive rights to drug an entire nation! According to the 1944 Jewish Encyclopedia: "He (David Sassoon) employed only Jews in his business, and wherever he sent them he built Synagouges and schools for them. He imported whole family of fellow Jews…and put them to work."

AFGHANISTAN'S ROLE IN IRAN'S DRUG PROBLEM

The recent boom in Afghan opium production, propelled by a resurgent Taliban, has had an increasing impact on Iranians—both young and old—across the border. Iran has an estimated 3 million drug users and "by many accounts, the world's worst heroin problem," says Peter Reuter, a drug expert and professor at the University of Maryland. The rise in drug use and smuggling has strained Iran's police forces and prisons, as well as its economy, and aggravated rifts along the population's main fault lines: young versus old, religious versus secular, modernist versus traditional. Drug abuse in Iran often gets overshadowed by other issues—namely Tehran's nuclear program—but experts say, if left unchecked, it may leave Iran with large social, demographic, and health problems for generations.

What is the status of opium production in Afghanistan?

Afghanistan has long been the world's leading producer of opium, accounting for 89 percent of total global production. Despite falling in 2005 for the first time in four years—mirroring worldwide trends—Afghanistan's opium production crept upward in unruly southern provinces like Kandahar (from roughly 12,000 acres in 2004 to 32,000 acres in 2005). This was partly due to the resurgent Taliban, which boosted cultivation levels even higher in early 2006. "Everybody was taken aback," Reuter says of the recent spike in production. Experts say farmers are rebuilding their inventory from 2000-2001, when the Taliban, then in control of Afghanistan, imposed a brief moratorium on production (but not on opium exports). The ban resulted in a huge collapse in total world output of opium. "Stockpiles were way down and prices remained high by historic standards," he says. Afghanistan's opium trade—the majority of it routed through Iran, Pakistan, and Tajikistan—has since blossomed. The head of the UN Office of Drugs and Crime (UNODC), Antonio Maria Costa, presenting his findings to the Afghan government in early September, called the trend "very alarming."

How has Afghanistan's rise in opium production affected Iran?

The UNODC estimates 60 percent of Afghanistan's opium is trafficked across Iran's border (much of it in transit to Europe). Seizures of the narcotic by Iranian authorities in the first half of this year are up 29 percent from the same period last year, according to the country's police chief, as reported by Radio Free Europe/ Radio Liberty (RFE/RL). Experts say the rise in poppy cultivation in Afghanistan will have some effect on Iran's opium prices but not a significant one. The *Washington Post* reports that Iran has the world's highest per capita number of opium addicts. After the Bam earthquake in 2003, among the emergency supplies brought in was methadone, a synthetic drug used to treat heroin and morphine addicts. Experts say those affected most are the millions of unemployed Iranians and youth chafing under the restrictions placed on them from the Islamic government and *basij*, or civilian morals police.

Has drug use contributed to a rise in HIV/AIDS in Iran?

Yes. The *Washington Post* reported last July a 25 percent HIV infection rate among heroin users in Iran. Of the estimated 20,000 Iranians with HIV/AIDS, two-thirds of them were infected through sharing contaminated needles, reports the UNODC. In Iran, talk of sex, drugs, and AIDS has remained taboo for two decades. But there are signs of progress, experts say. As reported cases of HIV/ AIDS became more prevalent in Iran, especially during the latter years of President Mohammed Khatami (1997-2005), the government took steps to counter the spread of the disease. A reformist, Khatami allocated more monies to drug treatment plans, increased subsidies for needle-exchange programs, and sponsored methadone centers. It is also now forbidden for doctors to turn away HIV-infected patients.

How has Iran's poor economy affected drug use?

Unemployment in Iran is somewhere between 11 percent (the official level) and 25 percent (the estimate given by some outside economists). One in four Iranians lives in poverty, despite high oil prices. Experts say because of these dire economic conditions—particularly among those under thirty, who comprise 70 percent of Iran's population—people turn to drugs. "This grievance combines with general boredom and a lack of options," writes Bill Samii of RFE/RL in the *Brown Journal of World Affairs*(PDF). A government poll shows almost 80 percent of Iranians detect a direct link between unemployment and drug addiction, reports the *Washington Post*. Further, according to the UK-based Beckley Foundation, because of Iran's poor economy " here has been a rise in internal migration, urbanization, crime, and social problems, providing a breeding ground (PDF) for the development and spread of drug problems."

Which addictive drugs pose the biggest problem in Iran?

Opium has long been the narcotic of choice among Iranians. "At least parts of the [Iranian] population have always used opium the way the West uses alcohol," says Francisco Thoumi, economics professor and expert on the global drug trade at the Bogotá-based Universidad Del Rosario. When opium prices soared after the Taliban cut poppy production in 2000, many Iranian drug users switched to heroin, a slightly cheaper derivative. The increase in heroin use also reflects the government's clampdown on drugs. "As countries get tougher on drugs, there's an increased incentive to use heroin because it's less conspicuous and more highly concentrated," Reuter says. RFE/RL's Samii, who has written extensively about drug abuse in Iran, reports that young Iranians, restricted from drinking alcohol in pubs, are increasingly switching to synthetic "club drugs" like methamphetamines (crank) and LSD, in addition to cannabis, ecstasy, and crystal (concentrated heroin). Iran's state welfare organization tells RFE/RL that an estimated 8 percent of the adult population is addicted to drugs, with 90,000 Iranians becoming drug addicts—most of them hooked on heroin or opium—each year. "Drugs are symptomatic of a people's social problems," Thoumi says, "[In Iran] it's a conflict between pre-modern and modern Iranians."

How has the Iranian government responded to the drug crisis?

Originally, government authorities, not unlike America's drug czars in the 1980s, mainly addressed the supply side of Iran's drug problem. Law-and-order policies with zero tolerance led to the arrest of tens of thousands of addicts and the execution of thousands of narcotics traffickers. "Iran is the only country I know of that had a similar rate of imprisonment for drug users as America," Reuter says. There are an estimated 68,000 Iranians imprisoned for drug trafficking and another 32,000 for drug addiction (out of a total prison population of 170,000, based on 2001 statistics), according to RFE/RL's Samii. Tehran also has spent millions of dollars and deployed thousands of troops to secure its porous 1,000-mile border with Afghanistan and Pakistan. Experts say a few hundred Iranian drug police die each year in battles with smugglers. "You have drug groups like guerrilla forces," the head of Iran's UNODC office, Roberto Arbitrio, told the *Times of London* last year. "They shoot heavily with rocket launchers, heavy machine guns, and Kalashnikovs." Under Khatami, the government's attitude on drugs changed and more emphasis was placed on prevention and addiction-treatment programs. Yet since President Mahmoud Ahmadinejad, a conservative hard-liner, came to power last year, Samii says Iran's drug policy has been reconsidered and shifted back toward supply interdiction and boosting border security.

What international efforts has Iran pursued to address its drug problem?

The bulk of the country's drug control and interdiction efforts are conducted between the Drug Control Headquarters and the Interior Ministry. However, because Iran lies on a popular transit corridor between opium producers in Afghanistan and opium consumers in Europe, the country faces added pressure to secure its borders and seize more incoming drug shipments. European countries like France, Spain, and Britain have provided some financial support, as well as counter-narcotics equipment like drug-sniffing dogs, but Iranians complain it is not enough. "Iranians repeatedly complain they are at the forefront of the battle on narcotics traffickers and they're the ones whose young people are druggies," Samii says. Iran has counter-narcotics agreements with several European, Asian, and Central Asian states. In addition, Tehran participates in a number of multilateral agencies involved in controlling drug abuse, including the Drug Control Coordination Unit of the Economic Cooperation Organization and the 6+2 group (comprising six Central Asian states plus Russia and the United States). Iran is a party to two UN treaties aimed at counter narcotics.

What steps has Washington taken to curb opium production in Afghanistan?

According to the 2001 Bonn Agreement, which laid out Afghanistan's postwar reconstruction plan, Britain was put in charge of opium eradication. In addition, the United States has provided the Afghan government with public-information campaigns, $135 million per year in financial aid for farmers to grow alternate crops, and technical assistance with eradication programs. In August, a group of Colombian police officers visited Afghanistan on a tour organized by Henry J. Hyde (R-IL), chair of the House International Relations Committee. Hyde has been critical of the Pentagon's eradication efforts and favors more attacks against drug kingpins, production labs, and trafficking routes.The head of UNODC has also pushed for "robust military action" from NATO forces to take out poppy farms but NATO has resisted such a role.

A new report by the Senlis Council, a Europe-based think tank, cautions against mixing counter-narcotics campaigns with military counterterrorism operations. The report finds that poverty drives Afghan farmers to cultivate poppies. "By focusing aid funds away from development and poverty relief, failed counter-narcotics policies have hijacked the international community's nation-building efforts and undermined Afghanistan's democratically elected government," the report concludes. U.S.eradication efforts have increased skepticism among local Afghans of Kabul's ability to administer and provide poverty relief for its far-flung provinces and thereby driven many Afghans to support the Taliban. Thoumi agrees with this assessment. "The factors that lead to production [of opium] are very much structural, institutional, and cultural," he says. "Countries that produce plant-based drugs are those with deep unresolved social problems and central states with no control of their territories."

3

End of the Afghan War: New Challenges to Regional Security

The allied forces 13 years prolong war in Afghanistan formally came to an end with the flag-lowering ceremony in Kabul. The U.S led forces marked the transition of fighting to Afghan forces. This happened as a result of the NATO conference held in Chicago in May 2012; the Obama Administration formally announced the end of combat operations by the International Security Assistance Force (ISAF) at the end of 2014 and a focus of operations until that time upon Security Force Assistance (SFA) to the Afghan National Security Forces (ANSF).

In fact, Afghanistan is influenced from every side of the map, for example from its West by the Iran, in the South Pakistan and in its North by the Central Asia. However, by the withdrawal of US led NATO forces, there are many speculations which arise, whether the Afghan forces are that much capable to handle their internal security issues without any external support?

Certainty the Afghan forces does not seem in a position of own capability to take over the Afghanistan's security responsibility. Apart from NATO claims that, the Afghan forces are ready to take over the security matters, the most important concern remains unanswered that is how much are Afghan forces capable to fully ensure their national security because the Afghan forces lack in many areas such as air defence capability, modern weaponry and strong real-time intelligence network. Afghan political and military elite is aware that such setbacks will strain the ability of forces which demonstrate their vulnerability in countering the insurgency. Though, the US military involvement will continue in Afghanistan under the terms of security pacts with the Afghan government which allows US led NATO forces role in two broad areas of training of Afghan forces and limited combat role against the terrorism. The NATO is also planning to set up a new civilian mission in 2015 that will train, assist and advise the Afghan security forces. But the Afghan forces are deeply overwhelmed by corruption; political affiliations and their incapability handle the insurgency. And consequently the Drug money will be generated by the smuggling and trade of drugs and ultimately will be used for the purposes of Warlords and terrorism.

In addition, while apparently there is a pretense of a unified government in Kabul, but in practice, the country has fractured into many small fractions of powerful local warlords and ethnic diversity. In the post-Taliban era, the warlord-ship has increased with a greater pace and in the wake of post- withdrawal, the future of Afghanistan seems much violent, anarchic and conflict ridden ultimately, an Afghanistan pondered to the new civil war and therefore, the future of Afghanistan seems uncertain after the withdrawal of the NATO, US and the ISAF forces. At public level the current scenario at government point is rarely trusted by the local population due to massive level of corruption and bribe in everyday affairs. At the other hand, the Taliban rebellions in Afghanistan are believed to be more trustworthy to common masses but are hardly supported by the International Community.

However, by the security vacuum after NATO's withdrawal, regional countries like Pakistan, Iran, China and Russia are rays of hope. The best that can be hoped for a stable Afghanistan is its relations and the support of regional specially neighbouring countries commitment to enable Afghanistan more firmly standing on its own feet.

RECENT HISTORY (2001–PRESENT)

On 9 September 2001, Ahmad Shah Massoud was assassinated by two Arab suicide attackers inside Afghanistan and two days later about 3,000 people were killed in the September 11 attacks in the United States. The US government identified Osama bin

Laden, Khalid Sheikh Mohammed and the Al-Qaeda organization based in and allied to the Taliban's Islamic Emirate of Afghanistan as the perpetrators of the attacks. From 1990 until this date over 400,000 Afghan civilians had already died in the wars in Afghanistan. The Taliban refused to hand over bin Laden to US authorities and to disband al-Qaeda bases in Afghanistan. In October 2001, Operation Enduring Freedom was launched as new phase of the War in Afghanistan (1978-present) in which teams of American and British special forces worked with ground forces of the United Front (Northern Alliance) to remove the Taliban from power and dispel Al-Qaeda. At the same time the US-led forces were bombing Taliban and al-Qaida targets everywhere inside Afghanistan with cruise missiles. These actions led to the fall of Mazar-i-Sharif in the north followed by all the other cities, as the Taliban and al-Qaeda fled over the porous Durand Line border into Pakistan. In December 2001, after the Taliban government was toppled and the new Afghan government under Hamid Karzai was formed, the International Security Assistance Force (ISAF) was established by the UN Security Council to help assist the Karzai administration and provide basic security to the Afghan people.

While the Taliban began regrouping inside Pakistan, more coalition troops entered the escalating US-led war. Meanwhile, the rebuilding of war-torn Afghanistan kicked off in 2002. The Afghan nation was able to build democratic structures over the years, and some progress was made in key areas such as governance, economy, health, education, transport, and agriculture. NATO is training the Afghan armed forces as well its national police. ISAF and Afghan troops led many offensives against the Taliban but failed to fully defeat them. By 2009, a Taliban-led shadow government began to form in many parts of the country complete with their own version of mediation court. After U.S. President Barack Obama announced the deployment of another 30,000 soldiers in 2010 for a period of two years, Der Spiegel published images of the US soldiers who killed unarmed Afghan civilians.

At the 2010 International Conference on Afghanistan in London, Afghan President Hamid Karzai said he intends to reach out to the Taliban leadership (including Mullah Omar, Sirajuddin

Haqqani and Gulbuddin Hekmatyar). Supported by NATO, Karzai called on the group's leadership to take part in a loya jirga meeting to initiate peace talks. These steps have resulted in an intensification of bombings, assassinations and ambushes. Some Afghan groups (including the former intelligence chief Amrullah Saleh and opposition leader Dr. Abdullah Abdullah) believe that Karzai plans to appease the insurgents' senior leadership at the cost of the democratic constitution, the democratic process and progess in the field of human rights especially women's rights. Dr. Abdullah stated:

"I should say that Taliban are not fighting to be accommodated. They are fighting to bring the state down. So it's a futile exercise, and it's just misleading.... There are groups that will fight to the death. Whether we like to talk to them or we don't like to talk to them, they will continue to fight. So, for them, I don't think that we have a way forward with talks or negotiations or contacts or anything as such. Then we have to be prepared to tackle and deal with them militarily. In terms of the Taliban on the ground, there are lots of possibilities and opportunities that with the help of the people in different parts of the country, we can attract them to the peace process; provided, we create a favorable environment on this side of the line. At the moment, the people are leaving support for the government because of corruption. So that expectation is also not realistic at this stage."

Over five million Afghan refugees were repatriated in the last decade, including many who were forcefully deported from NATOcountries. This large return of Afghans may have helped the nation's economy but the country still remains one of the poorest in the world due to the decades of war, lack of foreign investment, ongoing government corruption and the Pakistani-backed Taliban insurgency. According to a report by the United Nations, the Taliban and other militants were responsible for 76% of civilian casualties in 2009, 75% in 2010 and 80% in 2011. In 2011 a record 3,021 civilians were killed in the ongoing insurgency, the fifth successive annual rise.

After the May 2011 death of Osama bin Laden in Pakistan, many prominent Afghan figures began being assassinated, including Mohammed Daud Daud, Ahmed Wali Karzai, Jan

Mohammad Khan, Ghulam Haider Hamidi, Burhanuddin Rabbani and others. Also in the same year, the Pak-Afghan border skirmishes intensified and many large scale attacks by the Pakistani-based Haqqani Network took place across Afghanistan. This led to the United States warning Pakistan of a possible military action against the Haqqanis in the Federally Administered Tribal Areas. The U.S. blamed Pakistan's government, mainly Pakistan Army and its ISI spy network as the masterminds behind all of this.

"In choosing to use violent extremism as an instrument of policy, the government of Pakistan, and most especially the Pakistani army and ISI, jeopardizes not only the prospect of our strategic partnership but Pakistan's opportunity to be a respected nation with legitimate regional influence. They may believe that by using these proxies, they are hedging their bets or redressing what they feel is an imbalance in regional power. But in reality, they have already lost that bet." —Admiral Mike Mullen, *Chairman of the Joint Chiefs of Staff*

U.S. Ambassador to Pakistan, Cameron Munter, told Radio Pakistan that "The attack that took place in Kabul a few days ago, that was the work of the Haqqani Network. There is evidence linking the Haqqani Network to the Pakistan government. This is something that must stop." Other top U.S. officials such as Hillary Clinton and Leon Panetta made similar statements. On 16 October 2011, "Operation Knife Edge" was launched by NATO and Afghan forces against the Haqqani Network in south-eastern Afghanistan. Afghan Defense Minister, Abdul Rahim Wardak, explained that the operation will "help eliminate the insurgents before they struck in areas along the troubled frontier".

In anticipation of the 2014 NATO withdrawal and a subsequent expected push to regain power by the Taliban, the anti-Taliban United Front (Northern Alliance) groups have started to regroup under the umbrella of the National Coalition of Afghanistan (political arm) and the National Front of Afghanistan (military arm).

Governance

The government of Afghanistan is an Islamic republic consisting of three branches, executive, legislative and judicial.

The nation is currently led by the Karzai administration with Hamid Karzai as the President and leader since late 2001. The National Assembly is the legislature, a bicameral body having two chambers, the House of the People and the House of Elders.

The Supreme Court is led by Chief Justice Abdul Salam Azimi, a former university professor who had been a legal advisor to the president. The current court is seen as more moderate and led by more technocrats than the previous one, which was dominated by fundamentalist religious figures such as Chief Justice Faisal Ahmad Shinwari who issued several controversial rulings, including seeking to place a limit on the rights of women.

According to Transparency International's corruption perceptions index 2010 results, Afghanistan was ranked as the third most-corrupt country in the world. A January 2010 report published by the United Nations Office on Drugs and Crime revealed that bribery consumes an amount equal to 23 % of the GDP of the nation. A number of government ministries are believed to be rife with corruption, and while President Karzai vowed to tackle the problem in late 2009 by stating that "individuals who are involved in corruption will have no place in the government", top government officials were busy stealing and misusing hundreds of millions of dollars through the Kabul Bank. Although the nation's institutions are newly formed and steps have been taken to arrest some, the United States warned that aid to Afghanistan would be reduced to very little if the corruption is not stopped.

Elections and parties

The 2004 Afghan presidential election was relatively peaceful, in which Hamid Karzai won in the first round with 55.4% of the votes. However, the 2009 presidential election was characterized by lack of security, low voter turnout and widespread electoral fraud. The vote, along with elections for 420 provincial council seats, took place in August 2009, but remained unresolved during a lengthy period of vote counting and fraud investigation.

Two months later, under international pressure, a second round run-off vote between Karzai and remaining challenger Abdullah was announced, but a few days later Abdullah announced that he is not participating in the 7 November run-off because his demands for changes in the electoral commission had not been met. The next day, officials of the election commission cancelled the run-off and declared Hamid Karzai as President for another 5-year term. In the 2005 parliamentary election, among the elected officials were former mujahideen, Islamic fundamentalists, warlords, communists,reformists, and several Taliban associates. In the same period, Afghanistan reached to the 30th nation in terms of female representation in parliament. The last parliamentary election was held in September 2010, but due to disputes and investigation of fraud, the sworn in ceremony took place in late January 2011. After the issuance of computerized ID cards for the first time, which is a $101 million project that the Afghan government plans to start in 2012, it is expected to help prevent major fraud in future elections and improve the security situation.

Administrative divisions

Afghanistan is administratively divided into 34 provinces (*wilayats*), with each province having its own capital and a provincial administration. The provinces are further divided into about 398 smaller provincial districts, each of which normally covers a city or a number of villages. Each district is represented by a district governor.

The provincial governors are appointed by the President of Afghanistan and the district governors are selected by the provincial governors. The provincial governors are representatives of the central government in Kabul and are responsible for all administrative and formal issues within their provinces. There are also provincial councils which are elected through direct and general elections for a period of four years. The functions of provincial councils are to take part in provincial development planning and to participate in monitoring and appraisal of other provincial governance institutions.

According to article 140 of the constitution and the presidential decree on electoral law, mayors of cities should be elected through free and direct elections for a four-year term. However, due to huge election costs, mayoral and municipal elections have never been held. Instead, mayors have been appointed by the government. As for the capital city of Kabul, the mayor is appointed by the

President of Afghanistan. The following is a list of all the 34 provinces of Afghanistan in alphabetical order and on the right is a map showing where each province is located:

Foreign relations and military

The Afghan Ministry of Foreign Affairs is responsible for managing the foreign relations of Afghanistan. The nation has been a member of the UN since 1946, and has maintained goodrelations with the United States and other NATO member states since the signing of the Treaty of Rawalpindi in 1919.

The United Nations Assistance Mission in Afghanistan (UNAMA) was established in 2002 under United Nations Security Council Resolution 1401 to help the nation recover from decades of war and establish a normal functioning government. Today, more than 22 NATO nations deploy about 140,000 troops in Afghanistan as part of the International Security Assistance Force (ISAF). Apart from close military links, Afghanistan also enjoys strong economic relations with NATO members and their allies.

Afghanistan also has diplomatic relations with neighbouring Pakistan, Iran, Turkmenistan, Uzbekistan, Tajikistan, the People's Republic of China, including regional states such as India, Turkey, Kazakhstan, Russia, United Arab Emirate, Saudi Arabia, Iraq, Egypt, Japan, South Korea, and others. Afghanistan's relationship with Pakistan has often fluctuated since 1947. They have cultural, security and economic links with each other but disputes between the two states remain. Afghanistan continues to reject the porous and poorly marked Durrand Line as its international border with Pakistan, and has repeatedly accused Pakistan of supporting the Taliban insurgents, Haqqani Network, and other anti-Afghanistan terrorist groups. Economically, Afghanistan is highly dependent on Pakistan in terms of imports, supplies and trade routes. Conversely, Pakistan considers Afghanistan as an important trade route for access to Central Asian resources.

Pakistan harbours concerns over the growing influence of its rival India in Afghanistan. Relations between the two states were strained further after recent border skirmishes. Afghan officials allege that Pakistani intelligence agencies are involved in terrorist attacks inside Afghanistan. Pakistan has denied supporting the

Taliban and claimed that a stable Afghanistan is in its interest. India and Iran have actively participated in reconstruction efforts in Afghanistan, with India being the largest regional donor to the country. Since 2002, India has pledged up to $2 billion in economic assistance to Afghanistan and has participated in multiple socio-economic reconstruction efforts, including power, roads, agricultural and educational projects. There are also military ties between Afghanistan and India, which is expected to increase after the October 2011 strategic pact that was signed by President Karzai and Prime Minister Manmohan Singh.

The military of Afghanistan is under the Ministry of Defense, which includes the Afghan National Army and the Afghan Air Force. It currently has about 180,000 active soldiers and is expected to reach 260,000 in the coming years. They are trained and equipped by NATO countries, mainly by the United States Department of Defence. The ANA is divided into 7 major Corps, with the 201st Selab ("Flood") in Kabul being the main one. The ANA also has a commando brigade which was established in 2007. The National Military Academy of Afghanistan serves as the main educational institute for the militarymen of the country. A new $200 million Afghan Defence University (ADU) is under construction near the capital.

Crime and law enforcement

The National Directorate of Security (NDS) is the nation's domestic intelligence agency, which operates similar to that of the United States Department of Homeland Security (DHS) and has between 15,000 to 30,000 employees. The nation also has about 126,000 national police officers, with plans to recruit more so that the total number can reach 160,000.The Afghan National Police (ANP) is under the Ministry of the Interior, which is based in Kabul and headed by Bismillah Khan Mohammadi. The Afghan National Civil Order Police is the main branch of the Afghan National Police, which is divided into five Brigades and each one commanded by a Brigadier General. These brigades are stationed in Kabul, Gardez, Kandahar, Herat, and Mazar-i-Sharif. Every province of the country has a provincial Chief of Police who is appointed by the Ministry of the Interior and is responsible for law enforcement in all the districts within the province. The police are being trained by NATO countries through the Afghanistan Police Program. According to a 2009 news report, a large proportion of police officers are illiterate and are accused of demanding bribes. Jack Kem, deputy to the commander of NATO Training Mission Afghanistan and Combined Security Transition Command Afghanistan, stated that the literacy rate in the ANP will rise to over 50% by January 2012. What began as a voluntary literacy program became mandatory for basic police training in early 2011. Approximately 17 % of them test positive for illegal drug use. In 2009, President Karzai created two anti-corruption units within the Interior Ministry. Former Interior Minister Hanif Atmar said that security officials from the U.S. (FBI), Britain (Scotland Yard) and the European Union will train prosecutors in the unit.

The south and eastern parts of Afghanistan are the most dangerous due to the flourishing drug trade and militancy. These areas in particular are often patrolled by Taliban insurgents, and in many cases they plan attacks by using suicide bombers and planting improvised explosive devices (IEDs) on roads. Kidnapping and robberies are also often reported. Every year many Afghan police officers are killed in the line of duty in these areas. The Afghan Border Police are responsible for protecting the nation's airports and borders, especially the disputed Durand Line border which is often used by members of criminal organizations and terrorists for their illegal activities. Reports in 2011 suggested that up to 3 million people are involved in the illegal drug business in Afghanistan, many of the attacks on government employees and institutions are carried out not only by the Taliban militants but also by powerful criminal gangs. Drugs from Afghanistan are exported to Iran, Pakistan, Russia, India, the United Arab Emirate, and the European Union. The Afghan Ministry of Counter Narcotics is dealing with this problem.

Economy

Afghanistan is an impoverished and least developed country, one of the world's poorest due to the decades of war and nearly complete lack of foreign investment. The nation's GDPstands at about $27 billion with an exchange rate of $15 billion, and the GDP per capita is about $900. Its unemployment rate is 35% and roughly the same percentage of its citizens live below the poverty line. About 42 % of the population live on less than $1 a day, according to a 2009 report. On the positive side, the nation has a very lowexternal debt and is recovering by the assistance of the world community.

The Afghan economy has been growing at about 10% per year in the last decade, which is due to the infusion of over $50 billion dollars in international aid and remittances from Afghan expats. It is also due to improvements made to the transportation system and agricultural production, which is the backbone of the nation's economy. The country is known for producing some of the finest pomegranates, grapes, apricots, melons, and several other fresh and dry fruits, including nuts. While the nations's current account deficit is largely financed with the donor money, only a small portion is provided directly to the government budget. The rest is provided to non-budgetary expenditure and donor-designated projects through the United Nations system and non-governmental organizations. The Afghan Ministry of Finance is focusing on improved revenue collection and public sector expenditure discipline. For example, government revenues increased 31% to $1.7 billion from March 2010 to March 2011.

Da Afghanistan Bank serves as the central bank of the nation and the "Afghani" (AFN) is the national currency, with an exchange rate of about 47 Afghanis to 1 US dollar. Since 2003, over 16 new banks have opened in the country, including Afghanistan International Bank, Kabul Bank, Azizi Bank, Pashtany Bank, Standard Chartered Bank, First Micro Finance Bank, and others.

One of the main drivers for the current economic recovery is the return of over 5 million expatriates, who brought with them fresh energy, entrepreneurship and wealth-creating skills as well as much needed funds to start up businesses. For the first time since the 1970s, Afghans have involved themselves in construction, one of the largest industries in the country. Some of the major national construction projects include the $35 bn *New Kabul City* next to the capital, the *Ghazi Amanullah Khan City* near Jalalabad, and the *Aino Mena* in Kandahar. Similar development projects have also begun in Herat in the west, Mazar-e-Sharif in the north and in other cities.

In addition, a number of companies and small factories began operating in different parts of the country, which not only provide revenues to the government but also create new jobs. Improvements to the business-enabling environment have resulted in more than $1.5 billion intelecom investment and created more than 100,000 jobs since 2003. The Afghan rugsare becoming popular again and this gives many carpet dealers around the country to expand their business by hiring more workers.

Afghanistan is a member of SAARC, ECO and OIC. It is hoping to join SCO soon to develop closer economic ties with neighbouring and regional countries in the so-called *New Silk Road* trade project. Foreign Minister Zalmai Rassoul told the media in 2011 that his nation's "goal is to achieve an Afghan economy whose growth is based on trade, private enterprise and investment". Experts believe that this will revolutionize the economy of the region. Opium production in Afghanistan has soared to a record in 2007 with about 3 million people reported to be involved in the business but then declined significantly in the years following. The government started programs to help reduce cultivation of poppy, and by 2010 it was reported that 24 out of the 34 provinces were free from poppy grow.

Mining and energy

Michael O'Hanlon of the Brookings Institution explains that if Afghanistan generates about $10 bn per year from its mineral deposits, itsgross national product would double and provide long-term funding for Afghan security forces and other critical needs. The United States Geological Survey (USGS) estimated in 2006 that northern Afghanistan has an average 1.6 billion (bn) barrels (bbl) of crude oil, 15.7 trillion cubic feet (440 bn m^3) of natural gas, and 562 million bbl of natural gas liquids. In December 2011, Afghanistan signed an oil exploration contract with China National Petroleum Corporation (CNPC) for the development of three oil fields along the Amu Darya river in the north.

Other reports show that the country has huge amounts of lithium, copper, gold, coal, iron ore and other minerals.

TheKhanashin carbonatite in Helmand Province contains 1,000,000 metric tons (1,100,000 short tons) of rare earth elements. In 2007, a 30-year lease was granted for the Aynak copper mine to the China Metallurgical Group for $3 billion, making it the biggest foreign investment and private business venture in Afghanistan's history. The state-run Steel Authority of India won the mining rights to develop the huge Hajigak iron ore deposit in central Afghanistan. Government officials estimate that the country's untapped mineral deposits are worth between $900 bn and $3 trillion. One official asserted that "this will become the backbone of the Afghan economy" and a Pentagon memo stated that Afghanistan could become the "Saudi Arabia of lithium". In a 2011 news story, the *CSM* reported, "The United States and other Western nations that have borne the brunt of the cost of the Afghan war have been conspicuously absent from the bidding process on Afghanistan's mineral deposits, leaving it to mostly to regional powers."

Transport and communications

Afghanistan has about 53 airports, with the biggest ones being the Kabul International Airport, serving the capital and nearby regions followed Kandahar International Airport in the south, Herat International Airport in the west, and Mazar-i-Sharif Airport in the north. Ariana Afghan Airlines is the national carrier, with domestic flights between Kabul, Kandahar, Herat and Mazar-i-Sharif. International flights include to United Arab Emirate, Saudi Arabia, Germany, Turkey, India, Iran, Pakistan and a number of other Asian destinations.

There are also domestic and international flight services available from the locally owned Kam Air, Pamir Airways and Safi Airways. Airlines from a number of regional nations such asTurkish Airlines, Gulf Air, Air Arabia, Air India, PIA and others also provide services to Afghanistan. Flights between Dubai and Kabul take roughly 2 hours to reach.

The country has limited rail service with Uzbekistan and Turkmenistan in the north. The government plans to extended the rail line to the capital and then to the eastern border town of Torkham by 2014, connecting with Pakistan Railways. Long distant road journeys are made by older model company-owned Mercedes-Benz coach buses or carpool and private cars. Newer automobiles have recently become more widely available after the rebuilding of roads and highways. They are imported from the United Arab Emirates through Pakistan and Iran. As of 2012, vehicles that are older than 10 years are banned from being imported into the country. The development of the nation's road network is a major boost for the economy due to trade with neighbouring countries. Afghanistan's postal and package services such as FedEx, DHL and others make deliveries to major cities and towns.

Telecommunication services in the country are provided by Afghan Wireless, Etisalat, Roshan, MTN Group and Afghan Telecom. In 2006, the Afghan Ministry of Communications signed a $64.5 million agreement with ZTE for the establishment of a countrywide optical fibre cable network. As of 2011, Afghanistan has around 17 million GSM phone subscribers and over 1 million internet users. It only has about 75,000 fixed telephone lines and little over 190,000 CDMA subscribers.

Health

According to the Human Development Index, Afghanistan is the 15th least developed country in the world. The average life expectancy was estimated in 2012 to be 49.72 years.Afghanistan has the 9th highest total fertility rate in the world, at 5.64 children born/woman (according to 2012 estimates). Afghanistan has the highest maternal mortality rate in the world, estimated in 2008 at 1,400 deaths/100,000 live births, and the highest infant mortality rate in the world (deaths of babies under one year), estimated in 2012 to be 121.63 deaths/1,000 live births.

Data from 2010 suggests that one in 10 children in Afghanistan dies before they are five years old. While these statistics are tragic, the government plans to further cut the infant mortality rate to 400 for every 100,000 live births by 2020. The country currently has more than 3,000 midwives with an additional 300 to 400 being trained each year.

A number of new hospitals and clinics have been built over the last decade, with the most advanced treatments being available in Kabul. The French Medical Institute for Children and Indira

Gandhi Childrens Hospital in Kabul are the leading children's hospitals in the country. Some of the other main hospitals in Kabul include the 350-bed Jamhuriat Hospital and the Jinnah Hospital, which is still under construction. There are also a number of well-equipped military controlled hospitals in different regions of the country.

It was reported in 2006 that nearly 60% of the population lives within two hours walking distance of the nearest health facility, up from 9% in 2002. Latest surveys show that 57% of Afghans say they have good or very good access to clinics or hospitals. The nation also has one of the highest incidences of people with disabilities, with an estimated one million handicapped people. About 80,000 citizens have lost limbs, mainly as a result of landmines. Non-governmental charities such as Save the Children and Mahboba's Promise assist orphans in association with governmental structures. Demographic and Health Surveys is working with the Indian Institute of Health Management Research and others to conduct a survey in Afghanistan focusing on Maternal death, among other things.

Education

Education in the country includes K-12 and Higher Education, which is supervised by the Ministry of Education and Ministry of Higher Education. The nation's education system was destroyed due to the decades of war, but it began reviving after the Karzai administration came to power in late 2001. More than 5,000 schools were built or renovated, with more than 100,000 teachers being trained and recruited. It was reported in 2011 that more than seven million male and female students were enrolled in schools.

As of 2011, about 82,000 students are enrolled in different universities around the country. Kabul University reopened in 2002 to both male and female students. In 2006, the American University of Afghanistan was established in Kabul, with the aim of providing a world-class, English-language, co-educational learning environment in Afghanistan. The capital of Kabul serves as the learning center of Afghanistan, with many of the besteducational institutions being based there. Major universities outside of Kabul include Kandahar University in the south, Herat

University in the northwest, Balkh University in the north, Nangarhar University and Khost University in the eastern zones, as well as a number of others.

The National Military Academy of Afghanistan, modeled after the United States Military Academy at West Point, is a four-year military development institution dedicated to graduating officers for the Afghan armed forces. The $200 million Afghan Defence University is under construction near Qargha in Kabul. The United States is building six faculties of education and five provincial teacher training colleges around the country, two large secondary schools in Kabul and one school in Jalalabad.

Literacy rate of the entire population is low, around 28%. Female literacy may be as low as 10%. In 2010, the United States began establishing a number of Lincoln learning centers in Afghanistan.

They are set up to serve as programming platforms offering English language classes, library facilities, programming venues, Internet connectivity, educational and other counseling services. A goal of the program is to reach at least 4,000 Afghan citizens per month per location. The military and national police are also provided with mandatory literacy courses. In addition to this, Baghch-e-Simsim (based on the American Sesame Street) was launched in late 2011 to help Afghan children learn from preschool and onward.

Demographics

As of 2011, the population of Afghanistan is around 29,835,392, which includes the roughly 2 million Afghan refugees still living in Pakistan and Iran. In 1979, the population was reported to be about 15.5 million. The only city with over a million residents is its capital, Kabul. The other largest cities in the country are, in order of population size, Kandahar, Herat, Mazar-i-Sharif, Kunduz, Jalalabad, Lashkar Gah, Taloqan, Puli Khumri, Khost, Ghazni, Sheberghan, Sar-e Pol, and Farah. Urban areas are experiencing rapid population growth following the return of over 5 million expats. According to the Population Reference Bureau, the Afghan population is estimated to increase to 82 million by 2050.

POST-NATO AFGHANISTAN: IMPLICATIONS FOR REGIONAL SECURITY

Afghanistan is a land of extreme diversity. Fractured along various fault lines – geographic, ethnic, tribal, linguistic, and sectarian – it would not have emerged as a single unified state but for a "grand bargain" struck between its major communities. And that would not have happened without compelling reasons.

Arnold J. Toynbee, the famous British historian, described the territory that roughly covers today's Afghanistan as the "eastern crossroads of history." Indeed, the country lies at a junction of three distinct large regions: Central Asia, South Asia, and the Middle East (sometimes called 'West Asia'). Any venture into this vast area worth its while – invasion of the subcontinent, trade with China, attempts to gain access to the Indian Ocean or to the region's natural resources – would unmistakably involve Afghanistan. Whole civilizations have passed through it and armies have trampled over its territory. So the "grand bargain" came as the only way to ensure the territory's collective security. It was brokered in 1747 by Ahmed Shah Durrani, who has since been rightly called the "father of the nation."

Once unified, Afghanistan could no longer be controlled or dominated by foreign forces: they were unable to secure the grand consensus that formed the country, while that could be the only reason for making the Afghans agree to the occupation. Even before Afghanistan emerged as a state, three powerful Asian empires – the Uzbek Khanate, the Safavid Iran and the Mughal India – struggled vainly for influence in Afghanistan. After its creation, when two European powers – Britain and Russia – got engaged in the so-called "Great Game" for as long as the entire 19th century, the political astuteness of the Afghan emirs saved it as a buffer state. After NATO's withdrawal, this model may well appear to be most helpful for the Afghans seeking stability.

Afghanistan's stability as a function of a broad consensus is not just a wishful ideal. Its topography and demographic structure make it possible for the major factions – ethnic or tribal – to reign supreme in their chosen areas. Any of them not on board can make enough mischief to cause instability. That was exactly the reason for Pakistan's pleading for the formation of an interim government to be represented by all Afghan major factions in 1989 when the Soviet troops were to withdraw from Afghanistan. (The failure to do so eventually led to the civil war.) Now the same rationale stands behind the need to establish an intra-Afghan dialogue to work out modalities of the transfer of power before NATO forces leave the country.

REGIONAL CHALLENGES

Bringing all the major Afghan factions to the negotiating table is indeed a daunting task. The baggage of the past – especially of the period when the Taliban ruled the country – is one reason. More importantly, the Taliban, who in 2002 offered to cooperate with the Kabul regime but were denied any role as it believed that they no longer counted, are now a formidable force. Besides expanding their areas of influence and conducting some spectacular operations against heavily guarded targets, the Taliban presently receive money from NATO for safe passage of its convoys (which last year amounted to $150 million). But the most serious obstacle to starting a reconciliation process is Washington's plan to maintain a large combat presence in the country after 2014.

The Afghans (generally) and the Taliban (most certainly) would rail against this presence. Their neighbours, too, would prefer Afghanistan to be vacated at the earliest possible time. Pakistan is obviously a country most affected by the events in Afghanistan. Since many Afghans would resist the retention of foreign military bases, the frontier areas of Pakistan would remain in the war zone and a target of U.S. retaliation. Iran has its own valid reasons to be worried about the continued retention of American military assets in the region. Russia and China, too, are wary of this powerful extra-regional existence which could adversely affect the power game in this geo-strategic pivot. Due to the worsening relations with Pakistan, NATO is shifting its focus to the Northern Distribution Network to supply its troops in Afghanistan and to their eventual drawdown. Some of these concerns have become especially acute.

The Central Asian states, which are still in a state of flux after the breakup of the Soviet Union, will face an even more uncertain future after the withdrawal of foreign forces from Afghanistan. Their borders, drawn back in Stalin's time during their establishment as Soviet republics, severed traditional trading zones and settled areas. Stalin's idea was to split the region's Muslim ethnic groups and make them less of a threat to Moscow. Seeds of this ethnic divide began to sprout when these republics got independence while remaining within the unnatural borders. This situation made Zbigniew Brzezinski describe the region as a "hotbed of conflict" and the "Eurasian Balkans." While in the past the Central Asian countries were swept into the vortex of the Great Game between the British and the Russian empires, today they are being wooed by major powers seeking to gain influence and set up military bases there.

Tajikistan seems most vulnerable to any major change in the status quo. Facing a strong Islamic opposition, it seeks external help. As NATO is reducing its presence in the area, the fragile balance is likely to give way to fresh violence. Its Gorno-Badakhshan region, having only three percent of the country's population but spreading over forty-five percent of its territory, has cultural, religious and ethnic ties with the Afghan province of Badakhshan. It is virtually inaccessible and has traditionally served as a sanctuary for militants. Tajikistan's long border with Afghanistan, once patrolled by Russian troops, is too porous to be sealed. The main foreign countries vying for influence in Tajikistan are: Iran (which has strong cultural links with it), India (which is upgrading a former Soviet air base there), and China (which is trying to use economic incentives to reduce trans-border links between militant groups).

Kyrgyzstan is a country where both the U.S. and Russia have military presence. Washington uses the base at Manas to supply its troops in Afghanistan and has most of its tanker fleet stationed there. It pays the Kyrgyz government $60 million a year for this favor. Russia has a base near Bishkek that also maintains its 6,000 strong contingent in Tajikistan.

As for China, it has an agreement with Ashgabat under which Turkmenistan will supply Beijing with up to 40 billion cubic meters of gas in four years. Beijing shares Central Asia's fears of Islamist movements. To control its restless Muslim majority province of Xinjiang, it seeks help from the Central Asian neighbours. China also believes it has a vision for the future – the "New Silk Road" project which involves the construction of pipelines, highways from the region to its East Coast, and railway links from Beijing to Tashkent and on to Europe.

Furthermore, a declaration of intent for the construction of a giant pipeline through Afghanistan to Pakistan and India has been signed (although the plan will remain a pipedream until the security situation in the region becomes favorable).

And, of course, one should not forget that narco-trafficking routes controlled by the Islamists pass through Central Asia.

PRUDENT RESPONSE

The regional response to all the above challenges has been enhanced over the last decade.

The first to respond was probably the Shanghai Cooperation Organization (SCO). Established with the goal of fighting terrorism, it essentially aims to promote regional cooperation to counter the external ingress in the wake of the U.S.-led invasion of Afghanistan. It is evolving at a deliberate pace. In the meantime, some of the regional powers, such as Russia, China, Iran and Pakistan, are trying to coordinate their policies to cope with the fallout of the war in and around Afghanistan. This may eventually reinforce the SCO's objectives, but as of now these efforts seem to be taking their own course. Indo-Pakistani rapprochement, for example, is a strictly bilateral affair.

Relations between India and Pakistan have had their feel-good moments in the past, but never before did the two countries match their expressions of goodwill with such firm action. In early 2011, a major Indian military exercise close to the Pakistani border hardly made anyone in Pakistan raise an eyebrow. On a similar occasion in 1987, Islamabad mobilized for war. After dragging its feet for over a decade, rationale apart, Pakistan has eventually granted India the MFN status that is obligatory under the WTO. This move was followed up by a liberal trade and visa agreement. Soon after the murder of the former Afghan President, Burhan-ud-Din Rabbani, which produced plenty of ill-will against Pakistan in Kabul, Karzai visited Delhi and signed a "strategic agreement" providing for increased economic cooperation and India's assistance in training the Afghan military. In earlier times, it would have created uproar in Pakistan. Significantly, Pakistan has dropped its objections to India's participation in the second round of the Istanbul Process, indicating that it is now prepared to engage the "archrival" on Afghanistan in a regional setting.

India, on its part, no longer blames Pakistan for unrest in Kashmir or for that matter anywhere else in the country. Both countries have supported each other's candidature for the UNSC. They may still be reluctant to meaningfully cooperate on Afghanistan (even though a significant opinion in India is in favor of granting Pakistan the lead role), but the relationship has clearly turned a corner.

India's interests in the region are indeed not merely linked to its equation with Pakistan. It wants to compete with China to exploit Afghanistan's mineral resources and is planning to revive airstrips and military hospitals in Central Asia. Pakistan believes that India could legitimately pursue these projects.

The two South Asian countries have also improved their bilateral ties with Iran. In a joint operation, Pakistan and Iran decimated Jandullah, an anti-Iran militant group that used to operate from Pakistani Balochistan with America's help. After a five-year hiatus, India has revived cooperation with Iran, with Tehran reciprocating positively, despite Delhi's past support for the U.S.-led sanctions against the Mullah regime. Since India's improved relationship with Pakistan is still in a nascent phase, it seeks access to Afghanistan through Iran, but at the same time remains mindful of U.S. sensitivities.

There has been a remarkable turnaround in Russia's relations with Pakistan. Moscow firmly endorses the latter's full membership of the SCO, and has offered to help modernize the Karachi Steel Mills which uses Soviet technology of the 1970s. It has also pledged to support a project that would bring electricity from Tajikistan to Pakistan. Since the transmission lines are to run through the non-Pashtun areas of Afghanistan, the people there would have a stake in this relationship. It will be an important gesture to Tajikistan, as well.

The most significant step that the two countries have taken together is their clear stand on the U.S.-sponsored project nicknamed the "New Silk Road." Ostensibly, it is aimed at developing the region's economy with Afghanistan as the hub. However, the regional countries regard it as a ploy to perpetuate American influence, justify the retention of its military bases in the region, and diminish the role of Iran, China, and Russia. Except for the Kabul regime, no regional country supported the proposal when it was presented in Istanbul on November 7, 2011. China and India kept a low profile: the former firmly believing that the others would effectively scuttle it, and the latter fearing it could harm its relations with the U.S. India's "hedging" was no surprise to Russia, still a power with significant political clout. With Europe in the throes of a financial crisis, Russia, possessing some surplus cash, has a good chance to regain influence in the former Soviet states of Central Asia.

China's location and economic prowess provide it with probably the best cards in the game, and it seems to be playing them well. Its pipeline projects with Russia and investments in Afghanistan's infrastructure and minerals are on track. The sixty-billion-dollar trade with India effectively deters the latter from undertaking any "containment" role on behalf of the U.S. And it happily transports oil from Iran through the straits of Hormuz unmindful of the American armada or embargo. But indeed it is worried about the prospects of an open-ended American military presence in the region, which will continue to adversely affect China's strategic interests in Pakistan – developing and securing communications lines to the Indian Ocean and investments in the resource-rich province of Balochistan – and in due course threatens China's freedom of action in the region. (But of course, China keeps investing in the U.S. treasury bonds.)

The SCO, comprising Russia, China, and four of the five Central Asian states, is likely to grant India and Pakistan full membership, and has added Afghanistan as an observer and Turkey as a dialogue partner. It is indeed uniquely placed to provide a regional canopy under which India and Pakistan could work together on issues of regional security such as Afghanistan. The problem is that both India and Pakistan remain mindful of their relations with the U.S. and therefore tend to drag their feet on issues that might draw flak from Washington (a pipeline from Iran, for example). Moreover, along with Australia, Japan and South Korea, India is tempted to cooperate with NATO on the latter's ABM project. Of course, if India does that, it will adversely affect its standing in the region.

THE ENDGAME: PLAYING TOGETHER

Essentially, the policies and measures that the regional state and non-state actors have taken so far makes one believe that they will cope with any situation that might emerge. Since the outcome of Afghanistan's "endgame" is not clear, the Central Asian states, faced with many unresolved internal and external problems, are trying to clinch the best bargains available under the circumstances.

Yet to get the optimum benefits in the long term, the region can do better than that.

A few years after the Cold War ended, Strobe Talbott, an American academic, diplomat and an expert on Soviet affairs, wrote that a "new Great Game" could either be played together or by no one at all. Like Afghanistan, the broader region, too, cannot function without an overarching consensus. When there are too many actors who can throw a spanner in the works, nothing works till all or most of them are on board. Insurgents or saboteurs can only blow up pipelines; cross-alignments among competing centers of power may keep the region in turmoil for decades to come.

India and Pakistan may have changed camps after the Cold War – from East to West in case of the former and the other way around in case of the latter. The environment in the new great game is so complex that they still need help from each other. India has many advantages due to its size, economic clout and historical linkages with the region, but it cannot fully realize its potential unless Pakistan, which comes in the way, cooperates. Pakistan claims more leverage in Afghanistan, mainly because of its geography and role in helping the Afghan resistance during the last decades. Today it is facing the consequences of this policy both inside the country and on its western borders, and it needs India's help to keep the eastern front quiet. It seems both countries have just begun to extend the minimum essential relief.

Of course, there are many multilateral arrangements under which the countries of the region can cooperate and contribute towards a bigger objective. Besides their essentially useful bilateral relationship, India and Pakistan may be inching towards a quadrilateral framework to include Iran and Afghanistan. A Chinese strategist has proposed to form a Pamir Group comprising China, Afghanistan and Pakistan. The Collective Security Treaty Organization (CSTO), established to bring some of the former Soviet states together, may serve a similar, and perhaps even more useful, purpose. The SCO umbrella has an obvious advantage: it already has all the big regional players – Russia, China and even India – principally on board.

One goal towards which all of them can start working right away is the formation of a consensus government in Afghanistan. Besides ensuring security within the country (something no military force could, and the Afghan National Army can ever achieve), it would enable the country to make independent decisions in its relations with other nations. Afghanistan's policies during its "buffer" years provide a good example of delicate balancing without posing threats to any of its neighbours.

Playing together, as advised by Talbott, will definitely work for the region, but may place his home country at a disadvantage. The U.S. does not belong in the region, it no longer has money to invest, and in fair play its main rivals in the region – even in Europe – stand to gain more. However, it has enough hard power and global reach to act as a spoiler. Long time back, another American, Eisenhower, had warned that the U.S. military-industrial complex could keep the country in a state of perpetual war. A collective approach from within the region can thus be the panacea for many of its security woes.

TALIBAN ATTACKS ON SUPPLY LINES THROUGH PAKISTAN

In November and December 2008, there were multiple incidents of major theft, robbery, and arson attacks against NATO supply convoys in Pakistan. Transport companies south of Kabul have also been reported to pay protection money to the Taliban. In an attack on 11 November 2008, Taliban fighters in Peshawar hijacked a convoy carrying NATO supplies from Karachi to Afghanistan. The militants took two military Humvees and paraded them in front of the media as trophies.

The area east of the Khyber pass in Pakistan has seen very frequent attacks. Cargo trucks and Humvees have been set ablaze by Taliban militants. A half-dozen raids on depots with NATO supplies near Peshawar destroyed 300 cargo trucks and Humvees in December 2008. The Taliban destroyed an iron bridge on the highway between Peshawar and the Khyber pass in February 2009.

Coalition issues with Pakistan

An unnamed senior Pentagon official told the BBC that at some point between 12 July and 12 September 2008, President George W. Bush issued a classified order to authorize U.S. raids against militants in Pakistan. Pakistan however said it would not allow foreign forces onto its territory and that it would vigorously protect its sovereignty. In September, the Pakistan military stated that it had issued orders to "open fire" on American soldiers who crossed the Pakistan border in pursuit of militant forces.

On 25 September 2008, Pakistani troops shot towards ISAF helicopters, which belonged to American troops. This caused confusion and anger in the Pentagon, which asked for a full explanation into the incident, and they denied that American choppers were in Pakistani airspace. Pakistani President Asif Ali Zardari was quick to deny that shots were fired but instead insisted that the Pakistani troops shot flares to warn the Americans that they were in Pakistani airspace.

A further split occurred when American troops apparently landed on Pakistani soil to carry out an operation against militants in the Khyber Pakhtunkhwa Province but 'Pakistan reacted angrily to the action, saying 20 innocent villagers had been killed by US troops'. However, despite tensions between Pakistan and the U.S., the United States has continued to increase the use of remotely piloted drone aircraft in Pakistan's border regions, in particular the Federally Administered Tribal Regions (FATA) and Balochistan; as of early 2009, drone attacks were up 183% since 2006. By the end of 2008, the Taliban apparently had severed remaining ties with al-Qaeda. According to senior U.S. military intelligence officials, there are perhaps fewer than 100 members of al-Qaeda remaining in Afghanistan.

In a meeting with General McChrystal, Pakistani military officials urged international forces to keep their fight on the Afghan side of the border to prevent militants from fleeing into Pakistan. Pakistan noted that it has 140,000 Pakistani soldiers on its side of the border with Afghanistan to monitor and address militant activities, while the Coalition only has 100,000 soldiers to police the Afghanistan side of the border.

2009: Southern Afghanistan

In response to the increased risk of sending supplies through Pakistan, work began on the establishment of a Northern Distribution Network (NDN) through Russia and several Central Asian republics. Initial permission for the U.S. military to move troop supplies through the region was given on 20 January 2009, after a visit to the region by General Petraeus. The first shipment along the NDN route left on 20 February from Riga, Latvia, then traveled 3,212 miles (5,169 km) to the Uzbek town of Termez on the Afghanistan border. In addition to Riga, other European ports include Poti, Georgia and Vladivostok, Russia. U.S. commanders have stated their hope that 100 containers a day will be shipped along the NDN. By comparison, currently 140 containers a day are shipped through the Khyber Pass. By 2011, the NDN handled about 40% of Afghanistan-bound traffic, compared to 30% through Pakistan.

On 11 May 2009, Uzbekistan president Islam Karimov announced that the airport in Navoi, Uzbekistan was being used to transport non-lethal cargo into Afghanistan. Due to the still unsettled relationship between Uzbekistan and the United States following the 2005 Andijon massacre and subsequent expulsion of U.S. forces from Karshi-Khanabad airbase, U.S. forces were not involved in the shipment of supplies. Instead, South Korea's Korean Air, which is currently involved in overhauling Navoi's airport, officially handles logistics at the site. Originally only non-lethal resources were allowed on the NDN. In July 2009, however, shortly before a visit by President Obama to Moscow, Russian authorities announced that U.S. troops and weapons could use the country's airspace to reach Afghanistan.

Additionally, human rights advocates are concerned that the U.S. is again working with the government of Uzbekistan, which is often accused of violating human rights. Nevertheless, U.S. officials have promised increased cooperation with Uzbekistan, including further assistance to turn the Navoi airport into a major regional distribution center for both military and civilian ventures.

Azerbaijan, which has sent its peacekeeping forces to be a part of ISAF, also provided its airspace and airports for transportation of vital supplies for the U.S. Army in Afghanistan. Apart from usage of Azerbaijani airspace by U.S. Air Force, over one-third of all of the nonlethal equipment including fuel, clothing, and food used by the U.S. military in Afghanistan travels through Baku.

Increase in U.S. troops

In January, about 3,000 U.S. soldiers from the 3rd Brigade Combat Team of the 10th Mountain Division moved into the provinces of Logar and Wardak. Afghan Federal Guards also fought along with U.S. Troops. The troops were the first wave of an expected surge of reinforcements originally ordered by George W. Bush and increased by Barack Obama.

In mid-February, it was announced that 17,000 additional troops would be deployed to the country in two brigades and additional support troops; the2nd Marine Expeditionary Brigade of about 3,500 from the 7,000 Marines, and the 5th Brigade, 2nd Infantry Division, a Stryker Brigade with about 4,000 of the 7,000 U.S. Army soldiers. The U.S. commander in Afghanistan, General David McKiernan, had called for as many as 30,000 additional troops, effectively doubling the number of troops currently in the country.

On 23 September, NBC News reported that a classified assessment of the war in Afghanistan by General McChrystal included his conclusion that a successful counterinsurgency strategy would require 500,000 troops and five years of fighting.

In November, the U.S. ambassador in Kabul sent two classified cables to Washington expressing deep concerns about sending more U.S. troops to Afghanistan until President Hamid Karzai's government demonstrates that it is willing to tackle the corruption and mismanagement that has fueled the Taliban's rise. Ambassador Karl W. Eikenberry, a retired three-star general who in 2006–2007 commanded U.S. troops in Afghanistan, also expressed frustration with the relative paucity of funds set aside for spending on development and reconstruction in Afghanistan. In subsequent cables, Ambassador Eikenberry repeatedly cautioned that deploying sizable American reinforcements would result in "astronomical costs" – tens of billions of dollars – and would only deepen the dependence of the Afghan government on the United States.

On 26 November 2009, Afghan President Hamid Karzai made a public plea to the United States to engage in direct negotiations with the Taliban leadership. In an interview with CNN's Christiane Amanpour, Karzai said there is an "urgent need" for negotiations with the Taliban, and made it clear that the Obama administration had opposed such talks. There was no formal American response.

On 1 December 2009, President Barack Obama announced at The United States Military Academy in West Point that the U.S. will be sending 30,000 more troops to Afghanistan. Antiwar organizations in the United States responded quickly, and cities throughout the U.S. saw protests on 2 December in response. Many protesters compared the decision to deploy more troops in Afghanistan to the expansion of the Vietnam War under the Johnson administration.

Kunduz Province campaign

In April, German forces stepped up their efforts to retake some rebellious areas of Kunduz province, considered to be the most dangerous part of Northern Afghanistan by ISAF commander McChrystal. The fighting centres upon the areas to the west and south of the city of Kunduz with a main focus on an area between the town of Chahar Dara in the West and the Kunduz river in the east. Up to now this campaign consisted of several large offensives linked by countless skirmishes and gunfights. Operations of

German, Afghan, U.S., and Belgian troops were still ongoing as of December 2009. Insurgent militias suffered more than 650 casualties in this period. At least 86 coalition troops were wounded or killed. On 4 September, a devastating NATO air raid was conducted 7 kilometres to the southwest of Kunduz where Taliban fighters had hijacked civilian supply trucks, killing Up to 179 people including over 100 Afghan civilians.

Operation Khanjar and Operation Panther's Claw

We're doing this very differently. We're going to be with the people. We're not going to drive to work. We're going to walk to work. — Brig. Gen. Lawrence D. Nicholson, commander of the 2nd Marine Expeditionary Brigade, July 2, 2009.

On 25 June 2009, American officials announced the launch of Operation Khanjar ("strike of the sword").About 4000 U.S. Marines from the 2nd Marine Expeditionary Brigade and 650 Afghan soldiers are currently involved in Operation Khanjar, which will be staged on the Helmand River. Khanjar follows a British-led operation named Operation Panther's Claw in the same region. Officials call it the Marines' largest operation since the 2004 invasion of Fallujah, Iraq. Operation Panther's Claw was aimed to secure various canal and river crossings to establish a permanent International Security Assistance Force(ISAF) presence in the area.

Initially, Afghan and American soldiers have been moving into towns and villages along the Helmand River to secure the civilian population from the Taliban. The main objective of the operation is to push troops into insurgent strongholds along the river. A secondary aim was to bring security to the Helmand Valley in time for presidential elections, set to take place on 20 August. The first aggressive phase will last 36 hours, where the secondary aim will be achieved first.

Taliban's gains

According to a 22 December 2009, briefing by Major General Michael T. Flynn, the top U.S. intelligence officer in Afghanistan, "The Taliban retains required partnerships to sustain support, fuel legitimacy and bolster capacity." The 23-page briefing states that "Security incidents projected to be higher in 2010." Those incidents are already up by 300 percent since 2007 and by 60 percent since 2008, according to the briefing. NATO intelligence at the time also indicated that the Taliban had as many as 25,000 dedicated soldiers, almost as many as before 9/11 and more than in 2005. On 10 August 2009, Stanley McChrystal, the newly appointed U.S. commander in Afghanistan, said that the Taliban had gained the upper hand. In a continuation of the Taliban's usual strategy of summer offensives, the militants have aggressively spread their influence into the north and west Afghanistan, and stepped up their attack in an attempt to disrupt 20 August presidential polls. Calling the Taliban a "very aggressive enemy", he added that the U.S. strategy in the months to come is to stop their momentum and focusing on protecting and safeguarding the Afghan civilians, while also calling it "hard work".

The Taliban's claim of disrupting 20 August elections is largely disputed, claiming over 135 incidents of violence; media was asked to not report on any violent incidents, however, causing many outlets to hail the elections as a success, even though some estimates give the voter turn out as much less than the expected 70 percent. In southern Afghanistan where the Taliban holds the most sway, there was a low voter turnout and sporadic violence directed at voters and security personnel. The chief observer of the European Union election mission, General Philippe Morillon, said the election was "generally fair" but "not free".

Western groups and election observers had difficulty accessing the southern regions of Afghanistan, where at least 9 Afghan civilians and 14 security forces were killed in attacks intended to intimidate voters. The Taliban released a video days after the elections, filming just up the road between Kabul and Kandahar, a major route in Afghanistan on election day, stopping buses, cars, and asking to see their fingers. The video went on to showing ten men who had voted, being talked to by a Taliban militant, they went on to say they may pardon the voters because of the Holy month of Ramadan The Taliban also attacked towns with rockets and other means of indirect fire. Amid claims of widespread fraud, both of the top contenders, Hamid Karzai and Abdullah Abdullah, claimed victory in the election. Reports also suggest that the turnout was lower than the last election, and there are fears that a results dispute can turn violent, even though both candidates vowed not to incite violence in case of a loss.

After Karzai's alleged win of 54 per cent, which would prevent a run off with his rival, Abdullah Abdullah, over 400,000 votes had to be discounted for Karzai, and many more with hundreds of thousands of votes and polling ballots being accused of fraud. Making the real turnout of the elections much lower than the official numbers, many nations criticizing the elections as "free but not fair". In December, an attack on Forward Operating Base Chapman, used by the Central Intelligence Agency to gather information and to coordinate drone attacks against Taliban leaders, killed at least six CIA officers and was a major setback for the agency's operations in the region.

2010: American/British offensive and Afghan peace initiative

In January 2010, American officials said privately that the Pakistanis are reluctant to go after the Afghan Taliban and the Haqqani network because they see them as a future proxy against Indian interests in Afghanistan when the Americans leave. In their public statements U.S. officials had previously praised Pakistan's military effort against the militants during its offensive in South Waziristan in November 2009. Afghan President Hamid Karzai also started peace talks with Haqqani network groups in March 2010. Pakistan's President Asif Ali Zardari said that Pakistan has lost over 35 billion U.S. dollars during the previous eight years as a result of the fight against militancy. According to the Afghan government, approximately 900 Taliban were killed in operations conducted during 2010. Due to increased use of IEDs by insurgents there was a significant increase in the number of injured coalition soldiers, mainly Americans, losing one limb or more or suffering major injury to their genital and pelvic areas.

Peace Initiatives

In October 2008 Defence Secretary Gates asserted that a political settlement with the Taliban was the endgame for the Afghan conflict. "There has to be ultimately – and I'll underscore ultimately – reconciliation as part of a political outcome to this," Gates stated.

By 2010 peace efforts began. In early January, Taliban commanders held secret exploratory talks with a United Nations special envoy to discuss peace terms. Regional commanders on the Taliban's leadership council, the Quetta Shura, sought a meeting with the UN special representative in Afghanistan, Kai Eide, and it took place in Dubai on January 8. It was the first such meeting between the UN and senior members of the Taliban.

On 26 January 2010, at a major conference in London which brought together some 70 countries and organizations, Afghan President Hamid Karzai told world leaders that he intends to reach out to the top echelons of the Taliban within a few weeks with a peace initiative. Karzai set the framework for dialogue with Taliban leaders when he called on the group's leadership to take part in a "loya jirga" – or large assembly of elders – to initiate peace talks. Karzai also asked for creation of a new peacemaking organization, to be called the National Council for Peace, Reconciliation and Reintegration. Karzai's top adviser on the reconciliation process with the insurgents said that the country must learn to forgive the Taliban.

In March 2010, the Karzai government held preliminary talks with Hezb-i-Islami, who presented a plan which included the withdrawal of all foreign troops by the end of 2010. The Taliban declined to participate, saying "The Islamic Emirate has a clear position. We have said this many, many times. There will be no talks when there are foreign troops on Afghanistan's soil killing innocent Afghans on daily basis."

In July 2010, *The Guardian* newspaper reported that the campaign to "win hearts and minds" of Afghan civilians by U.S. troops has been proving more difficult than expected. One U.S. Army report read: "It seems to always be this way when we go there [to meet civilians]. No one wants anything to do with us." And a report on meeting up with school representatives mentioned students throwing rocks at soldiers and not welcoming their arrival, as has been reported on several occasions elsewhere.

In September 2010 General David Petraeus commented on the progress of peace talks to date, stating, "The prospect for reconciliation with senior Taliban leaders certainly looms out there...and there have been approaches at (a) very senior level that hold some promise."

Marja offensive

In early February Coalition and Afghan forces began highly visible plans for an offensive, codenamed Operation Moshtarak, on the Taliban stronghold near the village of Marja. It began on 13 February and, according to U.S. and Afghan officials, was the first operation where Afghan forces led the coalition. The offensive involves 15,000 US, British and Afghan troops. It is the biggest joint operation since the 2001 invasion that ousted the Taliban. The troops are fighting over an area of less than 100 square miles (260 km^2), with a population of 80,000.

Troop surge

Deployment of additional U.S. troops continued in early 2010, with 9,000 of the planned 30,000 in place before the end of March and another 18,000 expected by June, with the 101st Airborne Division as the main effort. The Pentagon anticipates that U.S. troops in Afghanistan will outnumber those in Iraq for the first time since 2003. The CIA, from a request by General McChrystal, the commander of NATO forces in Afghanistan, is planning to increase teams of operatives, including their elite paramilitary officers from Special Activities Division (SAD), with U.S. military special operations forces. This combination worked well in Iraq and is largely credited with the success of that surge. The CIA is also increasing its campaign using Hellfire missilestrikes on Al-Qaeda in Pakistan. The number of strikes in 2010, 115, more than doubled the 50 drone attacks that occurred in 2009.

The surge in troops also meant a sixfold increase in Special Forces operations. There were 700 air strikes in September 2010, alone versus 257 in all of 2009. From July 2010 to October 2010, 300 Taliban commanders and 800 foot soldiers were killed. Hundreds more insurgent leaders were killed or captured as 2010 came to a close. General David Petraeus characterized the damage Special Forces were inflicting on the insurgents this way: "We've got our teeth in the enemy's jugular now, and we're not going to let go."

The CIA created what would be called Counter-terrorism Pursuit Teams (CTPT) at the beginning of the war. This force grew to over 3,000 soldiers by 2010 and is considered one of the "best Afghan fighting forces". According to Woodward·book *Obama's War,* Firebase Lilley as one of the nerve centers for the covert war conducted by the CIA's SAD. These units have not only been highly effective in operations against the Taliban and al-Qaeda forces in Afghanistan, but have expanded their operations into Pakistan. They were also important factors in both the "counterterrorism plus" and the full "counterinsurgency" options discussed by the Obama administration in the December 2010 review.

Taliban offensive

The Taliban announced an offensive for the spring and launched several attacks against ISAF and Afghan government forces. Attacks include a car bomb against a NATO convoy in Kabul which killed 18 people including six NATO soldiers and separate attacks against two of the largest ISAF bases in Afghanistan, Bagram and Kandahar Air Bases. Overall, 2010 saw the most insurgent attacks of any year since the war began, peaking in September at more than 1,500. Insurgent operations increased "dramatically" in two-thirds of Afghan provinces.

Wikileaks disclosure

On 25 July 2010, the release of 391,832 classified documents from the Wikileaks organization was made public. The documents cover U.S. military incident and intelligence reports from January 2004 to December 2009. Some of these documents included sanitised, and "covered up", accounts of civilian casualties caused by Coalition Forces. The reports also included many references to other incidents involving civilian casualties like the Kunduz airstrike and Nangar Khel incident.

The leaked documents also contain reports of Pakistan collusion with the Taliban. According to *Der Spiegel,* "the documents clearly show that the Pakistani intelligence agency Inter-Services Intelligence (usually known as the ISI) is the most important accomplice the Taliban has outside of Afghanistan." *The New York*

Times was especially alarmed by the level of collusion with the Taliban, having concluded that Pakistan "allows representatives of its spy service to meet directly with the Taliban in secret strategy sessions to organize networks of militant groups that fight against American soldiers in Afghanistan, and even hatch plots to assassinate Afghan leaders." *The Guardian*, however, did not think there was "a convincing smoking gun" for complicity between Pakistan intelligence services and the Taliban.

Kandahar offensive

A U.S. and Afghan military offensive, called Operation Hamkari, focusing on the Afghan province of Kandahar was launched soon after the Muslim holiday of Ramadan, which ended September 10. The Kandahar offensive was originally planned to be launched during July, but was delayed for further preparations. The offensive did not begin as one specific operation, but rather a series of operations in Kandahar City and its surrounding districts throughout the late summer and fall in 2010. Places where operations were conducted included Malajat, Zhari, Arghandab and the Horn of Panjwayi. Operations conducted in 2010 is credited with putting severe pressure on insurgent operations and increasing security in some key areas such as in Panjwayi. Unlike operations of previous years, Operation Hamkari featured the extensive use of Afghan National Security Forces, including the Afghan Border Police (ABP), led by Spin Boldak ABP Commander Gen. Abdul Razziq.

Operation Bawaar was the Canadian aspect of the 2010 Kandahar offensive. It involved the hold and build in the district of Zangabad as well as the Ground Line of Communication (GLOC) project to Mushan – all in an area known as the Horn of Panjwai.

Pakistan and U.S. tensions

Tensions between Pakistan and the U.S. were heightened in late September after several Pakistan Frontier Corps soldiers were killed and wounded. The troops were attacked by a U.S. piloted aircraft that was pursuing Taliban forces near the Afghan-Pakistan border but for unknown reasons opened fire on two different Pakistan border posts. In retaliation for the strike, Pakistan closed the Torkham ground border crossing to NATO supply convoys for an unspecified period. This incident followed the recent release of a video allegedly showing uniformed Pakistan soldiers executing unarmed civilians. After the Torkham border closing, the Pakistani Taliban attacked the NATO convoys carrying supplies, killing several of the drivers and destroying around 100 tankers.

Raids on Taliban leaders

Beginning in May 2010 NATO special forces began to concentrate on surgical operations to capture or kill specific Taliban leaders. As of March 2011, according to the U.S. military, the operations had resulted in the capture or killing of more than 900 low and mid-level Taliban commanders. The effectiveness of the operations in defeating the Taliban was not yet known.

2011: U.S. AND NATO DRAWDOWN

Battle of Kandahar

The Battle of Kandahar was part of an offensive named after the Battle of Bad'r that took place on 13 March 624, between Medina and Mecca. The Battle followed an announcement, April 30, 2011, that Taliban would launch their Spring offensive throughout the country. On 7 May 2011, the Taliban launched a major offensive on Government buildings in Kandahar. Around 12:30 pm local time, the Taliban unleashed a major assault on government buildings throughout the city. The Taliban said their goal was to take control of Kandahar city. At least eight locations were attacked: the governor's compound, the mayor's office, the NDS headquarters, three police stations and two high schools.

The battle continued onto a second day, 8 May 2011. The BBC's Bilal Sarwary called it the worst attack in Kandahar province since the fall of the Taliban government in 2001, and a embarrassment for the Western-backed Afghan government.

Death of Osama bin Laden

On 1 May 2011, U.S. officials announced that al-Qaeda leader Osama bin Laden was killed in a Special Operation to kill or capture Osama Bin Laden, conducted by the CIA and United States Navy SEALs, in Pakistan. Crowds gathered outside the

White House in Washington, DC, chanting "USA, USA" after the news emerged, and President Barack Obama addressed the nation and the world from the East Room of the White House to tell the world of the operation.

Withdrawal

On 22 June, President Obama addressed the nation from the White House and announced that 10,000 troops would be withdrawn by the end of 2011 and an additional 23,000 troops will leave the country by the summer of 2012. After the withdrawn of 10,000 U.S. troops, only 80,000 left are participating in the war. In July 2011 Canada withdrew all of its combat troops, and has transitioned to a training role.

Following suit, other NATO countries announced reductions in troop numbers. The United Kingdom has stated that it will gradually start withdrawing some of its troops, however it has not yet specified numbers or dates. France has announced that it would withdraw roughly 1,000 soldiers by the end of 2012, with 3,000 soldiers remaining in Afghanistan at that point. Several hundreds would gradually come back at the end of 2011 and in the beginning of 2012, when the Afghan National Army takes control of the Surobi district. The remaining troops will continue to operate in Kapisa, and their complete withdrawal is expected by the end of 2014 or earlier if the security in this district is considered good enough.

Belgium announced they would withdraw half of their force starting January 2012. Norway announced it had started a withdrawal of its near 500 troops, and would be completely out of Afghanistan by 2014. Equally, the Spanish Prime Minister has announced the withdrawal of troops beginning in 2012 with a target of up to 40 percent of the current force withdrawing by the end of the first half of 2013, and complete withdrawal by 2014.

U.S. helicopter shot down

On 6 August 2011, Taliban fighters shot down a U.S. Chinook helicopter which caused the death of 30 U.S. Soldiers, including 17 Navy Seals who were part of the Naval Special Warfare Development Group (DEVGRU). It was the same unit who killed

Osama Bin Laden, although none of the deceased partook in the operation. Seven Afghan troops and one civilian interpreter were also killed.

ANA/Australian incidents

On 30 October 2011, an ANA soldier opened fire on Australian forces at a patrol base in northern Kandahar Province, shooting 11 people. This attack killed three Australian soldiers and an Afghan Army interpreter and severely wounded seven Australians. The ANA soldier responsible for the attack was killed during the gunfight. It was the bloodiest incident for Australian forces since 2001, and the worst for the ADF since the Vietnam war. The incident raised questions of Australia's commitment to the war in Afghanistan and if success with working alongside the ANA was even possible. The attack weakened trust between Australian and ANA forces and led to weapons being confiscated from some ANA elements for several days. The Australian Prime Minister Julia Gillard later reaffirmed her government's support for Australian involvement. A similar attack occurred just 10 days later on 9 November 2011, when an ANA soldier opened fire wounding three Australians and two Afghan soldiers before escaping.

2011 U.S.-NATO ATTACK IN PAKISTAN

On the Peak of Tensions after "Operation Neptune Spear", an accidental, direct attack on Pakistan's armed forces by ISAF forces occurred on 26 November 2011, killing 24 Pakistani soldiers. Pakistan blocked NATO supply and ordered Americans to leave Shamsi Airfield. NATO Secretary General Anders Fogh Rasmussen said the attack was 'tragic' and 'unintended'. "This (regret) is not good enough. We strongly condemn the attacks and reserve the right to take action," said DG ISPR Major General Athar Abbas, while speaking to the national and international media from abroad on Monday. "This could have serious consequences in the level and extent of our cooperation.

Coordinated attacks against Shiites civilians

A series of terrorist attacks in the Afghan cities Kabul, Kandahar and Mazar-i-Sharif killed 60 Shiite worshippers including many children and wounded an estimated 200 on the Day of Ashura on December 6, 2011. The highly coordinated attacks which nearly went off simultaneously were considered to be among the war's deadliest attacks against civilians. Lashkar-i-Jhangvi, a Pakistan-based Deobandi extremist group allied to al-Qaeda, claimed responsibility. Lashkar-i-Jhangvi is known for its systematic attacks against Shiites in Pakistan. According to the Washington Post and New York Times, the Pakistani Inter Services Intelligence (ISI) had ties to Lashkar-i-Jhangvi in the past. The Afghan Taliban, which were allied to Lashkar-i-Jhangvi in their fight against Afghanistan's anti-Taliban United Front in from 1996 to 2001, denied any role in the attacks.

2012: STRATEGIC AGREEMENT

Reformation of the United Front (Northern Alliance)

In late 2011 the National Front of Afghanistan (NFA) was created by Ahmad Zia Massoud,Abdul Rashid Dostum and Haji Mohammad Mohaqiq in what many analysts have described as a reformation of the military wing of the United Front (Northern Alliance) to oppose a return of the Taliban to power. Meanwhile, much of the political wing has reunited under theNational Coalition of Afghanistan led by Abdullah Abdullah becoming the main democratic opposition movement in the Afghan parliament. Former head of intelligence, Amrullah Saleh, has created a new movement, Basej-i Milli (Afghanistan Green Trend), with support among the youth mobilizing about 10,000 people in an anti-Taliban demonstration in the capital Kabul in May 2011.

In January 2012, the National Front of Afghanistan raised concerns about the possibility of a secretive and untransparent deal between the US, Pakistan and the Taliban during a widely publicized meeting in Berlin. U.S. Congressman Louie Gohmert wrote, "These leaders who fought with embedded Special Forces to initially defeat the Taliban represent over 60-percent of the Afghan people, yet are being entirely disregarded by the Obama and Karzai Administrations in negotiations." After the meeting with US congressmen in Berlin the National Front signed a joint declaration stating among other things:

"We firmly believe that any negotiation with the Taliban can only be acceptable, and therefore effective, if all parties to the conflict are involved in the process. The present form of discussions with the Taliban is flawed, as it excludes anti-Taliban Afghans. It must be recalled that the Taliban extremists and their Al-Qaeda supporters were defeated by Afghans resisting extremism with minimal human embedded support from the United States and International community.

The present negotiations with the Taliban fail to take into account the risks, sacrifices and legitimate interests of the Afghans who ended the brutal oppression of all Afghans. —National Front Berlin Statement, *January 2012*

High-profile U.S. military incidents

During the first four months of 2012 four incidents involving US troops occurred which were described by The Sydney Morning Herald as "a series of damaging incidents and disclosures involving American troops in Afghanistan." These incidents created fractures in the partnership between Afghanistan and the NATO troops operating in the country, raised the question wether discipline within U.S. troops is breaking down and strained the relations between Afghanistan and the United States. In the following sections these "high-profile U.S. military incidents in Afghanistan" are described.

Urination video

In January 2012 a video of US troops urinating on Taliban fighters was posted on YouTube and other websites. The video shows four men in U.S. Marine combat gear laughing and joking as theyurinate on what appear to be dead men somewhere in a rural part of Afghanistan. News sources describe the dead men as Taliban insurgents. The video caused outrage in Afghanistan, the Middle East and across the world. Officials from the United States Department of Defence have identified all four U.S. Marines in the video and launched a criminal investigation. The released video eroded, alongside with the burning of the Muslim holy book Koran by US troops and Panjwai shooting spree, relations between the United States and Afghanistan, has "cast American soldiers in the harshest possible light before the Afghan public" and "strongly motivated" an Afghan soldier to kill 4 French soldiers and wound 17 others in January 2012 after seeing the footage of "foreign soldiers urinating on Afghan corpses."

Afghan revolt for U.S. Koran burnings

On 22 February 2012, US troops at Bagram Base set fire to copies of the Muslim holy book Koran. Afghan forces working at the base reported this, resulting in outraged Afghans besieging Bagram AFB, raining it with petrol bombs and stones.

Large demonstrations also massed in Kabul, to which NATO security forces dispatched reinforcements in a bid to stop the violent demonstrations from spiraling out of control in the fiercely conservative Islamic Republic. The U.S. commander in Afghanistan, General John Allen publicly apologized and ordered an investigation.

On 24 February 2012, US President Barack Obama was forced to apologize over the mass burnings of Koran, to help stem the violent demonstrators. Furious Afghans attacked French, Norwegian and US bases, as thousands more besieged NATO bases at Mihtarlam and Kapisa. The Taliban exploited the anti-US sentiment by stating;

"You should bring the invading forces military bases under your brave attack, their military convoys, kill them, capture them, beat them, and teach them a lesson that they will never again dare to insult the Holy Koran."

After five days of protest which are continuing, 30 people have been killed, including four Americans. Over 200 people have been wounded.

In early April 2012 two investigations into the incident were completed. As of May 7, 2012 it is however unclear whether the ISAF commander General John Allen undertook actions against the in the incident involved U.S. military personnel. His options inluded to take no action, to recommend criminal charges or to issue written reprimands. No U.S. military persons, be it officers or enlisted personnel, have been disciplined as of April 19, 2012 for their roles in the incident according to The Atlantic magazine.

Panjwai shooting spree

On 11 March 2012, US Army Staff Sergeant Robert Bales allegedly left his base and killed 16 civilians inPanjwai District, Kandahar Province. Initially, about 300 local Afghans responded by protesting at the military base. Leaders demanded accountability. Shukria Barakzai, a member of parliament, said, "Afghan blood cannot be spilled in vain We really need a proper, very official court for that guy We really, really need it." The Taliban vowed revenge. American and ISAF forces have apologized and promised a full investigation, with Secretary of Defence Leon Panetta stating that the soldier "will be brought to justice and be held accountable," and that the death penalty "could be a consideration." Except US Army Staff Sergeant Robert Bales no U.S. military persons, be it officers or enlisted personnel, have been disciplined as of April 19, 2012 for their roles in the incident according to The Atlantic magazine.

Insurgents' bodies incident

The Insurgents' bodies incident is an incident involving US troops who posed with body parts of dead insurgents during the Afghanistan war.Concerns by the US military that the photos could provoke violent unrest in Afghanistan did not come true because the Afghan society holds suicide bombers in contempt.

4

Pakistan and Iran's Dysfunctional Relationship

Iranian president Mahmoud Ahmadinejad visited Pakistan as part of a whistle-stop tour of South Asia. The meeting was cordial but tense. While the two neighbours were once staunch Cold War allies, the Islamic Revolution, Afghanistan's civil war, and Pakistan's nuclear development have transformed the relationship into one of tense rivalry. As Afghanistan's stability has become a U.S. strategic concern, preventing Pakistan-Iran tensions from again transforming Afghanistan into a proxy battlefield should be a U.S. interest. Unfortunately, so long as the Iranian and Pakistani governments remain concerned with the defense of Shi'i and Sunni sectarian interests respectively, U.S. and NATO forces in Afghanistan may not be able to bring stability but at best may remain referees in a struggle that extends far beyond that country's borders.

A TROUBLED TRIANGLE

Pakistan and Iran are bound by cultural, tribal, and religious bonds. Pakistan gained its independence in 1947 at the beginning of the Cold War. Iran became the first state to recognize the new nation, and the two neighbours soon developed a strong partnership, signing a treaty of friendship in 1950. Some of this was geopolitical. Pakistan was born amidst great bloodshed and a transfer of population with India, a country with which Pakistan has territorial disputes to the present day. Pakistan found a natural partner in Iran after the Indian government chose to support Egyptian president Gamal Abdel Nasser who sought to export a pan-Arab ideology that threatened many Arab monarchies, a number of which were favored by the Iranian shah. Iran was a natural ally and model for Pakistan for other reasons as well. Both had majority Muslim populations but remained secular, centralized, and Western-oriented in practice. Both countries granted the other most-favored nation status for trade purposes; the shah offered Iranian oil and gas to Pakistan on generous terms, and the Iranian and Pakistani armies cooperated to suppress the rebel movement in Baluchistan.

Both countries also became major bulwarks of U.S. policy in the Middle East. Both were firm U.S. allies and members of the anti-Soviet Baghdad Pact. In 1971, however, the geopolitical situation began to shift. The withdrawal of British forces from the Persian Gulf left the United States to fill the vacuum, making Saudi Arabia far more important in U.S. strategic calculus. Pakistan's defeat in its 1971 war with India—and the loss of half its territory with Bangladesh's independence—led it to court China as a means to balance India. Pakistan also sought closer ties with the Arab states in order to isolate India, and thus weakened its ties to Iran, even though Islamabad-Tehran relations remained cordial.

The shah's fall in 1979 was a blow to Pakistan. Ayatollah Ruhollah Khomeini's anti-American posture worried the Pakistani authorities, as did the prospect of any export to Pakistan of Khomeini's radical views. After all, in 1979, perhaps 20 percent of Pakistan's population was Shi'i and, at the same time, Khomeini's religious rhetoric sparked radicalism across the sectarian divide. Nevertheless, Islamabad offered an olive branch to Tehran. Pakistan was among the first countries to recognize the new Islamic Republic and was among very few countries in the region that refrained from supporting Iraq during the Iran-Iraq war.

The 1979 Soviet invasion of Afghanistan brought the Soviet Union to Pakistan's doorstep, transforming the geostrategic environment further, all the more so given India's close ties to Moscow. For the United States, concerned about Soviet expansionism, Pakistan's importance rose. Ironically, Pakistan, Iran, and the United States all found themselves on the same side with regard to Afghanistan, even as Iran's revolutionary authorities continued to hold U.S. diplomats hostage. Though Iran was preoccupied with domestic turmoil and its war with Iraq in the 1980s, it supported the Afghan resistance and provided limited financial and military assistance to groups who supported the Iranian vision of revolutionary Islam.

Meanwhile, Pakistan emerged as the frontline state in the U.S. struggle to expel the Soviets from Afghanistan. Here, the Pakistani military regime under General Zia ul-Haq did try to coordinate with the Islamic Republic but, in practice, Islamabad cooperated much more fully with Saudi Arabia, which bankrolled Pakistani military programs.

Pakistan became the transit point for weapons and aid to Saudi-funded, U.S.-equipped, and Pakistani-trained mujahideen who fought to drive the Red Army from Afghanistan. Pakistani authorities, however, put a filter on the aid. The loss of Bangladesh—formerly East Pakistan—in 1971 had led the Pakistani leadership to be very wary of ethnic nationalism. Pashtun nationalism in Afghanistan had challenged Pakistani cohesion for as long as Bengali nationalism. The Pakistani government, therefore, only allowed aid to flow to those groups who rallied around a sectarian rather than a nationalist identity.

The Iranian authorities, in contrast, miscalculated. While generous with aid to their allies, they had far fewer resources at their disposal because of the ongoing war of attrition with Iraq. That aid which Iranian officials could provide, they limited largely to Shi'i and ethnic Persian-speaking Tajik groups. This transformed a potential Afghanistan-wide influence into a far more localized interest. Nor, in contrast to the actions of the Pakistani leadership, did Iranian authorities properly cultivate or manage their population of Afghan refugees in order to spread their influence.

Tehran did not want to cede the advantage to Islamabad, though, and continued to fight for influence in Afghanistan, even as the Pakistani- and Saudi-backed Taliban consolidated control over 90 percent of the country. This proxy fight, however, polarized Afghanistan and brewed further Pakistan-Iran mistrust.

In August 1998, after an incident in which the Taliban sacked an Iranian consulate in Mazar-i-Sharif and murdered six Iranian diplomats and some agents, the Iranian military massed some seventy thousand troops on their border with Afghanistan and blamed Pakistan, claiming that Pakistan had assured the safety of their diplomats. Iranian president Mohammad Khatami, however, helped walk Iran back from the brink of war as he sought to thaw relations between Iran and both the United States and the Taliban.

The 9-11 terrorist attacks on the United States changed the foreign policy priorities of both Iran and Pakistan. The George W. Bush administration's tough stance forced president Pervez Musharraf to support Washington's "war on terror," which ended Taliban rule in Kabul. Though Iranian officials welcomed the move, they soon found themselves encircled by U.S. forces in Pakistan, Afghanistan, Central Asia, and the Persian Gulf. President Bush's inclusion of the Islamic Republic as part of an "Axis of Evil" also led some Iranian officials to presume that Tehran might be next in line for regime change and ended whatever détente had occurred in U.S.-Iranian ties under Khatami. Bush's emphasis on transformative diplomacy and democratization worried Iranian leaders further.

Tehran and Islamabad sought to improve bilateral relations after the Taliban's 2001 fall. Iran supported the Bonn agreement which, under U.N. auspices, brought prominent Afghans together to plan for the future governance of their war-ravaged nation. In December 2002, Iran signed the Kabul Declaration on Good Neighborly Relations along with Pakistan and other regional states. Khatami visited Islamabad in December 2002, the first visit by an Iranian head of state since 1992. Iran has tried to project itself as a responsible regional actor since the fall of the Taliban in 2001, urging the Afghan Northern Alliance to accept the Bonn agreement for the formation of a new broad-based government in Kabul and offering aid and loans as well as training Afghan soldiers. It is investing in construction projects in the western parts of Afghanistan, building roads, rail links, and border posts. It played a major role in restarting the post-Taliban political process in Afghanistan and has pledged $560 million in aid and loans to Afghanistan. However, other interests are also at play as Iran supports conservative Shi'i religious schools and warlords and is increasing its intelligence activities across Afghanistan. Iran has viewed itself traditionally as the guarantor of the security of Afghanistan's Shi'a.

However, the situation in Afghanistan continued to overshadow the relationship. Tehran moved promptly to establish diplomatic ties with Hamid Karzai's new government. Iranian authorities supported Karzai's attempts to exert authority over the entire territory of Afghanistan, encouraging the Hazara, for example, to support Karzai, despite his Pashtun background. Tehran's links to Ismail Khan, the former Herat governor, were especially strong. However, Iranian officials supported the U.S. and Afghan central government's efforts to subordinate Khan—who acted as Iran's proxy in Afghanistan—to Kabul's authority.

SOFT AND HARD POWER IN THE AFGHANISTAN RIVALRY

While Karzai's government is nominally supported by both Tehran and Islamabad, neither neighbor has been willing to sacrifice its own interests. With time, tension has increased. Iran retains its special interests in Afghanistan's western Herat region, until 1857 part of Iran, and Pakistan considers the Pashto-speaking southern sections of Afghanistan to be within its sphere of influence. Kabul remains a contested area within that sphere. The deterioration in Afghan security, perhaps sparked by one or both, has also created a dynamic of increasing tension between Iran and Pakistan. Increasingly, as a perception of U.S. weakness spreads, Iran has raised its rhetoric against the presence of U.S. and NATO troops in Afghanistan, which Islamabad nominally supports, at least publicly. Tehran continues to blame the U.S. presence in Afghanistan for continuing instability in the region.

Both Iran and Pakistan have adopted strategies of using soft power influence to provide cover for their more traditional hard power approach vis-à-vis Afghanistan. Though Musharraf committed Pakistan to support efforts to stabilize Afghanistan after the fall of the Taliban and agreed to strengthen the Karzai administration, doubts remain as to Islamabad's capacity and commitment to crack down on terrorists and militants. Kabul is suspicious of Pakistan, on whom its security largely depends. Pakistan's Inter-Services Intelligence (ISI) agency has long supported the Taliban and has aided its resurgence. The rejuvenation of the Taliban bolsters Pakistan's role as a frontline state in the war on terrorism, securing often lucrative assistance from the United States. The ISI and Pakistani military elite also see Pakistan as engaged in a proxy war for influence in Afghanistan. The Taliban may be a concern to both Kabul and Washington, but Islamabad is more willing to tolerate jihadist violence so long as it is focused outward on Afghanistan, Kashmir, or other parts of India. The brazen terror assault on Mumbai in November 2008 that has increased tensions between the two nuclear armed states in the subcontinent is just the latest case of Islamabad continuing to direct Islamist extremism towards its neighbours.

Iran, meanwhile, has taken a multi-pronged approach towards Afghanistan, focusing its economic, social, and educational efforts on the western provinces of Herat, Farah, and Nimruz, perhaps to seek a zone of influence in western Afghanistan and to prevent the West and the Karzai administration from adopting a coherent, countrywide strategy. While Iran has focused its development aid on portions of Afghanistan it considers its near-abroad, Tehran has learned a political lesson from the past and now cooperates with any Afghan group, regardless of sect and language, so long as they oppose the U.S. presence in Afghanistan. The perception that Pakistan and the United States would gain an upper hand in the evolving political environment in Afghanistan has pushed Iran into charting a proactive course towards its eastern neighbor. Iran's strategy toward Afghanistan seems geared toward hastening the withdrawal of U.S. forces, preventing the Taliban from regaining power, and trying to keep Afghanistan under Tehran's sway.

As a result of this policy, some Iranian groups appear to have reached out to the Taliban. U.S. and NATO forces have repeatedly intercepted shipments of Iranian weaponry to the Taliban. The Taliban are already using Iranian-made improvised explosive devices (IEDs) as well as heat seeking missiles and rifles to deadly effect against Western forces. Though the Iranian government has denied any such involvement, sections of the Iranian establishment, in particular the Quds Force, are seen as behind such moves. Several media reports from Afghanistan suggest that Iran has been increasing its operations in Afghanistan in an effort to gain influence with the contending insurgent factions and to hasten the departure of U.S. troops from the country. Growing tensions between Afghanistan and Pakistan are also working to Iran's advantage with Kabul increasingly dependent on Tehran for its transit trade routes. The Karzai government cannot pick fights with both its vital neighbours and so tries to keep Iran in good humor. While Washington maintains that Iran is funneling weapons into Afghanistan, the Afghan government continues to say that Iran is a close friend and ally.

Will a Pakistani-Iranian Rivalry Erupt?

There is little common ground between Iran and Pakistan on a solution to the Afghan crisis, and history may repeat itself with both states once again funding proxy wars between Shi'a and Sunnis in each other's countries as well as in Afghanistan, increasing the likelihood of a major sectarian explosion in the region.

Communities of some five million Baluch tribesmen stretch across southwestern Pakistan and southeastern Iran. Baluchis on both sides of the border feel neglected, on sectarian grounds in Iran and on ethnic grounds in Pakistan, and nationalist sentiments have long simmered, sometimes erupting into open insurrection. While the shah helped the Pakistani army crush Baluch insurgencies in the days prior to his ouster, today insurgency has again erupted with both Pakistani and Iranian officials accusing each other of aiding the insurgents. Tehran has also repeatedly accused the U.S. Special Forces of using their bases in Pakistan to pursue undercover operations inside Iran designed to foment Baluch opposition to the Islamic regime. In June 2008, Jundallah terrorists, an insurgent Baluchi group operating from Pakistan, kidnapped sixteen members of Iran's paramilitary Law Enforcement Forces (*niru-ye entezami*) and, over the course of months, executed all of their hostages. Tehran blames the Pakistani government for sheltering the group even though Pakistan has also declared Jundallah to be a terrorist organization and, on occasion, Pakistani troops have killed Jundallah terrorists.

Sectarian tension has also complicated relations. In the 1980s, several radical groups sponsored by Pakistani intelligence began a systematic assault on Shi'i symbols and mosques in Pakistan. Pakistani Shi'a, with Iranian assistance, responded by forming their own militias. The continued targeting by Sunni terrorists of Pakistani Shi'a remains an Iranian concern. This Shi'i-Sunni strife in Pakistan has provoked Iran to provide clandestine support to its co-religionists there.

However, Pakistan and Iran have worked to improve security cooperation. In 2001, the two states established the Pakistan-Iran Joint Ministerial Commission on Security to enhance cooperation on security issues such as terrorism, drug trafficking, and sectarian violence. Top Iranian political and intelligence officials regularly engage their Pakistani counterparts, but engagement does not necessarily equate to trust.

The nuclear issue also complicates Pakistani-Iranian ties. Pakistani and Western officials sometimes say that Pakistani nuclear scientist Abdul Qadir Khan operated outside the law when he provided assistance to Tehran's nuclear weapons program; however, evidence also suggests that the Pakistani military was not only aware of Khan's nuclear transactions with Iran but also tacitly approved of his activities. Nevertheless, there remains a sense of rivalry between Islamabad and Tehran on the nuclear issue, given Pakistan's unique position as the sole Muslim country with the bomb. Interestingly, one of the drivers of Iran's nuclear weapons ambitions is fear of a "Sunni bomb." Rumors of an oil-for-nukes pact between Riyadh and Islamabad have exacerbated such concerns.

An Economic Solution?

Is it possible to ameliorate Iran-Pakistan ties to prevent the development of a dynamic that will undercut Afghan security and, by extension, the safety and security of U.S. and NATO troops present in that country? Here, economics may provide a solution. Trade between Pakistan and Iran remains in the range of $500 million, and both governments hope to double it. Absent much trade, however, political and security tensions will continue to exercise a negative effect on ties.

It is in this context that the impetus comes for the so-called "peace pipeline" that would transport Iranian gas to Pakistan and onward to India. Should the pipeline project come into operation, then trade will become the defining feature of Iran-Pakistan ties. Rising energy demand in both India and Pakistan, at least until the 2008 worldwide recession struck, have led both to consider collaborating on a gas pipeline from Iranian fields through Pakistan to India. Such a pipeline might in theory create mutual economic interests and bring Islamabad perhaps $500 million annually in royalties. However, there has been little progress, largely because of disagreements about pricing and the methods to be used to supply gas to India. India and Iran signed the $22 billion deal in 2005 before Mahmoud Ahmadinejad assumed the presidency and while the crude oil price was low. India considers the pricing deal final while Iranian officials have sought an upward revision in price, arguing that the contract is not valid until the Iranian Supreme Economic Council ratifies it. There are also differences between the national oil companies of Iran and India over the legal interpretation of the contract for the export of five million tons of liquefied natural gas to India.

Both India and Pakistan have contended that Tehran should offer a price for gas in line with global practices for long-term contracts and have rejected Iran's gas pricing formula, whereby the gas price is linked to Brent crude oil with a fixed escalating cost component. The Indian government also argues that it should only pay for gas upon delivery, and opposes Tehran's demand for price revision every three years. The three states decided by consensus to refer the matter to an independent consultant, but Tehran continued to maintain that the consultant's opinion should not be binding, causing tensions among the three parties. As with many pipeline projects, the bickering has led to much recrimination but little construction. Other points of contention include Pakistan's costs for security and transit and U.S. government opposition to any investment in an Iranian project, alongside Iranian worries that tensions between Pakistan and India could disrupt operations and undermine economic viability.

Conclusion

Notwithstanding some tentative recent attempts by Pakistan and Iran to improve their bilateral ties, the two countries' relationship remains strained. Rather than bringing the two states together, the situation in Afghanistan has provided a stage where their rivalry is once again played out. Though the vacuum resulting from the fall of the Taliban government is the main factor behind the rising turmoil in Afghanistan, the problem there also remains a regional one. The more the United States and its NATO allies fail to secure Afghanistan, the more neighbouring states will revive their ties to ethnic and ideological proxies, creating a dynamic that will further undermine Afghanistan.

While both Pakistan and Iran seem to have concluded that a stable, independent, and economically strong Afghan state is preferable to a weak and troubled one, they remain very sensitive to their relative gains vis-à-vis each other.

Regardless of who runs Afghanistan, Tehran's and Islamabad's conflicting interests over Afghanistan have played a pivotal role in the formation of their foreign policies toward each other. Afghanistan's predicament is a difficult one. The country may like to enhance its links with its neighbouring states, yet, peace and stability will continue to elude it so long as its neighbours view it through the lenses of their regional rivalries and as a chessboard on which to play out the game of their regional power and influence.

In many ways, it is a paradox. The situation in Afghanistan can only improve if Tehran and Islamabad revise their attitudes, but any deterioration in Afghanistan's security situation will instead compound suspicions and force them to prioritize their own security interests in a way which intensifies regional rivalries.

Iran will only play a positive role in Afghanistan if it feels its vital interests are not under threat, and a deteriorating security environment in Afghanistan will only make Iran feel more vulnerable, forcing it to take steps to safeguard its interests, letting the conflict spiral further.

Pakistan, meanwhile, is reluctant to cede the preeminent position it has enjoyed for the last several decades in determining Afghanistan's political trajectory. And as the security environment in Afghanistan deteriorates further, Islamabad will view this as an opportunity to maintain its presence in its neighbor's territory in order to secure its larger strategic interests.

By no means does this suggest that the United States or its NATO allies should abandon Afghanistan. However, U.S. policymakers should recognize that they are not the only players in the sand box nor that their struggle to stabilize the Karzai regime and battle the Taliban is the only fight going on in the country. Indeed, until there is fundamental change in either Tehran or Islamabad, Afghanistan will remain a crossroad if not for armies, then for their proxies.

Harsh V. Pant is a lecturer in the defense studies department at King's College London and an associate at the King's Center for Science and Security Studies.

IRAN AND PAKISTAN – IT'S COMPLICATED

The recent kidnapping of 5 Iranian soldiers serving along Iran's border with Pakistan, and their subsequent alleged captivity in Pakistani territory has shed light on the complex relationship between the two states. With western media analysis firmly focused on continued negotiations over Iran's nuclear programme and Pakistan's internal troubles, there is little written about the relations between the two neighbours who share a 900km border running through the heart of the Baluchi cultural region. This is a relationship that contains myriad complexities and the potential for conflict and cooperation, ranging from tackling Baluchi separatism and drug trafficking to pipeline politics, Afghanistan and the ever present spectre of US and Saudi interests in the Middle East and beyond.

Despite the complexities, relations have been good up until now, showing the pragmatism of both states and the importance both place on the relationship. However, the recent comments of Iranian Interior Minister Abdolreza Rahmani Fazli, who has threatened unilateral action inside Pakistani territory as a means of maintaining Iran's security and that of its soldiers serving along the border, demonstrate the potential for a rupture and the necessity for pragmatism to prevail.

HISTORICAL BACKDROP

Iran and Pakistan have maintained formal diplomatic relations since the latter's independence, with Iran being the first state to recognise Pakistan's independence in 1947. Relations remained positive throughout the 50s and 60s with both states falling under the US defence umbrella as signatories to the Baghdad Pact and subsequent creation of CENTO.

The Iranian revolution in 1979 coincided with the strengthening of the nominally Islamist Zia ul-Haq regime in Pakistan and the two sides maintained a practical working relationship despite the anti-US stance of the new government in the Islamic Republic. Both states cooperate in shared multi-lateral initiatives, such as the Economic Cooperation Organisation, Non-Aligned Movement and D8 group of developing nations, and share a number of joint regional concerns as highlighted below.

Baluchi separatists

The issue of Baluchi separatism is a good starting point in light of recent events in the region. The Baluchi ethnic group are split between Iran, Afghanistan and Pakistan, and there has been separatist agitation resulting in open conflict several times in Pakistan's history since independence. In Iran, Baluchi separatists have been less prominent historically, but armed groups have stepped up attacks in the last 10 years. The armed group Junduallah carried out several attacks on Iranian forces stationed in Iran's Sistan-Baluchistan province from 2004, prior to their leader Abdolmalek Rigi being captured and executed by Iran in 2010.

The capture of Iranian border guards earlier this month, along with the killing of 14 Iranian soldiers in November, was claimed by the hitherto little known group Jaish ul-Adl, formed in January 2012. In keeping with the previous statements of Jundullah, their actions are framed within the wider sectarian divide that is resurgent across the Middle East. Claims of discrimination against Sunni groups within Iran are often given as a pretext for the actions of groups such as Jaish ul-Adl as a means of garnering wider support.

Iran has frequently raised concerns with harbouring of Jundullah and Jaish ul-Adl militants on Pakistani territory, and it is within this context that recent Iranian comments regarding unilateral actions across the border to maintain its security have been made. Despite the potential for conflict, the subsequent talks held between Iranian and Pakistani representatives since the kidnappings have been largely cordial, with a focus on joint measures aimed at securing the hostages' release and further cooperation in enhancing the security of the border region. Iranian unilateral action will most likely be held off providing they receive assurances from Pakistan that they are taking the matter seriously. At this time, the Iranian government has been assured by its Pakistani counterparts that they are taking the matter seriously and that troops will be sent by Pakistan to Baluchistan to search for the hostages.

Sectarianism

This brings us to the sensitive issue of sectarianism and its place in relations between Iran and Pakistan. The Islamic Republic has historically favoured a pragmatic quiescence on sectarian tensions within Pakistan, seeing it as a domestic issue. This should come as no great surprise to Iran watchers, as despite the media focus on its patronage of Hezbollah in Lebanon and attempts to depict the avowedly secular Assad regime in Syria as 'co-religionists,' Iran has displayed pragmatism on a number of issues that defy its image as a revolutionary actor supporting its Shi'i brethren. Its support for Christian Armenia over predominantly Shi'i Azerbaijan in their conflict over the disputed Nagorno-Karabakh region (in part an outcome of the need to dampen potential separatist agitation amongst its own Azeri population) is a case in point.

Furthermore, Pakistan's Shi'i community is not involved in any notable separatist agitation, and thus Iran has been able to build on its confessional linkages in a more benign manner, primarily through its cultural centres and the work of the Islamic Culture and Research Organisation (ICRO). The ICRO runs Iran's cultural bureaus abroad, and is directly accountable to the Supreme Leader, thus providing a useful diplomatic tool and an extension of Iranian soft power right from the most important centre of power in the Iranian political system.

It's worth noting that Pakistan is home to the largest number of Iranian cultural bureaus in the world, with 8 centres in total run by the ICRO, providing cultural activities such as Persian language classes, religious commemorations and joint activities with Pakistani cultural organisations. Persian culture, particularly in art and literature, has a strong tradition in Pakistan, and the cultural links between the nations are an oft-repeated theme returned to time and again in official meetings between the two states.

Afghanistan

On Afghanistan, there has long been potential for disagreement as both sides have supported different sides in that state's protracted internal conflict.

Iran has long provided material support to the often persecuted Shi'i Hazara minority in Afghanistan, and was a key ally, along with Russia, of the Northern Alliance in its fight against the Pakistan-backed Taliban prior to the arrival of coalition forces in 2001.

Despite this, there is not any sense of any kind of war by proxy being fought here and both states are served far better by a stable Afghanistan, particularly in light of the huge number of refugees that they have both absorbed over the last 35 years.

Although they have historically backed different sides, the arrival of coalition forces and Pakistan's ongoing internal struggle with its own Taliban wing in the form of the TTP has necessitated a shift in its direct patronage of the Afghan Taliban.

Since the Taliban's ouster in Afghanistan, the Islamic Republic has gradually increased its influence in the country, particularly in the East and North which are culturally and linguistically proximate to Iran. Furthermore, while Iran-Afghan relations have been broadly positive, the Karzai government has had a tricky relationship with Pakistan in light of its links with the Taliban regime. Thus, any incorporation of moderate Taliban elements in a future Afghan government may well serve Pakistan's interests. To this end, accommodation through recognition of informal spheres of influence could serve relations between Iran and Pakistan well, with the latter extending its influence to Afghanistan's Pashtun heartlands as a means of enhancing control over its porous frontier with that country.

PIPELINE POLITICS

A further feature of Iran-Pakistan relations has been the long-running negotiations taking place over Iran's supplying of natural gas to Pakistan. The pipeline was initially billed as the 'peace pipeline' as it was due to transport Iranian natural gas to India, via Pakistan. However, negotiations predictably floundered, and Iran has focused instead on pursuing bi-lateral initiatives with each state in terms of providing access to its hydrocarbon resources. The Iran-Pakistan pipeline was signed off in 2009, with construction on the Iranian side now largely complete; however, the project has been beset by delays on the Pakistani side. A key concern is that this would mean Pakistani circumvention of the US-led sanctions regime against Iran, which would further complicate its already difficult current relationship with the United States. Keen to increase its export market, Iran had also offered to provide funding for the construction of the pipeline in Pakistan but had to withdraw this offer due to its own financial problems.

Both sides had recently been looking at ways to revive the stalled project, but Pakistan has now stated that it cannot continue with its side of the deal due to the sanctions currently in place against the Islamic Republic. For the time being, Pakistan has decided that the likely penalties for not complying with the sanctions regime outweigh access to Iran's natural gas. The current PML-N government in Pakistan also has particularly close relations with Saudi Arabia, which many feel has exerted pressure on Pakistan to abandon the project. This is where the current nuclear negotiations between Iran and the P5+1 become influential – if a deal is struck whereby sanctions are lifted, then Pakistan will have greater freedom to act, and may be less inclined to follow the advice of its Saudi allies.

Wider geopolitics

The last point takes us to the wider geopolitical currents that also have a bearing on relations between Iran and Pakistan, particularly in light of the US and Saudi positions. Although there was a noticeable détente in Iran's relations with Saudi Arabia under Rafsanjani and into the Khatami era, relations between the two states have dipped considerably in recent years. This is not only due to the recent entrenchment of the sectarian divide in the Middle East, and subsequent proxy battles for control among competing belligerents in its myriad conflicts, but also a result of increased Iranian confidence in its position in the region following the fall of two hostile neighbouring regimes in the form of Saddam's Iraq and Taliban Afghanistan. Pakistan-Saudi relations have been traditionally close, however, this has not significantly hampered relations thus far with Iran (the pipeline issue notwithstanding).

Indeed, Pakistan sees itself as something of a mediator between the two, and has given Iran assurances that it will not assist in Saudi nuclear arms development. Similarly, Iran's good relations with India are not a hugely destabilising force in the Iran-Pakistan relationship. Iran has trod a careful line on Kashmir, offering rhetorical support for the Muslim population there but little more as it desires good relations with India. Both sides therefore have potential bargaining chips, but pragmatism has prevailed.

Pakistan's at times troubled relationship with US, while a significant influence as noted above vis-à-vis the pipeline issue, has also been largely put to one side in dealings between the two states, with the focus being primarily on bi-lateral and regional concerns. Interestingly, the domestic unpopularity of Pakistan's historical alignment with US foreign policy objectives is borne out by the high esteem with which the Pakistani population holds the Islamic Republic. A 2013 global attitudes survey conducted by Pew saw 69% of Pakistanis surveyed as viewing Iran favourably, with Indonesia the only other country to record a majority holding a favourable view of the Islamic Republic with 55%.

A COMPLEX RELATIONSHIP WHERE COMMON-SENSE PREVAILS

The above points to a relationship that is fraught with potential difficulties and open to manipulation of competing agendas. Both states are, perhaps sometimes unfairly, painted as problem cases in the international system with powerful internal tendencies (be they official or unofficial) that seek to challenge the international status-quo. This, along with the above external and internal pressures makes the continued common-sense approach of both governments laudable at a time when opposing views, be they religious/sectarian in nature, or security-driven are sustaining some of the world's bitterest conflicts.

The relationship between the two states is founded on a pragmatic need to maintain a working relationship despite differing security alignments, more pressing concerns within their own 'regions,' and a lack of ideological confluence. Yes, there will always be competing pressures but the relationship has been largely characterised by tactful diplomacy when bellicosity could easily prevail. Despite the firm statements coming from Iran with regards to the recent kidnappings and Pakistan's responsibility for ensuring the soldiers' safe return, both sides have sought to work together on this issue. Furthermore, the recent upturn in the trajectory of Iran's relations with the West, although still dependent on a mutually agreeable outcome of the nuclear talks, will also help keep ties on a sound footing.

PAKISTAN-IRAN FOREIGN RELATIONS

In June 2009, the Pakistani government officially congratulated Iranian President Mahmoud Ahmadinejad on his re-election. Pakistani President Asif Ali Zardari stated that the electoral victory was a "an acknowledgment of [Ahmadinejad's] outstanding services." Allama Sajid Naqvi, the head of Tehrik-e-Islami, said that the results of the election demonstrate that Ahmadinejad enjoys the trust and support of the Iranian people and expressed hope that Iran and Pakistan will enjoy an increasingly strong bond in the future. Tehri-e-Islami is a Shia political party in Pakistan that the former Pakistani President Pervez Musharraf twice banned for ties to terrorism.

Nuclear

Pakistan has publicly defended Iran's right to nuclear technology. Some American analysts also suspect Pakistani scientists employed by the Pakistani military of helping Iran acquire nuclear technology, although Pakistan officially denies any involvement. Henry Sokolski, former deputy for nonproliferation policy in the Office of the Secretary of Defense, explained in 2003 that "the notion that Pakistan wasn't involved is getting less and less tenable." Since then, inspectors have found in Iran's possession documents from Pakistani scientist Dr. A.Q. Khan detailing how to shape uranium for nuclear warheads, while in 2004 then-Pakistani President Pervez Musharraf officially pardoned Dr. Khan for his sale of nuclear technology. According to a report by the Congressional Research Service published in 2005, Dr. Khan "could not have functioned without some level of cooperation by Pakistani military personnel, who maintained tight security around the key nuclear facilities, and possibly civilian officials as well." On March 15, 2010, Pakistan rejected a US media report asserting that Khan provided nuclear related information and material, including drawings, centrifuge components, and a list of suppliers, to Iran. Abdul Basit, a spokesman for the Pakistani Foreign Office, described the claims, published by the Washington Post, as "yet another repackaging of fiction, which surface occasionally for purposes that are self-evident."

Over the past several years, Pakistan has increasingly called for peaceful reconciliation on the international nuclear standoff, despite increasing concern from the UN and Washington.

In a February 2010 meeting with her Iranian counterpart, Pakistani National Assembly Speaker Fahmida Mirza said that "Pakistan is against any kinds of sanctions against Iran and believes that Iran's nuclear disputes should be resolved peacefully and through dialogue." In a separate meeting with Iranian President Mahmoud Ahmadinejad, Mirza reiterated her earlier remarks and assured him that Pakistan supports Iran's independence and progress in all the areas, especially in utilizing peaceful nuclear energy. She also highlighted Iranian-Pakistani commonalities in religion, history, and culture, and added that extremism and terrorism is a common threat to the stability and progress of the entire region.

Economic Relationship

The two countries initiated significant cooperation in the energy sector in 1991, when Iran began negotiating an oil deal with Pakistan and Qatar. This initial collaboration, however, was limited and did not progress meaningfully. Iran again attempted negotiating with Qatar regarding the construction of gas pipelines to Pakistan in

1995, however was unsuccessful. Cooperation regarding energy has nonetheless increased since the 1990s and helped provide the foundation for a more thorough bilateral trade network between Iran and Pakistan in recent years. By 2005, Pakistan was actively seeking Iranian investment in bilateral trade and energy cooperation. Pakistan and Iran have deepened their economic partnership to such an extent that, in a joint statement issued in May 2010, the two countries expressed satisfaction with an increase in bilateral trade, which surpassed $1.2 billion in the previous financial year. In 2009, Pakistan increased its non-oil exports to Iran by 80 percent, reaching $279 million. Similarly, Iranian non-oil exports to Pakistan increased by 11 percent, totaling $278 million for the year. Despite this growth, Karachi Chambeer of Commerce and Industry President Abdul Majid Haji Mohammad said the lack of a banking system remains a major obstacle to Iran-Pakistan trade.

Since 2005, Islamabad has increasingly turned to Tehran to supply Pakistan's growing energy needs. In August 2008, Iran agreed to finance a robust energy project that would allow Pakistan to import 1,000 megawatts of electricity to overcome its power shortage. The project, a $60 million endeavor, consists of running a 100-kilometer electric line to help augment the 40 megawatts of electricity Pakistan already receives daily from Iran. In April 2010, Iranian Ambassador to Pakistan Mashallah Shakeri spoke before the Rawalpindi Chamber of Commerce and Industry, stressing Iran's commitment to economic relations with Pakistan. According to the envoy, Iran intends to supply the 1,000 megawatts to Pakistan at a discounted rate.

Iran and Pakistan have long discussed the construction of a 2,600-kilometer, $7.5 billion Iran-Pakistan-India gas pipeline (IPI) that would pump gas from Iran's South Pars field to Pakistan and India. Tentative talks on the pipeline began in 1994, however tense political relations between India and Pakistan frustrated realization of the project. International concern over Iran's nuclear program further delayed agreement and in November 2007 Iran and Pakistan accused India of hesitating because of pressure from the United States. In February 2010, Iranian Foreign Minister Manouchehr Mottaki accused the US of interfering with the planned pipeline by attempting to sway New Delhi away from the IPI. Indeed, Washington has repeatedly urged India not to follow through with the deal while Iran faces sanctions for its nuclear enrichment program. Both Russia and China have taken significant interest in the pipeline, with Russia's Gazprom offering to help supply oil and China holding talks with Iran and Pakistan in 2008 to replace India in case New Delhi chose to reject the partnership.

In May 2009, Iran and Pakistan signed a purchase agreement stipulating that Iran will initially transfer 30 million cubic meters of gas to Pakistan per day, with the volume eventually increasing to 60 million. The deal, to which India was not a party, ensures gas supplies to Pakistan for a period of 25 years. On June 13, 2010, the two sides formally concluded the $7.5 billion agreement over the objections of US Special Representative for Pakistan and Afghanistan Richard Holbrooke, who cautioned that although the "US understands that Pakistan faces [a] major energy crisis... new sanctions on Iran can impact Pakistan." According to a previous Pakistani Petroleum Ministry statement in May 2010, "the capital cost for the Pakistan section is estimated at 1.65 billion dollars…[and] the first gas flow is targeted by end 2014" with Iran completing the project ahead of schedule.

During a July 30, 2009 interview with the Iranian Islamic Republic News Agency, Dr. Ashfaq Hassan Khan, a former economic advisor in Pakistan, insisted that while economic ties between Iran and Pakistan should expand at all levels, cooperation in the energy sector is vital for Pakistan. Khan further expressed his view that the planned Iran-Pakistan pipeline would likely greatly benefit both countries.

Iran-Pakistan cooperation on transportation issues expanded greatly in August 2009, when the two inaugurated an international freight rail line from Islamabad to Istanbul via Tehran. The line is a "pilot project" of the Economic Cooperation Organization (ECO), a Central Asian trade bloc. Although Iran and Turkey already enjoy extensive rail cooperation, transportation ties with Pakistan are weaker. According to Director of Pakistan Railways Shafiqullah Khan, Islamabad and Tehran are seeking outside credit to resolve differences in rail gauge in order to regularize rail service between the two. Officials expect to begin regular freight service along the 6,500 km line in August 2010.

In February 2010, Punjab Chief Minister Muhammad Shahbaz Sharif called for the creation of an economic free-trade zone among Pakistan, Iran, Turkey and other Islamic countries. During a celebration of the 31st Revolution Day of Iran, Sharif noted that "deep, friendly relations exist between Pakistan and Iran and it is the need of the hour that socio-economic cooperation should be promoted."

Iranian and Pakistani officials, in February 2010, signed the first memorandum of understanding (MoU) between the two countries on cross border trade. The MoU was penned during the two countries' first joint committee meeting on border trade in Iran's southeastern Sistan and Balouchestan province. Iraj Hassanpour, the head of Sistan and Balouchestan's trade organization, stated that "[b]ased on [the] MoU, [the] two countries are bound to hold public and specialized fairs at their common borders and in [the] capital of Sistan & Balouchestan province, Zahedan, and Quetta in Pakistan." Both sides also decided to establish large storehouses to facilitate the storage of trade commodities at their border customs.

Sardar Muhammad Latif Khan Khosa, a Pakistani advisor to the prime minister on information technology, has called for increased collaboration between Iran and Pakistan in telecommunications. During a June 2010 conversation with Iran's ambassador to Pakistan, Mashallah Shakeri, Khosa expressed his belief that increased bilateral activity in the sector has the potential to increase regional economic development and security.

DIPLOMATIC/MILITARY RELATIONSHIP:

Iran has developed deep economic and political ties with Pakistan, an ally of the United States and a nuclear neighbor. In 2007, the Prime Minister of Pakistan, Shaukat Aziz, said that Pakistan shares extensive ties with Iran "based upon faith, belief, joint history and culture. Expansion of cooperation in the fields of trade and investment can further strengthen the bilateral ties." Iran and Pakistan cooperate in a number of trade groups and agreed in June 2008 on a list of 300 tradable items in an effort to stimulate economic relations. Iran is active in the Economic Cooperation Organization (ECO)—a trade and investment group that includes all of the central Asian countries, founded by Iran, Turkey and Pakistan. Additionally, both Iran and Pakistan also hold observer status in the Shanghai Cooperation Organization (SCO)—an Asian regional economic and security group. China and Russia are reportedly considering inviting Iran and Pakistan to full membership in the SCO so as to participate in resolving the conflict in Afghanistan. "In the current global context, the top priority is finding a solution to the Afghan issue," Secretary-General Muratbek Sansyzbayevich Imanaliev said during a news conference in Beijing in February 2010.

Pakistan has helped encourage trilateral trade with Iran and Turkey in commercial goods and development of infrastructure beyond the programs administered by regional organizations such as the ECO.

Iran has involved itself in the political and military instability in Pakistan's Afghan and Iran border regions. In June 2009, the Iranian Embassy in Pakistan donated $250,000 as humanitarian aid for Pakistan's unstable Swat province. In a statement, the embassy said that "Iran denounces terrorist acts in Pakistan's northern areas and announces its readiness to renew support for peace and stability in Pakistan." In July 2009, Iranian Ambassador to Pakistan Mashaallah Shakeri called on the Pakistani government to secure the release of Heshmatollah Attarzadeh Niyaki, an Iranian diplomat kidnapped by gunman in Peshawar in 2008. While speaking before the Iranian parliament in July 2009, Iranian Foreign Minister Manouchehr Mottaki stated that he believed "that the current situations [in western Pakistan] are improving...criminal acts [have been] reduced and controlled in [the] last year." Mottaki further indicated that Iran had received a good degree of cooperation from the Pakistani government in implementing new security measures on the border.

Speaking in July 2009, Former Interior Minister and Chairman of the Pakistan People's Party Sherpao Aftab Ahmad Khan Sherpao praised an Iraqi security forces raid on a People's Mujahedin of

Iran camp located north of Baghdad. Iranian authorities reacted warmly to news of the raid, which targeted a militant Iranian exile group hostile to the Islamic Republic. Sherpao explained his support for the raid by stating that no country should permit its territory to be used for hostile acts against another sovereign state. He further added that "Iran is our brotherly country and we always want Iran to prosper."

In August 2009, Iran took part in a meeting of the "Friends of Democratic Pakistan." During the summit, which was held in Turkey and largely focused on the security situation in Pakistan, Foreign Minister Mottaki discussed the importance of bilateral ties with his Pakistani counterpart, Shah Mahmood Qureshi. The two also spoke about the need to combat terrorism and establish stability in Pakistan, with Mottaki adding that he considers Pakistan-Iran-Afghanistan relations to be an "appropriate model" for regional conflict resolution.

The two countries' 'brotherly' relations were threatened in October 2009 following attacks against the Iranian Islamic Revolutionary Guard Corps (IRGÑ) in Sistan-Baluchistan province. President Ahmadinejad publically accused "certain officials in Pakistan" of involvement in the attacks. Tehran further demanded the extradition of Abdolmalek Rigi, the chief of suspected terrorist group Jundallah. Pakistani officials denied any involvement in the attacks, rejecting Iranian Interior Minister Mostafa Mohammad Najjar's accusation that Jundallah received financial aid from Pakistan. Pakistan subsequently released 11 Iranian security officers accused of illegally crossing the border. Pakistani President Asif Ali Zardari met with Najjar in Islamabad a week after the attacks. Zardari stated that the attackers "were the enemies of both countries" and vowed to cooperate with Iran in their capture. At the beginning of November 2009, however, the IRGC accused Pakistan of releasing the leader of Jundallah immediately before the October 18 bombing in Sistan-Baluchistan, thereby implicating the Pakistani government in the attacks. According to the deputy head of the IRGC, Brigadier General Hossein Salami, the Jundallah leader, Abdolmakel Rigi, "was arrested on September 26 in Pakistan's Baluchistan province. But he was released after an hour with the intervention of the Pakistani intelligence service." In March 2010, upon receiving assurances from Islamabad that authorities would take measures to improve security in the area, Iran reopened its border with Pakistan. Iran had closed the border to trade four months prior in response to the October IRGC attack.

Deputy Foreign Minister of Iran Hassan Qashqavi said in January 2010 that the Pakistani government should take serious measures to stem terrorist activities across the border of the two countries. According to the minister, "the Pakistani government is expected to live up to its promises and take more serious measures to stem the terrorist and evil activities."

The same month, an Iranian Foreign Ministry official claimed there is a hidden agenda behind the recent destabilizing measures on Iran's eastern borders with Pakistan and Afghanistan.

On January 16, 2010, officials from Pakistan, Afghanistan, and Iran met to discuss regional security and terrorism, agreeing on a joint framework for cooperation in tackling political volatility in the area. The three agreed that regional stability and security could only be advanced through sincere adherence to the principle of national sovereignty and territorial integrity. Pakistani Foreign Minister Shah Mehmood Qureshi stated that "it is important to consult amongst ourselves so that we are on the same page and we have closer positions on different issues that confront our neighborhood." A joint declaration from the meeting called for Pakistan, Afghanistan, and Iran to coordinate efforts to combat extremism as well as drug and weapons smuggling. The ministers also raised Iranian concerns regarding the expanded presence of US forces in Afghanistan. A day after the meeting, the Iranian ambassador to Pakistan, Mashallah Shakeri, announced that the third Iran-Afghanistan-Pakistan summit will be held in Tehran in the near future.

In January 2010, Iranian First Vice-President Mohammad Reza Rahimi insisted that Iran considers durable security and stability in Pakistan to be of paramount importance to Iranian interests. Referencing recent efforts by Tehran to establish sustainable security in Pakistan, Rahimi stated that "Iran believes that comprehensive expansion of ties with Pakistan plays a major role in materializing the interests of the two countries and the region." He called for the fortification of the Iran and Pakistan's common borders and added that "terrorist groups should not be allowed to disturb security of the two countries' border regions."

During the first Meeting of the Heads of Interpol of the Economic Cooperation Organization, held on June 29, 2010, Interior Minister Nijjar urged the association's members to collaborate more closely on security issues. The minister proposed the creation of a regional police headquarters and encouraged more rapid sharing of information on criminal investigations.

Ambassador Shakeri has said that Iran is determined to continue its involvement in Pakistani development despite ever-increasing security challenges.

In a February 2010 message commemorating the 31st anniversary of the victory of the Islamic Revolution in Iran, the ambassador noted that "Pakistan, in its capacity as a Muslim neighbor, has a special status in the macro-strategy of the foreign policy of Iran, with durable security, stability and all-round development of Pakistan being Iran's desire."

During a six-day visit to Iran in February 2010, Pakistani National Assembly Speaker Fahmida Mirza met with Iranian President Mahmoud Ahmadinejad, Parliament Speaker Ali Larijani, and Foreign Minister Manouchehr Mottaki.

Mirza and Larijani issued a joint statement calling for the expansion of ties between Pakistan and Iran in the political, economic, and cultural spheres.

Iran and Pakistan also agreed to increase their parliamentary cooperation on global issues at international bodies. In addition, the two countries underlined the need to adopt a comprehensive political approach in the campaigns against terrorism, drug trafficking, and organized crime.

During an April 2010 appearance before the Rawalpindi Chamber of Commerce and Industry, Iranian Ambassador Shakeri reaffirmed his country's commitment to aiding Pakistan deal with its internal turmoil, saying that "Iran is fully aware of the problems currently facing Pakistan and our prime goal is to bring Pakistan out of the prevailing crisis."

According to a May 2010 joint statement following a meeting between Deputy Foreign Minister of Iran Seyed Ameer Mansoor Borghei'e and Pakistani Foreign Minister Shah Mehmood Qureshi, Iran and Pakistan support efforts by Afghan President Hamid Karzai to achieve national reconciliation in his country. The two countries further agreed to continue cooperate to help and achieve sustainable peace in Afghanistan.

On May 4, 2010, Pakistan's Senate Chairman Farooq Naek stressed the importance of parliamentary relations during a meeting with Iran's acting deputy foreign minister, Amir Mansour Borqaei. The two sides spoke of the possibility of exchanging parliamentary delegations and lauded the two countries' history of friendly relations.

5

Pakistan and Iran in Afghanistan

FROM SOVIET INTERVENTION TO THE FALL OF TALIBAN

It is the most important current issue which establishes the brotherly relationship between the three traditional friends, and neighbouring Muslim Countries, Iran, Afghanistan and Pakistan, which are connected with each other by close geographical proximity, common heritage and deep socio-cultural and ethno-linguistic affinities. All these factors have made Iran and Pakistan an eternal and enduring friends since the emergence of Pakistan in 1947. The paper analyzes their common interests and similar policies on various regional and international issues. But Pakistan's relation with its North-Western neighbor, Afghanistan remained at lowest ebb since its inception. This chapter discusses the Pakhtoonistan issue which proved an irritating factor in Pak-Afghan relations.

This chapter further highlights their common concerns and policies regarding the Soviet intervention in Afghanistan and its grave implication on both Pakistan and Iran. Their different geo-strategic perception and contradictory policies regarding Afghanistan since the Soviet's withdrawal also form the part of the paper. The paper mainly concentrates on the emergence of Taliban in Afghanistan which proves a suicidal factor in Pak-Iran relations. In addition, their conflicting interests and varying views and their support for the opposite factions in Afghanistan made them a virtual rivals, and strong competitors. And above all, the change in Pakistan's policy towards Taliban since 9//11 provided both the countries with an opportunity to mend their differences and to accommodate each other's interest in Afghanistan. The paper primarily focuses on the policy convergence of these two countries (Pakistan and Iran) in Afghanistan and the considerable improvement in their bilateral mutual relationship in the period cited above.

Research Method

An analytical method is used to determine the nature and significance of the various statements made by the public authorities of the two countries. In this respect, various issues, events and developments may be analyzed concerning the policies of the two countries (Pakistan and Iran) in Afghanistan. Moreover, the underlying factors have been examined and analyzed which resulted convergence and divergence in their mutual relationship and the pursuit of interests in Afghanistan.

HISTORICAL BACKGROUND

Since ancient period, Iran, Afghanistan and the areas now called Pakistan have been tied in a strong bond of friendship. Before Nadir Shah's Rule, Afghanistan was not an independent country with a present geographical status. Southern Afghanistan was the part of Iranian Province of Khurasan. Even before the advent of western imperialism in the 17th century, boundaries between Iran, Sub-continent and Afghanistan were loosely demarcated, and the demographic movements were quite frequent. Cultural, social traditional and religious bonds connected the people of these three countries. Over centuries, the relations between Iran and the areas now famed Pakistan are rooted in the same moral valves and common ideals of Islam, which provides the foundation of continued and perpetual cooperation between the two countries. Gandahara what may be described in modern times as Peshawar Valley including the district of Swat, Buner and extending up to Taxilla was the part of Iran. Active commercial relations between Iran and the Indo-Pak Sub-continent started during the time of Abbasid period which reached its zenith during the Mughal rule in India.

Iran, Afghanistan and Pakistan were the part of the historical Silk Route which provides trade route to the regional states, especially, the Central Asian States. The historical pattern of migration, market integration and interdependence of local communities and their trans-border networks have significance beyond the calculus of national interest. With the introduction of contemporary diplomatic system, which commenced after the World War-II, the three regions (Iran, Afghanistan and Indo-Pak Sub-continent) have revived their historical relations.

But Pakistan's relations with Iran became more strengthened and consolidated since its independence, in 1947. Shared geographical proximity, common history, and deep socio-cultural affinities were the numerous factors that brought these two countries close to each other. Iran was the first country which recognized Pakistan after its independence in 1947 and supported Pakistan's entry into United Nations. Diplomatic relations were established between the two countries when the Government of Pakistan appointed its first ambassador Raja Gazanfar Ali Khan to Iran in May, 1948. The first treaty of friendship and cooperation was signed between the two countries in February 19, 1950, providing for a good neighborly relations and for a most favored nation treatment between the two countries. From the very start of their relationship, the convergence of interests, common approaches and mutual understanding on most on the regional and international issues have made these countries a permanent friends, allies and partners. Collaboration with Iran is essential to Pakistan's defense strategy because Pakistan lacks depth and the only country which has provided depth was Iran. Friendship with Iran greatly enhanced Pakistan's position both at the regional and global level, and made stronger politically, diplomatically and militarily vis-à-vis it's over ambitious adversary, India.

But Pakistan's relations with Afghanistan have not been cordial in spite of the geographical contiguity, common religion, and same cultural and economic interests. It is the Pakhtoonistan issue—a legacy of the colonial role in Asia—that provides us a basis for understanding the strained relations between the two Muslim states. Afghanistan was the only country which voted against Pakistan's admission in the United Nation on the plea that it did not recognize NWFP as the integral part of Pakistan.

The relations between the two countries became tense on this issue that in 1949 the Afghan National Assembly passed a resolution repudiating all treaties, conventions and agreements concluded between Afghanistan and British India, thus rejecting the Durand Line formally.

In November 1955, the Afghanistan Grand National Assembly adopted a resolution stipulating the non-recognition of Pakhtoon territories as the part of Pakistan. Dr. Syed Salahuddin in his book, *The Foreign Policy of Pakistan, A Critical Analysis*, has remarked that the relations between Pakistan and Afghanistan became so tense and worse on this issue that in 1960 Pakistani Embassy in Kabul and Consulate in Qandahar, and Jalalabad were attacked and Pakistan's flag was molested.

In response, Pakistan imposed trade embargo on Afghan goods in the checkered history of the states.

Friendship of Iran proved constructive due to the mediation of Shah of Iran, who succeeded normalizing relations between the two countries, when he visited Islamabad and Kabul in June-July 1962, which was accepted the President of Pakistan Ayub Khan. Shah's good offices produced good and positive results when, in May-1963, trade relations between these two countries (Pakistan and Afghanistan) were restored.

Again Shah's effort brought positive results when he was succeeded to normalize the relations between Pakistan and Afghanistan which became deteriorated after the ascendancy of Sardar Mohammad Daud.

This time Shah increased its influence on Afghanistan by providing 2-billion $ economic aid to Afghanistan. An atmosphere was created in which the normalization of Pak-Afghan relations became imminent. Referring to Shah's initiatives in this respect S.R Chauri says, the Shah of Iran pushed Pakistani and Afghani leaders to the negotiating table to search for peaceful ways to end their 30-years old hostility.

SOVIET INTERVENTION IN AFGHANISTAN AND ITS IMPLICATIONS ON PAK-IRAN RELATIONS

The Soviet intervention in Afghanistan toward the end of 1979, produced the convergence of strategic purpose, as both the countries (Pakistan and Iran) received the flood of Afghan refugees. Geographically, Pakistan and Iran are the immediate neighbours of Afghanistan. Pakistan shares (2450-km) border with Afghanistan, it is the longest of the six countries encircling Afghanistan, while Iran shares (936 km) border with Afghanistan. Both countries have a common concerns and perceptions regarding Afghanistan. They shared a common stance in opposing Moscow's incursion into Afghanistan. The Soviet intervention in Afghanistan posed serious security, political, social, and economic problems for both Iran and Pakistan. The leaders of the two countries (Ayatollah Khomeini of Iran and General Zia-ul-Haq of Pakistan), raised an identical voice, calling for the immediate and the total withdrawal of Soviet forces, and the restoration of the Sovereign and Islamic Government in Afghanistan. The Government of Pakistan highly appreciated the moral and political support rendered by Iran in Afghan crisis, and stated that this was a resplendent chapter in the annals of their friendship and cooperation.

Iran strongly condemned the Soviet intervention in Afghanistan and declared its determination to help the Afghan Mujahideen. Khomeini denounced the Soviet move as a "brutal intervention".... by looters and occupiers, and a threat to Iran. He criticized the Soviet Union and urged the Muslim world to enter into defense pact in order to pull back Soviet Union from Afghanistan. Although, Iran did not played an active role in Afghanistan due to its internal problems, and also its pre-occupation with Iran-Iraq war, which lasted till 1988. However, situation in Afghanistan posed a serious danger to the security of Iran, as the result of direct military threat from Soviet Union.

Keeping in view, the prevailing anarchic political situation in Iran, many observers thought that Iran may possibly be the second Soviet target after Afghanistan. It was observed that Moscow had positioned its 80000 to 100000 troops in Afghanistan in the West along the Iranian border where there was a relatively minor resistance. The forces were highly equipped and were mobilized on Iranian border. One can hardly account for any other rationale of such a huge deployment of force. At the same time it was felt that once Russians consolidated themselves in Afghanistan, they would certainly move further. Importance of Afghanistan for Pakistan can hardly be underestimated. It is certainly Pakistan's first line of defense from the north. Pakistan was directly facing political, strategic, and economic consequences of Afghan war. Politically, it was facing immense pressure from Soviet Union for providing help to the refugees and Afghan Mujahideen. Economically, it was bearing a burden of more than two millions Afghan refugees, and strategically, it was facing a direct military threat from Soviet Union, often violating its space by Russian planes and helicopters.

In fact, in the wake of Afghan war Russia had been following a "Carrot and Stick Policy" towards Pakistan, sometimes offering economic and technical assistance, and other time, threatening its independence. Gromyko, the then Foreign Minister of Russia had warned Pakistan in clear words that "it will lose its independence if it continues its present policy of supporting of Afghan Mujahideen in Afghanistan." Contemporary changes in Afghanistan aimed at making Pakistan "an ideological spring boat" of Soviet for the region. Following its 'Carrot and Stick Policy' in a long run it would compel Pakistan to abandon long-standing support for Afghan Mujahideen, which will enable the Soviet Union to consolidate its hold on Afghanistan. Simultaneously, offering economic, military, and technical aid, paved way for the ideological encroachment with Pakistan under an apparent beneficial political, military and economic cooperation. Thus, in fact, the Soviet desired to bring Pakistan into the same trap in which Afghanistan had fallen.

The Soviet intervention in Afghanistan led the two countries (Pakistan and Iran) in a critical situation. Both were sailing in the same boat, the difference is only that Pakistan suffered a lot than Iran, and secondly, she played more active role than Iran in the Afghan war. Pakistan's security is very much important to Iran. For this purpose, Iran's interest in enhancing strategic cooperation with Pakistan with a view that Iranian borders are the borders of pace, love and friendship. Economically, both the countries suffered a lot due to the influx of Afghan refugees. During 1980-84, five million Afghans have migrated to Pakistan and Iran. Almost, the entire burden of sustaining the Afghan Jihad against the Soviet occupation had fallen on Pakistan, which had received a much larger number of Afghan refugees than Iran. The main organization of Afghan Mujahideen had their headquarters in Pakistan, which became the conduit for military equipment, as well as, humanitarian assistance to over three million Afghan refugees in the country.

The governments and the leadership of both Pakistan and Iran tried their best to seek the political solution of the problem; because their interests were at stake in the wake of Soviet intervention. In this regard, a frequent exchange of visits of the foreign ministers and high officials of the two countries took place from time to time with a view to identify their common views and opinions to find out ways and means for the political solution of the Afghan problem. To be contrary, Pakistan wanted to take Iran together in the resolution of the crisis. For that purpose, the Foreign Minister of Pakistan, Agha Shahi's visit to Iran, on February 2, 1981, to seek its endorsement of Pakistan initiative for dialogue with Kabul/ USSR, though a UN was a positive step. In addition, despite Iran's' refusal to take any part in the indirect Geneva talk on Afghanistan under the UN auspices since June 16, 1982, Pakistan made it a point clear that throughout the negotiations, Iran was kept fully informed about the developments in the said talks.

The visit of the Iranian Foreign Minister, Ali Akbar Velayati, to Pakistan on March 30, 1982 was a constructive step in this regard. A compete unanimity of views was found between the two parties on Afghan problem, during his two rounds of talks with his counterpart Sahibzada Yaqoob Khan, and also with President of Pakistan, General Zia-ul-Haq. Similarly, the visit of Foreign Minister of Pakistan, Sahibzada Yaqoob Khan to Iran on November 20, 1982 and again, on September 11, 1984, signified the wide ranging cooperation between the two countries in Afghanistan. Consequently, a consensus developed between Iran and Pakistan on this sensitive issue, the common objective of the two being the earliest possible withdrawal of Soviet forces from Afghanistan. The diplomatic efforts to bring international pressure on Soviet Union to withdraw from Afghanistan were coordinated by Islamabad, which finally culminated in the conclusion of Geneva Accords in 1988.

THE CONFLICT OF INTERESTS IN AFGHANISTAN

Since 1993, Afghanistan became a major area of concern for both Pakistan and Iran. Their varying perceptions and different approaches for the formation of the future Afghan government created misunderstanding, tension and confusion in Pak-Iran relations. At first, Iran played a minor role in Afghanistan due to its preoccupation with war with Iraq which lasted till 1988. But after the conclusion of Iran-Iraq war which coincided with the signing of Geneva Accord, Iran began to pay more attention to the developments inside Afghanistan. The Iranian activism vis-à-vis Afghanistan became a serious of tension between Islamabad and Tehran, which both the countries were trying hard to managed.

Pakistan played a leading role in promoting agreement among the different rival Afghan factions, first through Peshawar Accord of 1992, and then through Islamabad Accord of 1993. Both these accords were concluded with the support and participation of Iran, and Saudi Arab. The main objective of these accords was to end the strife among the different Afghan factions, thereby, creating a condition in which the Afghan refugees would return to their homes safely, and the task of reconstruction could be taken in their hands. But despite of these accords, factional fighting in Afghanistan continued, and more damages were done to the major Afghan towns as the result of the civil war during 1992-95, then during the long decade of Soviet occupation.

Divergence had already appeared in the policies of the two countries (Pakistan and Iran) since Peshawar Accord, which had been reinforced by Islamabad Accord. Professor Burhan-ud-din Rabbani was to relinquish the Presidency by the end of 1993, to replace by the multi-party administration, which was to hold the election of the democratic constituent government. The Iranian was complaining that until 1992, they were kept involved in the tripartite dialogue between Pakistan, Iran and Afghan Mujahideen. But later on, when the time came for discussion on the eve of Peshawar Accord of 1992, and especially, Nawaz Sharif's visit to Kabul on April 29, 1993, they were ignored. The presence of Al-Faisal, the Saudi Intelligence Chief, as the only foreign official to go with Prime Minister to Kabul, despite the fact, that Iranian had sent Mir Mahmood Masavi, the former Iranian ambassador to Pakistan, a week before this development took place, as an open insult. Even Khomeini had condemned the Peshawar accord "as exchanging Russian for American domination."

The policy makers in Islamabad believed that their need for depth in difference would be best served of the Pushtun speaking Afghan (Pukhtuns) kith and Kin of Pakistan's own Pushtun in NWFP dominated the new government in Kabul. But Tehran favored the Farsi speaking and Shia tribes in the Western and Northern Afghanistan. Iran recognized the Afghan government headed by Prof. Burhan-ud-din Rabbani, while Pakistan did not accept it as the legitimate one. The first difference between Pakistan and Iran arouse when Rabbani refused to step down at the end of 1993. Iran continued to back him mainly because he was Persian speaking Tajik, while Pakistan felt this was the total violation of the Islamabad Accord, which had been further confirmed in Makkah.

The authority of the Rabbani regime was rapidly eroded as Hikmatyar and the leaders of other faction challenge it, and the civil war broke out between them. The situation became chaotic, as anarchy prevailed in Afghanistan and as a result, more refugees left the country. The situation became more worse when the unknown faction, Taliban, under the leadership of Mullah Umer, emerged in Qandahar with the dual objective to save Afghanistan form further disintegration, and, to introduce a purely Islamic government based on the principles of Shariah.

THE TALIBAN STAKES OF PAKISTAN

As Ahmad Rashid has described so well, the Taliban (Islamic student) movement sprang from Pushtun refugees in Pakistan, concentrated in temporary camps in western Pakistan. Pushtun young men who had grown up in these camps were drawn back to the Afghan homeland after the Soviet exit, but under civil war conditions in their country. These youths had been trained in the use of small arms (carrying weapons was a natural legacy of their culture) and taught to believe they could impose a peaceful, Islamic moral order on their country. Most had no deep memory of traditional social life in Afghanistan itself, many had lost their parents and, being displaced, few were accustomed to the valued roles women played in Afghan society. The Taliban religious outlook was a product of the free, but largely Quranic, obscurantist education available to boys in the austere camp environments. Their teachers themselves typically were religious leaders (*maulvis* or *mullahs*) from Deobandi or Wahabi brands of fundamentalist Islam who ran traditional religious schools (*madrassas*) with hostels, frequently using them as recruiting grounds for political ends.

When the Soviet forces withdrew from Afghanistan in 1989, the United States essentially washed its hands of responsibility for the future of that debilitated country. Having defeated Soviet power and installed a weak Islamic republic under Tajik cleric Burhanuddin Rabbani in Kabul, Afghan mujahideen groups increasingly quarreled among themselves on ethnic and tribal lines and most of Afghanistan succumbed to internal warfare. Pakistan's elected, bureaucratic and armed leaders could not so easily ignore this turbulence and groped for a strategy that would restore civil order beyond Pakistan's borders in Afghanistan.

Under liberal Prime Minister and Interior Minister in 1993, the government of Pakistan worked out a two-fold strategy toward Afghanistan: (a) to support the revival of traditional Pushtun rule in the hope of extinguishing inter-tribal war, suppressing banditry, reopening roads, reviving trade with Iran and Central Asia, and securing Afghanistan for Western-financed pipeline projects that could provide Afghanistan revenue while transporting natural gas from Turkmenistan to Pakistan and on to India; and (b) to preempt Pushtun revival of the demand for a separate Pushtun state (Pakhtunistan) that had threatened Pakistan's integrity in the northwest tribal belt for many years after Independence, by ensuring the primacy of Pushtun stakes in Afghanistan's future.

The Taliban association emerging from the refugee settlements provided a natural political vehicle for this Pakistani strategy. It depended on the cooperation of the Islamist political parties that sponsored the Taliban in the camps. The task merely involved lightly arming and training Taliban cadres, and negotiating their entry through Quetta to join those Pushtun militia leaders inside Afghanistan who deplored the country's internal disintegration and aspired, however crudely, to pacify, reunify and rebuild Afghanistan.

The Pakistani armed intelligence arm, the Inter-Services Intelligence agency (ISI)—which had served as the main American and Saudi conduit for training, financial support, and transferring arms to the Afghan mujahideen—became the overseers and managers of Pakistan's assistance to the Taliban. This ISI role was secretive, but it was no rogue operation—as some in Pakistan and the United States may now wish to believe. Rather, it was the policy of Pakistan's elected governments from 1993, including that of the Harvard- and Oxford-educated Benazir Bhutto, Pakistan's first female prime minister.

The Taliban gained a local foothold around Kandahar in 1994 and then rapidly spread within southern and eastern Afghanistan, seizing Kabul and asserting a claim to govern Afghanistan in 1996, with all but a northeastern tenth of the country falling under their sway by 1998. Some financial support for the Taliban came from Saudi Arabia and other Gulf states. The Taliban regime was formally recognized by Saudi Arabia, Pakistan, and United Arab Emirates as the government of Afghanistan. Other governments and the United Nations either continued to recognize the first mujahideen (Rabbani) government even after it fled Kabul, or declined to recognize the Taliban regime, hoping that diplomacy and United Nations relief could patch together a workable, coalition government more representative of the country as a whole.

Almost imperceptible to Westerners at the start, the Taliban project at first was not considered objectionable in Washington. The Taliban became anathema only later, after word of its brutality spread. Having seized power in Kabul, the Taliban's inhumane governing practices undercut its once positive reputation for disarming warlord factions and bringing peace in one locality after another. From Kabul, the new regime imposed uniquely harsh judicial procedures and tried to force the surviving remnants of Afghanistan's battered urban society to give up music and entertainment. On pain of beating or even execution, men were forced to grow beards and wear traditional clothes, and women to leave jobs and whenever outdoors to wear the head-to-toe covering known as *burqas*. Western revulsion was aroused by media reports of the Taliban's draconian interpretation of Islamic law, confinement of women, suppression of female education, arbitrary arrests, mutilation or execution as punishments, and intolerance of non-Muslim religious minorities.

However a great deal the Taliban was eventually despised in the West, it was not the offspring of, nor originally associated with, al-Qaeda. Osama bin Laden apparently left Sudan in 1996 and moved back to Afghanistan some time in 1997. Thereafter, al-Qaeda gradually extended influence over the Taliban by spending its own resources to win the favour of senior Taliban leaders. Al-Qaeda also provided armed support and guidance to Taliban fighters who were fighting the Northern Alliance forces and other autonomous factions elsewhere in the country. The United States focused only on the significance of the Taliban's grant of sanctuary to al-Qaeda after its bombing of U.S. Embassies in East Africa in 1998.

Toward the end of its tenure, the Clinton administration put considerable pressure on Pakistan to arrange communication with Taliban officials, hoping to persuade them to expel Osama bin Laden and his associates. But the Taliban's counter demand was that it be recognized as Afghanistan's de jure government. This price the United States was unwilling to pay. How deeply the Taliban depended on al-Qaeda for armed operations against the Northern Alliance was not apparent to ordinary observers until after 9/11. What was clear, however, was that Pakistan had a major stake in the Taliban's claim to govern Afghanistan, was opposed to the Northern Alliance, and could not disengage from those positions in Afghanistan, short of a world-shaking crisis. September 11 brought just that crisis.

This analysis indicates that Pakistan's stakes in the Taliban were not based on a ordinary religion or on matters or Islamic principle, per se. Pakistan was interested in geopolitical objectives, not in the religious aims of the Taliban or its parochial justification of a strict Islamic discipline. Pakistan hoped to foster order through a client regime in a war-torn country on its borders. In doing so, it aimed to promote the revival of trade, to link Central Asian energy resources with the subcontinent, and to extinguish any Pushtun impulse to tear part of Pakistan away as a separate Pushtun state.

Exploiting reservoirs of Afghan Islamic fervor was useful to Pakistan (as well as to the United States) against the Soviet forces in Afghanistan, and useful again to Pakistan in helping the Taliban come to power, but the Taliban movement's Islamic fundamentalist orientation was never for Pakistan's government an end in itself. Only a smattering of individual Pakistanis and fundamentalist groups—mainly Pushtun tribes and Islamic political parties with roots in the Pushtun tribal regions—identified with the Taliban cause emotionally or ideologically. For the Pakistani authorities, the Taliban's religious appeal was only a tool.

Far more basic for Pakistan's government, and painful to abandon, was the aim of Pushtun dominance within Afghanistan as a means of resolving the civil war and opening the way to the trans-Afghanistan energy project. In achieving this aim, to cut off the Taliban even after George W. Bush threw down the gauntlet was tantamount to sacrificing Pushtun interests in Afghan politics and undermining Pakistan's interests in Afghanistan's stability and its own security. Pakistan's view of the power of the Northern Alliance, perhaps mistakenly, was that it jeopardized stability in Afghanistan. Thus, when Pakistani chief Pervez Musharraf turned against the Taliban under U.S. pressure, the decision was acutely difficult. Because Pakistan's strategy toward Afghanistan—and its own security on its western borders—was based on a successful Taliban campaign for power, it required accepting a fundamentally different calculation of Pakistan's national interests.

The new calculation was that Pakistan could not afford to be stigmatized by the West as a terrorist state. Once the Taliban refused to dissociate itself from al-Qaeda, Islamabad recognized that the United States would regard the Taliban as a de facto "terrorist" regime, and a legitimate object of armed attack. For Pakistan to be associated with the Taliban political cause after that would not only put Pakistan on a slippery slope toward international ostracism but could be used, potentially, to justify armed attack on Pakistan itself. Indeed, it was exactly this sensitivity that India latched onto when it initiated a armed confrontation with Pakistan after the attack on parliament in December 2001. But before we examine that crisis, the dramatic progress of the U.S. war in Afghanistan and the potential effects on the Kashmir side of Pakistan's Afghanistan-related entanglement need separate discussion.

ARMED MOVEMENT AGAINST THE TALIBAN AND AL-QAEDA

Pakistan had to make a decision very quickly whether it would support the U.S. armed effort in Afghanistan. Senior Pakistani officials announced on September 15, *within four days* of the 9/11 terrorist attacks on the United States, that they had agreed to give "full support" to U.S. efforts to combat international terrorism. President Musharraf 's address in Urdu to the nation three days later informed his people that the United States had demanded armed overflight rights, logistical support, and intelligence cooperation against three targets—Osama bin Laden, the Taliban, and international terrorism. Musharraf noted that the United States had won United Nations support and confided to the nation that neighbouring India had offered its armed facilities to the United States in the hopes of isolating Pakistan and getting it declared a terrorist state. Musharraf made it clear to his countrymen that Pakistan had to assist the United States; otherwise four vital interests of Pakistan would be in jeopardy—its sovereignty, its economy, its strategic (nuclear and missile) assets, and its cause in Kashmir. Musharraf and his advisors apparently drew the line, however, at inserting Pakistani armed forces into Afghanistan.

Despite concerns about a violent domestic backlash from political parties and groups that had links with the Taliban as well as the threat of al-Qaeda or Taliban attacks across the border, Pakistan thus committed itself almost overnight to give the United States valuable flight corridors over its territory and access to stage U.S. search and rescue forces at facilities near Karachi in the south and closer to Afghanistan at the Pakistani armed airfield near Jacobabad.

Pakistani forces also provided backstopping for U.S. operations against al-Qaeda and the Taliban later, by attempting to seal the mountainous borders so as to prevent hostile units fleeing across the border into Pakistan. Pakistani intelligence and security forces also cooperated with covert U.S. forces in efforts to hunt down those al-Qaeda and Taliban elements that succeeded in entering Pakistan to take refuge, or to slip out of the country.

Operation Enduring Freedom against al-Qaeda and Taliban forces in Afghanistan began with air strikes on October 7, 2001. Saudi Arabia had vetoed U.S. use of amenities on its soil for the attack and Iran denied access through its airspace. This put a much greater burden on U.S. aircraft carriers and other naval forces that assembled in the Arabian Sea, on bombers that had been flown to Diego Garcia and some that flew all the way from the United States, and on the prodigious use of aircraft refueling capabilities. But to the surprise of most observers, Russian President Putin gave his blessing to the U.S. counterterrorist effort and the leaders of three post-Soviet Central Asian states neighbouring Afghanistan—Uzbekistan, Tajikistan, and Kyrgizstan—provided the United States air access and staging facilities near Afghanistan in the north and west. Use of these facilities greatly eased U.S. cooperation with the Afghan Northern Alliance and the Uzbek elements that had reestablished a presence under General Rashid Dostum and that would retake Mazar-i-Sharif.

As a result, not merely was the United States able to use its own infiltrated ground spotters and air strikes to destroy exposed Taliban armed assets and installations—there were relatively few big targets— but it was also able to use airborne firepower to break down the front lines of the Taliban forces opposite the Northern Alliance, enabling the alliance and the other anti-Taliban forces that reemerged to advance, taking Mazar-i-Sharif, Kabul, Herat and Konduz in succession. Mazar-i-Sharif fell on November 9. Kabul was retaken on November 12, and Herat fell the same day. Konduz, where a combined force of about twenty thousand al-

Qaeda and Taliban forces put up a fierce resistance, fell on November 24.

A thousand U.S. marines were airlifted on November 26 into a remote landing strip (dubbed Camp Rhino) fifteen miles southeast of Kandahar to provide protection for a buildup of helicopters, armored personnel carriers, and the entry of additional special operations units. This also provided the United States with a staging area inside Afghanistan to pursue operations in the Pushtun areas to the north and east, including near the border with Pakistan. Coupled with well-targeted air raids, the ground presence of U.S. combat forces helped break the main, residual Taliban resistance in the south, stimulated defections, and forced the hard core to disperse into hiding. Kandahar fell on December 7.

Aided by the Rome political process of negotiating a new Afghan government, Hamid Karzai's leadership had begun by this time to make significant headway among Pushtun elements in the south and east that could absorb defectors and accommodate the Northern Alliance in forming a new government in Kabul. The U.S.-assisted Afghan meetings in Rome helped negotiate agreed steps to constitute a new, representative government in stages—and made the level of international commitment to rehabilitating Afghanistan clearer.

Special combat operations shifted once Kandahar had fallen to the White Mountains, near Khost, adjoining Pakistan, where al-Qaeda and Taliban forces had taken refuge in fortified and well-provisioned mountain caves and bunkers. The Tora Bora operations heavily bombed the cave complexes and ground units then cleared most of them on the ground by early January 2002. Several hundred al-Qaeda and Taliban prisoners were taken, with many shipped to Guantanamo Bay in Cuba for interrogation. A significant number of the al-Qaeda Arabs at Tora Bora evidently slipped through into Pakistan, however. In March, U.S. and allied forces gathered in Operation Anaconda to attack a well-dug-in al-Qaeda/Taliban force of about 1,500 fighters in the Shah-e-Kot Mountains south of Gardez in northeastern Afghanistan. Anaconda produced the largest number of U.S. casualties in a single Afghan operation, but apparently took a heavy toll on the enemy, killing an estimated four hundred to eight hundred opponents. Again, some of the fighters melted away into Pakistan, although in this case Pakistani forces intercepted and fought small units, capturing and turning over a number of al-Qaeda members to the United States for interrogation.

In roughly six months U.S. and allied armed intervention, coupled with the residual anti-Taliban forces in Afghanistan, had radically transformed the situation. Momentum increasingly favored the formation of a new Afghan government—although it was clear that such a government would be hard put to establish order throughout the country and develop the capacity, even with international assistance, to conduct a far-reaching economic and social rehabilitation program. Pockets of Taliban and al-Qaeda resistance remained, with a capacity to harass the emerging Karzai government and foment perceptions of disorder, but by summer 2002, these isolated elements no longer held the capacity to counter-attack the U.S. and allied presence in any major way.

During that armed campaign, the radical Islamic backlash that the Musharraf government had feared would erupt within Pakistan launched a handful of demonstrations but then largely subsided during the remainder of 2001. Considerable anti-American feeling and anger with Musharraf's decisions percolated below the surface but potentially massive, violent agitation was contained. Meanwhile, the level of violence in Kashmir rose to a degree. Then on December 13, 2001, halfway through the armed campaign, terrorists struck the Indian parliament and precipitated a full Indian armed mobilization against Pakistan.

PAK-IRAN RELATIONS UNDER THE SHADOW OF TALIBAN IN AFGHANISTAN

The relations between the two countries entered into rough and abnormal phase when an unknown faction, Taliban, emerged in Afghanistan, and within a short span of two years, became a leading political and military power of the country. According to Professor Dani, "the Taliban received their early education at Deeni Madrasas in Pakistan and were being supported by the religious elements in Pakistan. Dani claimed that the young students were being prepared for Jihad against whom; it was observed were not adhering to the moral code of Islam.

Regarding the origin of Taliban, two points of view are widely circulated. The first is 'the Islamic point of view', which highlights the rise of Islamic fundamentalism, and the second, is the 'the US point of view'. According to the Islamic point of view, Taliban had first come into force under the leadership of Mullah Umer, a well-known and respected Mujahid leader of the area, who successfully fought against the Soviet Union. After the fall of Najib, he got much popularity and assumed the religious role as the head of Madarsa. What followed than is better explained by Ralph Magnus and Eden Naby, in these words, "the chaos and lawlessness of the local lords, bandits, and drug dealers disrupted Mullah Umer and a number of like minded Mullahs and former Mujahideen.In July, 1994, a particular highway robbery and assault on women made Mullah Umer to assemble a force of his own group Taliban and former Afghan Mujahideen to punish criminals who were responsible for this inhume action. The effect of his action was electrifying public opinion, and other local commanders rallied round Taliban. They captured the Afghan border town Spin Boldak in October and Qandahar in November 1994, respectively after been invited by the local residents.

As for as the US point of view, it is generally believed the United States was a master-minded the creation of Taliban for serving its own interests in Afghanistan, most, on the similar pattern which it followed in organizing and training of Afghan Mujahideen to fight against Soviet Union in Afghanistan. This point of view, is however, credibly substantiate by Richard Mackenzie, Editor in Chief of Global News Services and a regular visitor of Afghanistan, who in his paper "the United States and Taliban" has successfully pointed out many realities behind the scene of US policy regarding Taliban. He asserted that "long before the Taliban began their thrust towards Kabul, the US officials had high aspirations." They hoped that Taliban would serve the US supreme interest in Afghanistan.

The ideological difference between Iran and Taliban made them a natural rivals and strong competitors in Afghanistan. The

Taliban was highly orthodox Sunni Islamic Movement while Iran is a Shia majority country. Hence, the emergence of Taliban is Afghanistan was mentally and psychologically unacceptable to Iran, and tried its best to crush and to root out their lasting influence from Afghanistan once for all. The emergence of Taliban in Afghanistan led a major divergence in Pak-Iran relations. Both (Pakistan and Iran) had different policies, perceptions, and approaches, with regard to Afghanistan. Pakistan was supporting the cause of Taliban, while Iran was a staunch supporter of Anti-Taliban Northern Alliance. Their support for apposite factions made them natural rivals in the affairs of Afghanistan.

Pakistan was supporting Taliban in hope that they would have become a strong military force and their determination to establish their control over the major parts of Afghanistan. Pakistan's policy of supporting Taliban, however, was based more on the anger and antagonism as they felt against Rabbani, who was instrumental in sacking Pakistan's embassy in Kabul, than the genuine love for Taliban whose doctrine of interpretation of Shariah did not coincide with Islamabad. Pakistan's moral, diplomatic, and material support to Taliban was based partly on the desire to protect and promote its own national interest. According to C. Plano and Roy Olton, "National interest is the fundamental objective and the ultimate determinant that guide the decision makers of the state, is typically a highly generalize conception of these elements that constitutes the state's most vital needs."

Dr. Goga an advisor to Foreign Minister of Uzbekistan remarked during a Press Conference in Peshawar in February, 1996, that Pakistan foreign policy was not very passive, implying that Pakistan was involved in the supply of arms and armaments to its favorite in Afghanistan. The main objective of Pakistan's Foreign policy vis-à-vis Taliban have been;

a. Durable peace in a war-ravaged land;
b. A friendly government across its western border;
c. Repatriation of Afghan refuges;
d. Access to Central Asian markets;
e. A safe route for oil and gas pipeline from Turkmenistan to Arabian Sea.

Dr. Iffat Malik is of the view, that Iran has a several reasons of opposing Taliban. Apart from the ideological factor, the Iranian concern for Shia living in Afghanistan, of whom the largest group was Hazaras. Taliban have been accused of targeting Hazaras, even carrying out massacres against them. The obvious example was the murder of a prominent Hizb-e-Wahdat leader, Abdul Ali Mazari, while in their custody. Iran has also been accused that the drug-trafficking increased with the emergence of Taliban. According to General Zaeri, the Iranian Police Chief, around 147 tons of drugs being smuggled by Taliban has been seized in March, 1996.

More important than this essentially 'human' reason for Iran's opposition to Taliban are geo-politics and economics. For Iran, Afghanistan is a gateway to Central Asia, while it would not wish to rule the country. Iran wanted the establishment of Pro-Iranian Government in Afghanistan, which allow it an easy and assured access to Central Asia. Hence, Iran did not recognize Taliban's supreme control over most parts of Afghanistan. The geo-political reason for Iranian opposition to Taliban is linked to the Caspian Sea region and will be considered in movement. According to Iran, a counter informal alliance of USA, Saudi Arab, and Pakistan was emerged which support Taliban in Afghanistan. Iran was apprehended that in case of Taliban's victory, they would defeat the pro-Iran Afghan factions, unify the country, and thus made Afghanistan an alternative gateway for Pakistan to Central Asia. This was the part of general policy of US to contain Iran. Hence Iran's initial reaction to Taliban victory was to condemn it as the handiwork of Pak-US-Saudi.

Pak-Iran differences were increased when Taliban occupied the city of Heart in early 1995, and expelled pro-Iranian commander Ismail Khan from Heart and forced him to take refugee in Iran. This was realized by Tehran as Pakistan's backed move to take over the area, which was traditionally within Iran's sphere of influence. Afterwards, Iran and Pakistan supported the rival parties in their struggles for power. Moreover, Taliban's success to capture of Kabul in September 1996, further strained Pak-Iran relations. After the capture of Kabul most parts of Afghanistan (about 90%)

adjoining Pakistani border; came under their control. The government in Islamabad had no option but to give de-facto recognition to Taliban Government in Afghanistan. However, Iran continued to support the so-called Northern Alliance consisting the faction of Rabbani, Dostum and Shia Hizb-e-Wahdat, which had it's headquarter at Mazar-i-Sharif.

The gulf between the two countries widened with the victories of Taliban and the defeat of pro-Iranian faction, Northern Alliance. The Iranian government and media openly criticized Pakistan for creating Taliban and stressing for the establishment of broad based multi-ethnic government in Afghanistan. Pakistan not only recognized the government of Taliban, but also pleaded for international community's recognition of Taliban government in Afghanistan on the basis of ground realities. While Iran continued to support and recognize the Rabbani Government. On October 23, 1996, the Iranian Foreign Minister, Ali Akbar Velayati at a Press Conference in Tehran made it absolutely clear that his country continued to recognize only the Rabbani Government. It also emphasized the need for the establishment of broad-based government upholding the sovereignty, and territorial integrity and political independence of Afghanistan.

THE TRAGEDY OF MAZAR-E-SHARIF AND PAK-IRAN RELATIONS

The differences between Iran and Pakistan touched their lowest ebb, in 1998, when the Taliban captured the Afghan city of Mazar-e-Sharif (the Stronghold and the Headquarter of Northern Alliance), and killed a scores of Iranian diplomats allegedly supporting the cause of the Northern Alliance. The Iranian reaction became harsh and severe and this led to the open confrontation between Iran and Taliban controlled Afghanistan. Pakistan was condemned by Iran for supporting Taliban. Iran blamed Pakistan for its considerable influence over Taliban in Afghanistan. However, Pakistani analysts were of the view that Pakistan's influence over Taliban in Afghanistan was exaggerated by Indian propaganda, whose objective was to project Pakistan as fundamentalist State by linking it with Taliban. The two armies (The Iranian and Taliban) stood eyeball to eyeball and there was grave possibility of conflict between them. What makes the situation so critical for Pakistan, is the opening warming of the Iranian Supreme leader Ayatollah Khamaini, asking Islamabad to stop backing the Taliban militia which has been told "to abandon its action which had led to catastrophe" In his statement from Radio Tehran, the Iranian Supreme leader said, "I have — so far prevented the lightening of fire in the region which would be hard to extinguish. But all should not that a very great and wide danger is quite near." It was really a strong reaction by the Iranian leader towards Pakistan. He called upon the people of Pakistan what he had said, was interference in Afghanistan by the segments of Pakistani Army.

M.S. Johari in his book, "the Taliban; Assent to Power" writes "that earlier the Iranian had seriously objected to not only to the political and diplomatic support to Taliban but also on the reports of the presence of Pakistani troops within Taliban militia. For instance, refugees from Mazar-e-Sharif reported that the Taliban were occupied by Pakistani fighter identifiable by their language and flag of the Muslim fundamentalist party aligned with Taliban." The Mazar-e-Sharif incident led dire consequences for Pak-Iran relations. The Iranian turned hostile against Pakistan. The Iranian anger and hostility was obvious from several demonstrations which occurred in Tehran and other major Iranian cities, in which thousand of people took part and raised a slogans "death to America, death to Taliban, and death to Taliban's backers."

It is something discouraging and disappointing that, in October 1998, the security forces prompted Iran to pull sixty of its diplomats out of Pakistan. The Iranian press had a great misgiving about Taliban. They considered Taliban as the offspring of ISI, puppet and stooge of Pakistan. The Iranian Foreign Minister, Kamal Kharazi told on Radio Tehran on his return from UN General Assembly that: "it is entirely natural to cut down the number of one diplomat in a country when their security is not assured."

In the words of Syed Abdul Hassan Raeissassadat, the Former Director General of Khan-e-Farhang, Peshawar, "the Taliban factor in Pak-Iran relations proved suicidal for the geo-strategic and the economic interests of both the countries (Iran and Pakistan). It was a serious challenge and a root cause of divergence in Pak-Iran relations, which in turn, gave birth to other problems, confusion and tensions in their mutual bilateral relationship. Of these, the sectarian conflicts in Pakistan, Pak-Iran tussle and competition in Central Asia, and Iran's growing and meaningful relations with India were outstanding. Of course Pakistan denied all the charges particularly its involvement of problem of some elements of its security agencies and official militia. The disagreement on Afghanistan was just one of the many jagged edges of a bilateral relationship that had been smooth more in 'myth than in reality; on this particular issue between Pakistan and Iran. But from the real political point of view, Pakistan support to Taliban was not because of its competition with Iran but primarily because of the India against which Pakistan, as a matter of defense policy, had always tried to avoid two front threats in its northeast and northwest. Thus, it was the compulsion of Pakistan to recognize a friendly regime in the shape of Taliban in Afghanistan which was more a geo-political rather than the ideological requirement for Pakistan.

Not only had this, but the government of Nawaz Sharif tried its best to diffuse the tension between Kabul and Tehran, and persuade them for negotiation. For this purpose, the Prime Minister sent his Foreign Minister, Sartaj Aziz, on a special mission to Tehran to resume the Iranian government that Pakistan would use all its influences with Taliban to obtain satisfaction of the Iranian demand for the return of its nationals and, the punishment of those guilty of the killing of Iranian diplomats in Mazar-e-Sharif. The Prime Minister Nawaz Sharif met President Khatami in New York a few days later, and their talks brought about a significant breakthrough in ending the tension between them. They agreed that brotherly relations between the two countries are "precious" and precondition for maintaining a complete regional peace and stability. The main points of agreement between the two countries were discussed. The external forces were shaping the situation in Afghanistan, and it was agreed that the efforts should be made under the UN auspices to promote durable peace. As the two sides agreed to build on positive signals, and to maintain mutual friendship and trust.

The developments since the historic meeting have witnessed the continuation of positive trends. During this period, Pakistan also coordinated closely with the neighbouring Iran with which it launched a joint mission to promote an Afghan peace process in June-July, 1998. Pakistan's Foreign Secretary Shamshad, accordingly, visited Tehran in the first week of January 1999, for bilateral consultation with his Iranian counterpart; during his meeting he was also received by Foreign Minister and President. But unfortunately, the Iranian response to our earnest desires and patient efforts to improve bilateral relations had been rather luck-warm. Apart from this, the eliciting reaffirmation of Tehran's support for UN Resolutions on Kashmir and reference to Afghan historical reality that discounts the utility of outside pressure in the evolution of government in Kabul, no convergence of views on Afghanistan seem to have emerged during these visits.

POST TALIBAN AFGHANISTAN AND PAK-IRAN RELATIONS

The scenario in Afghanistan took a dramatic turn after 9/11, when US declared war against Al Qaida and Taliban in Afghanistan, which resulted in the fall of Taliban rule in Afghanistan. Mullah Omer and Osama Bin Laden, most wanted to USA, succeeded in fleeing the country, and thus, the Pro-US Government of Northern Alliance was installed in Afghanistan. The fall of Taliban (anti-Iranian) removed a major irritant in Pak-Iran relations. The new trends in the regional strategic dynamics necessitated Pak-Iran relations. But, more than, it was change in Pakistani policy towards Taliban in the wake of US led attack against Afghanistan that paved the way for new upward trends in Pak-Iran relations. Pakistan sided with the international coalition against Taliban, who were soon removed from the government in Kabul. The Taliban retreat led Pakistan and Iran to end their decade old strained relations and work for accommodating each other's strategic and economic interests in Afghanistan.

Soon after the fall of Taliban in Afghanistan, the Iranian Foreign Minister, Kamal Kharazi, paid a to day visit to Islamabad, during which he confirmed that both the countries had come to close to each other's point of view on Afghan issue. Both agreed to help to each other for the establishment of broad based multi-ethnic government in Afghanistan under the auspices of United Nations. He said "we have removed our differences in our talks as we observe that Pakistan has changed its policy and agreed to play collective role in the reconstruction of Afghanistan." The fall of Taliban ushered a new era of cordiality, goodwill and cooperation in Pak-Iran relations. A statement of the then Foreign Minister of Pakistan, Abdul Sattar, in November 2001, "That the clouds are over and the sun is shinning over the skies of Pakistan and Iran" was meaningful and reflective of the new political development between them. Earlier, Iran has seriously objected to not only the political and diplomatic support of Pakistan to Taliban but also on the reports of the presence of Pakistani troops within Taliban militia.

Pakistan and Iran promised to forget their past differences in Afghanistan if any one and resolved to work jointly for the establishment of stable and durable government in Afghanistan, which would not only served the best interests of these countries, but, the interests of all the ethnic communities living inside Afghanistan. According to the Iranian scholar; "the 9/11 terrorist attack and the subsequent fall of Taliban in Afghanistan paved the way for mending of bilateral relations." Both the countries are against the US bombardment in Afghanistan and resolved that the same should come to an end. Both the countries desire for peaceful, prosperous and harmonious Afghanistan. Such an understanding suits both the nations and helps greatly to ensure a complete stability in Afghanistan as well. They also retreated to respect the sovereignty, territorial integrity and their full support for Hamid Karzai's interim government and Bonn Peace Process.

Pakistan and Iran are geo-politically important to the peace and stability in Afghanistan, a fact recognized not only by both countries but also by the extra-regional players. Thus, Pakistan and Iran in the context of new Afghan set up under Hamid Karzai can work together to be the real guarantors of Afghanistan's reconstruction and security, which itself is very important for peace and prosperity for these countries. In fact, the convergence of interests and the policies of these two countries on Afghanistan could serve a strong basis for their future bilateral relationship. However, the US-Iran rivalry, the presence of the American forces in Afghanistan and Central Asia, Pakistan support to the US policies in Afghanistan and the bases and ports facilities provided by Pakistan, still casts doubts on the prospects of any long tem strong relations between Pakistan and Iran.

Conclusion

The triangular relationship of Pakistan, Iran and Afghanistan was disrupted since the inception of Pakistan, when Iran became Pakistan's close friend and Afghanistan as its worse rival. The convergence of interests, common security concerns and policies, similar approaches and mutual understanding were the numerous factors which led Iran and Pakistan an enduring friends and allies. Moreover, Iranian help and full support to Pakistan on the issue of Kashmir and its two Indo-Pak wars proved a great source of courage, consolation, and satisfaction to Pakistan. Friendship with Iran proved time-tested which greatly enhance Pakistan's international dignity and prestige against its over-ambitious rival, India. On the other hand, Pakistan's relation with Afghanistan became strain on the issue of Pakhtunistan. This issue proved an irritating factor in Pak-Afghan relations which caused a deep mistrust, misunderstanding, discontent, disruption and dissatisfaction in their bilateral relationship. However, the Iran's mediating role and its constructive and meaningful effort proved a significant factor in bringing these countries (Pakistan and Afghanistan), close to each other.

The situation took a different turn in the wake of the Soviet intervention in Afghanistan. The intervention produced the homogeneity of interests between Pakistan and Iran as both countries were facing equally the political, social and the economic consequences of the Afghan problem. Generally speaking, the policies of the two countries (Pakistan and Iran) regarding Afghanistan were similar and cooperative despite of Iran's strong objective Pakistan's close association with USA (Iran's staunch enemy) and its role as a frontline state on the other side, Iran did not play a major role in the Afghan's conflict due to its preoccupation with its inter problems arising out Islamic

Revolution and its long eight years war with Iraq. But after the conclusion of Iran-Iraq War which coincided with the signing of Geneva Accord in 1988 that stipulated the withdrawal of Soviet Union from Afghanistan, Iran began to play an effective role inside Afghanistan.

The Iranian activism vis-à-vis Afghanistan became a serious source of friction, which in the time transformed into active rivalry. The representation of the rival Afghan factions in the formation of future government in Afghanistan became the bone of contention between Pakistan and Iran. More important, the emergence of Taliban in Afghanistan witnessed contradiction, confrontation, competition, disruption and dissatisfaction in Pak-Iran relations. Their divergent policies, different approaches on the issue of Taliban in Afghanistan made them a virtual rivals and strong competitors. Friendship with Iran is a cornerstone of Pakistan's foreign policy. But the warmth in their relations; unfortunately, gave way to active antagonism following Pakistan's overt backing for Taliban. Thus, their confrontationist stance in Afghanistan blocked all the chances of their good relationship. Their support for respective ethnic groups (Pakistan supported the cause of Taliban while Iran supported the anti-Taliban Northern Alliance) further widened the gulf between the two countries. The occupation of Kabul and Herat by Taliban in 1996 and 1997 respectively added fuel to fire to already strained relations. Furthermore, the Mazar-e-Sharif incident and the assassination of nine Iranian diplomats gave a final blow to Pak-Iran relations.

The killing of Iranian citizens and diplomats in Pakistan adversely affected their relations. And above all, the intensification of the sectarian strife and the failure of Pakistan's judicial process to comply with contributed negatively in Pak-Iran relations. The sectarian disharmony gave the feeling of insecurity to the Iranian nationals and officials in Pakistan. Effort on the part of the government of Pakistan to eradicate this menace from society did not materialize. Similarly, the Indian media campaign against Pakistan was yet, another factor, which led the two neighbours, and friends continued to draft apart on the sectarian issue.

The ouster of Taliban from Afghanistan removed a major irritant which provided both the countries with the opportunity to work jointly as the real guarantor of Afghanistan's peace, progress, prosperity and reconstruction. Above all, the statement of Pakistan's Foreign Minister Abdul Sattar in November-2002, further clarifies the situation that, "the clouds were over and the Sun is shinning over the skies of Pakistan and Iran was meaningful and reflective of the new political development between these two countries."

POST-2014 AFGHANISTAN: POLICY OPTIONS FOR INDIA AND IRAN

Today, Afghanistan is in a state of transition. While international support has been forthcoming, both in terms of financial aid and military assistance, it is Afghanistan's close neighbours who become crucial to the country's future. Pakistan, Iran and the Central Asian Republics (CAR) share borders with Afghanistan, forming the immediate neighbourhood, while China (though connected directly via the narrow Wakhan corridor), India and Russia form the extended neighbourhood.

Russia, owing to the bitter experience of its occupation during 1979-89, is unwilling to get directly involved in Afghanistan, and China appears focussed only on the economic arena. The CAR, themselves weak and prone to various threats are in no position to provide any direct help. Pakistan, with its known links to Taliban, its role in numerous terrorist attacks in Afghanistan, its quest for a weak and pro-Pakistan regime in Afghanistan, and its known involvement in harbouring top Taliban leaders, does not invoke confidence amongst Afghan policy makers.

This leaves India and Iran – both nations that have cordial relations with Afghanistan and are counted as reliable allies. As Afghanistan looks forward to 2015, two critical events take place this year: the presidential elections, and the security transition.

The present standoff with the US does not auger well for Afghanistan, for in the midst of all this, the Taliban remains strong and resolute. They have rejected peace talks stating that there cannot be any peace talks as long as foreign troops are present on Afghan soil. While hoping that the US and its allies will not abandon, Afghanistan has started considering the option of long term cooperation with India and Iran. Afghanistan considers India as it's "most trusted ally and an all-weather friend" and Iran is a part of its political and cultural history. Both countries enjoy cordial bilateral relations and share similar interests and concerns with regard to Afghanistan. With the signing of interim deal on Iran's nuclear program, there are indications of India shedding some restrictions and restraint in conducting business with Iran. Apart from the usual India-Iran oil and natural gas trade, Afghanistan could act as a crucial link in Indo-Iran relations – one that could offer opportunities for both countries and more importantly, lend a crucial lifeline to an Afghanistan that is currently desperately seeking support in the region.

This essay attempts to look at India and Iran's interests, concerns, vulnerabilities and options for engagement with Afghanistan in the coming decades.

IRAN AND AFGHANISTAN

Iran and Afghanistan share a 930 kilometer border and until the 1857 Treaty of Paris, Herat was an integral part of Iran. Given the history of cultural, economic and religious bonds between the two nations, a crossover of influence across either side is natural. Also, the legacy of the Persian Empire has left marks of influence in Afghanistan, especially in the western provinces. Religiously too, both nations enjoy proximity as Islamic nations. Although Afghanistan has a Sunni majority population (80 per cent), it does have a sizeable Shia minority (19 per cent) with the Hazaras, a Persian-speaking ethnic group constituting the majority Shia group. Iran and Afghanistan also share common languages. Dari, the Afghan version of Persian is one of the two official languages in Afghanistan.

Both nations witnessed turbulent histories in contemporary times. As the war in Afghanistan winds down and the ghost of economic and political sanctions on Iran promise to get diluted, both nations have the opportunity to emerge with new hope in coming times. In this context, Iran has the opportunity to open out towards Afghanistan, exploiting its past historical linkages and build a new partnership of mutual growth and prosperity. The journey, however, will be difficult and will come with its share of obstacles.

Iran and Afghanistan: A SWOT Analysis

As stated earlier, apart from sharing a common border with Afghanistan, Iran shares a rich history and cultural heritage with Afghanistan. Linguistic ties and a significant Shia Muslim population give Iran the required presence and acceptance within Afghanistan.

The common border is a source of major strength, especially as the two countries do not share any major border dispute. Also, Afghanistan's border management with Iran has always been better as compared to that with Pakistan. It could be attributed to better terrain on the Iran-Afghanistan border and to the efficient border control on the Iranian side. While Afghanistan's border with Pakistan has been notoriously porous and has facilitated easy infiltration/exfiltration of terrorists, its Iranian border has stable and peaceful for most part.

In 2001, Iran aided the Northern Alliance that overthrew the Taliban regime. Iran was also a significant actor in the Bonn I conference which led to the establishment of an interim government in Kabul. Tehran pledged $560 million at the 2002 Tokyo Conference on the Reconstruction of Afghanistan, and $100 million at the 2006 London Conference. Most of the aid has been spent on reconstruction projects, especially in Herat. Tehran has also endeavoured to create road links between Iran, Afghanistan, and the CAR – which includes a 120 kilometre-long road linking Herat in Afghanistan to Dogharoun in Iran. Iran is also in the process of linking Afghanistan to the Iranian port of Chabahar, which will provide access to maritime routes and also reduce Kabul's dependence on Pakistan. The Afghans acknowledge this assistance and aid and it acts as a major confidence-boosting measure in the future Iran-Afghanistan relations.

As a result of its support to the Northern Alliance, Iran has cultivated good relations with the Tajiks in Afghanistan. The Tajiks, who form the second largest population group in Afghanistan and dominate most positions in the government services, could become a good support base for Iran along with the Hazaras and other Shia communities in Afghanistan.

Iran and India share good relations and are likely to see greater bilateral engagements in the coming years. In the absence of any transit routes via Pakistan in the near future, India considers Iran as its gateway to Afghanistan and the CAR. Iran too appreciates Indian efforts towards stabilising Afghanistan. Both countries acknowledge that their national interests are better served with a politically stable and secure Afghanistan. These common concerns and interests could be a major motivation for Iran's outreach towards Afghanistan in coordination with India.

Iran's support to the Taliban is a major weakness in its efforts to coordinate efforts with India in Afghanistan. It is a paradox that Iran supported the Taliban, given its anti-Shiite ideology and the fact that the Taliban had killed nine Iranian diplomats in 1998, almost bringing Iran to war with the extremists. However, the Tehran-Taliban relationship had more to do with Iran despising the presence of the US to its Eastern flank.

The absence of a consistent policy towards Afghanistan has been another weakness. Again, Iran's on and off support to the Taliban is a major factor and is seen as adversarial by the Afghan government. It also fails to provide Iran the required leverage in Afghanistan despite the huge amount of economic aid and reconstruction projects undertaken by Tehran in the country.

The lack of resolve to take the lead in the resolution of the Afghan crisis is also seen as a weak spot in Iran's engagement with the country. While the Iran-US standoff over the nuclear issue can be attributed as one reason, Iran could have undertaken a more proactive role in the Afghanistan.

Furthermore, the lack of robust security cooperation with Afghanistan has been a hiccup for Iran in developing better bilateral relations with Afghanistan. It is only in August 2013 that the two countries signed the 'border and security agreement'.

The current Iran-US rapprochement on the Iranian nuclear program could be a great opportunity to enhance Iran's engagement in Afghanistan. Better ties with the US could open new, shorter routes for international aid and supply via Iran as an alternative to the presently used circuitous route through the CAR or the terror-infested routes in Pakistan. It would save money for the US and its allies, generate transit revenue for Iran, and ensure a healthy rate of supplies in Afghanistan.

With a possible deal on the nuclear issue and the retraction of sanctions, Iran and Afghanistan could also explore greater security cooperation, including possibly providing military equipment to the ANSF in at a later stage.

Iran's efforts in economic aid and reconstruction projects have been viewed positively, especially the western regions like Herat province. Iran could in fact be termed as critical to the economic revival of Afghanistan. Iran could well exploit this by pumping in more money and projects to win goodwill in Afghanistan.

Additionally, Iran has traditional ties with the CAR. With a significant Shia Muslim population, especially in Tajikistan, Iran has always strived to enhance its cultural ties with CAR. With Afghanistan as a bridge, it could well use good relations and connectivity to enhance not only cultural and religious ties but also use the territory to connect oil and gas pipelines towards China and to the Persian Gulf.

Prominent among the threats is the security and welfare of the Shiite population in Afghanistan. Iran has not forgotten the 1998 massacre of the Hazaras in Mazar-e-Sharif that almost led to a military conflict with the Taliban regime. Cases of Hazaras being targeted and prosecuted in Afghanistan remain a threat, especially so if there is a return of Taliban to Kabul post the withdrawal of international troops.

Also, Afghan refugees in Iran have been for long been a point of conflict between the two countries. According to the UN, there are over 2 million refugees in Iran. It is said to have an "adverse social and economic" impact on the Iranian society by draining Iran's economy by a sizeable measure, coupled with the threat of Taliban-like elements infiltrating into the country.

Water-sharing has been another point of contention between the two nations. With Afghanistan building a number of dams on Helmand River, the water supply into Iran, especially its southern and eastern provinces is threatened, which could be a cause of friction in the future. Drug-trafficking is another source of friction and a real threat to Iran-Afghanistan relations. Afghanistan is one of the largest producers of opium in the world. Iran, with its easy connectivity to Europe via Turkey is said to be a safe and convenient route of transit for almost 50 per cent of Afghan drugs. Drug addiction among Iranian youth too is becoming a major social problem and the Iranian government is reported to be incurring a loss of up to $10 billion in its anti-drug campaign.

Iran, unlike the US and its allies, does not have the luxury of leaving Afghanistan given the geographical construct. It equally realises Afghanistan's multiple and complex problems and the fact that they cannot be resolved soon. As Iran hopes to emerge from the shadows of international sanctions, Afghanistan presents an excellent opportunity to not only expand its influence eastwards but also be seen as a responsible regional player. Weaknesses in Iran-Afghanistan relations hover around Iran's on-off support to the Taliban. This too, in the context of the US withdrawal, would become redundant. The threats too, though significant, are not big enough to derail their bilateral relationship. On the contrary, Iran, building on its existing strengths, has a host of opportunities to be viewed as a major ally in Afghanistan.

INDIA AND AFGHANISTAN

India and Afghanistan share a long history of cultural, civilizational and economic ties. Both countries shared borders till 1947 when Pakistan was carved out of British India. Among the Afghan population, even today, India is considered the most popular country with most opinion polls giving over 70 per cent votes to India. India's support to the Afghan government and its consistent anti-Taliban stance has been always appreciated in Afghanistan.

Like Iran, India supported, funded and armed the Northern Alliance in the fight to overthrow the Taliban in 2001. Afghan President Hamid Karzai has called India as the "most trusted ally and an all-weather friend," and giving credence to the confidence that Kabul has in New Delhi, India was the first country Afghanistan signed its Strategic Partnership Agreement (SPA) with. India is popular not only among the Hazaras and Tajiks, but also among a large number of Pashtuns. It's over $2 billion aid to Afghanistan in reconstruction and welfare projects too have been well received.

Both nations share their concerns over terror and have been equally inflicted by it in the past decades; Afghanistan through the Taliban and India through Pakistan-sponsored terrorists in Jammu and Kashmir. Despite not committing militarily in Afghanistan, India has suffered from Taliban terror more than once, whether it was the hijacking of the Indian Airline flight IC814 to Kandahar in 1998, the multiple times the Indian embassy and missions have been targeted in Kabul, or even the attacks on Indian engineers working on reconstruction projects in Afghanistan.

Afghanistan appreciates the Indian sacrifices and commitment to the Afghan cause.

As the war in Afghanistan draws down by end of 2014, Afghanistan looks up to India as a major source of support. Similarly, India too is keen that a stable and peaceful transition takes place in Afghanistan. India thus has the opportunity to enhance its engagement with Afghanistan, building on its goodwill and support and create a new partnership. With no common borders and Pakistan in between, the journey is going to be difficult. It is therefore essential to run a SWOT analysis to examine India's future engagement with Afghanistan.

INDIA AND AFGHANISTAN: A SWOT ANALYSIS

India's historical links, its goodwill across the length and breadth of Afghanistan, as well as its reputation of being a benign power with no extra-territorial ambitions is the biggest strength in India's relations with Afghanistan. As mentioned above, the government and people in the country appreciate India's support to Afghan peace processes and the generous aid and assistance in reconstruction projects.

India's consistent stance vis-à-vis the Taliban is another source of strength in bilateral relations. India, despite being side-lined in the London Conference in 2010 for not recognising the difference between good and bad Taliban, has maintained its consistent anti-Taliban position, something that is well appreciated in Afghanistan.

India's aid to Afghanistan, and reconstruction projects too, are a major factor in the bilateral relationship. India is the fifth-largest donor in Afghanistan after the US, UK, Japan and Germany, and is the largest non-traditional donor in Afghanistan. This, coupled with the sacrifices made by Indians in building these projects too is great source of strength.

The absence of direct land or maritime connectivity with Afghanistan is perhaps the biggest obstacle to enhancing bilateral engagement between India and Afghanistan. With an unrelenting Pakistan and an isolated Iran given the international sanctions, India has felt often felt handicapped in transporting basic supplies, and/or equipment and manpower for reconstruction projects.

Another weakness labelled against India is that India has not been able to leverage its goodwill in Afghanistan. "Sitting on the side-lines," "service provider rather than a stake holder" are some of the accusations labelled against India.

India's failure to protect its embassy and missions in Afghanistan too has often been quoted as its weaknesses. India's reluctance to send regular troops after attacks on its embassy in 2008 and 2010, even to protect its mission, has been interpreted as a weak Indian stand.

India's formulation of its Afghan policy via the Pakistan prism is also seen as a weakness. Often, India has ceded to Pakistan's concerns not only in India's security engagement in Afghanistan, but also in its overall Afghan policy.

The SPA signed with Afghanistan is key opportunity for India. While signing the SPA, Indian Prime Minister Manmohan Singh stated that India would "stand by Afghanistan" when foreign troops withdraw from the country in 2014. The SPA promises to provide an institutional framework towards India's assistance towards Afghan capacity building in the areas of education, development, and people-to-people contacts, as also in the training, equipping and capacity building programmes for the Afghan National Security Forces. The SPA also promises a new dimension in economic relations. India has already started working on it by enhancing the scope of military assistance to Afghan Armed forces in the form of training and equipment.

India's investments in Afghanistan are another great opportunity in enhancing bilateral relations. The winning of the contract for estimated reserves of 1.8 billion tonnes of iron ore at Hajigak by a consortium of Indian firms led by the Steel Authority of India Limited (SAIL), as well as other projects and investments are ideal opportunities to galvanise Indian support in Afghanistan. The 'Heart of Asia' initiative by India to draw global finances and investments for Afghanistan presents one such opportunity.

India has for long sought good relations with the CAR. With Iran under sanctions and Afghanistan embroiled in war, India found it difficult to enhance its engagement with the CAR. With the possibility of both the issues to get resolved in the coming years, it presents an excellent opportunity for India to enhance its engagement with the CAR, especially in the context of energy supplies.

The 'New Silk Route' initiative proposed by the US to make Afghanistan a bridge for trade and transit between South, Central and West Asia offers a great opportunity for India. India has always felt left out in the great game of energy trade and transit of Central Asia, especially as the China-funded Central Asia Regional Economic Cooperation (CAREC) corridors (roads and pipelines) bypass India. If and when the New Silk Route initiative takes off, it would provide India an opportunity to seek its share in the Central Asian energy resources.

As mentioned in context of Iran too, good traditional ties between Iran and India coupled with possibility of lifting restrictions on Iran present a good opportunity to leverage their combined support in Afghanistan.

India has major concerns regarding the future of peace and security and Afghanistan. A weak government in Afghanistan is a threat to Indian interests. It may result in fragmented control of the government over the country, with parts of the country, especially the South and East under the Taliban influence. In the absence of US-led troops in the country, an unrelenting Pakistan and a resurgent Taliban, it could become a major concern for India, not only for its assets in in the country, but also its spill over effect on Indian territory. A political and security vacuum would thus constitute a direct threat to India. Any major attack on Indian missions or projects akin to the July 2008 attack on the Indian Embassy may force India, under pressure at home, to send an armed force contingent for protection or a decision to scale down its presence in Afghanistan. Both will not be in long term Indian interests in Afghanistan.

A return of the Taliban to power, though rather unlikely, could threaten Indian interests and result in an influx of foreign fighters and an upsurge in violence in Jammu & Kashmir, like in the 1990s. Also, any collaboration between the Taliban and Pakistan could relieve Pakistani forces deployed along the Af-Pak border, enhancing Pakistan's conventional military readiness and availability across Indian border.

India, like Iran does not have the option of abandoning Afghanistan. Despite the potential threats listed above, it is unlikely that the threats would manifest in the stated manner in near future. Afghanistan has come a long way since the days of the Taliban rule of the 1990s. The US and its allies are unlikely to abandon the country, and more importantly, Afghanistan as a nation has moved up in improving its socio-economic indicators to a degree that the return to the dark days of the Taliban rule is an unlikely option. India has the advantages of numerous opportunities, some already being implemented and some in the offing. The SPA with Afghanistan and the prospects of India and Iran jointly assisting Afghanistan hold promises for the future.

POLICY OPTIONS FOR INDIA AND IRAN IN AFGHANISTAN

Afghanistan presents a good opportunity, both for India and Iran. While India looks at Afghanistan more from the prism of regional peace and security, for Iran, Afghanistan presents an opportunity to establish its credentials as a responsible regional player.With Pakistan unlikely to provide direct land transit to Afghanistan, Iran becomes crucial to India's engagement in Afghanistan. Thus Iran, India and Afghanistan could engage fruitfully in a constructive regional engagement in the Afghan context, beyond 2014. Some of the policy options for India and Iran could be:

- India has already signed the SPA with Afghanistan. With the possible easing of economic sanctions as also rapprochement with the US, Iran could expedite the signing of a SPA with Afghanistan.
- India and Iran could then jointly work out a security cooperation arrangement for Afghanistan which could entail training, equipping and maintenance of the ANSF. With Iran in the loop, the question of connectivity would be overcome while India could get the required space to assist Afghanistan as per the SPA. Any tacit or overt support from the US would be welcome too. It could also result in exerting pressure on Pakistan in its support of the Taliban or efforts to undermine future Afghan governments.
- Iran and India could also explore a trilateral trade and transit agreement with Afghanistan. It would not only facilitate movement of goods through the Iran-Afghanistan land route but also make Pakistan's efforts to restrict the movement of Indian goods through Pakistani territory to Afghanistan, irrelevant.
- India and Iran could cooperate to expedite the development of Iran's Chabahar port as also the missing road link from Chabahar to Afghanistan that would facilitate quicker and efficient trade. India has already committed $100 million towards the development of the port.
- The Turkmenistan-Afghanistan-Pakistan-India gas pipeline and the Iran-Pakistan-India oil pipeline have been non-starters for India due to the Pakistan factor. With the existing dynamics unlikely to change soon, India could look at a new alignment to get Turkmen gas via Iran – explore a Turkmenistan-Iran-India (TII) pipeline. While Turkmenistan and Iran are connected in the wider pipeline network across West Asia, this connectivity would require an additional loop towards Chabahar which India and Iran could jointly explore. This would provide India with the CAR energy and Iran with an additional revenue from transit fees.
- India and Iran could also develop a rail link from Chabahar

to the Afghan border and further on to Hajigak mines in Bamiyan province. This 900-kilometer rail link would help India transport iron ore from Afghanistan and earn Iran substantial transit revenue.

- Both Iran and India have an excellent track record of reconstruction aid in Afghanistan, as well as cordial relations and good will among the population. As a conscious effort, India and Iran could, in conjunction with the Afghan government, identify suitable provinces or parts of them in Central, North or West Afghanistan, which could then be taken up by India or Iran or collectively for all round development. International aid, Afghan governmental support and aid from India and Iran could be routed through a consortium which will then undertake development projects and implement it as a model for modern development.

While Afghanistan looks at 2015 with cautious optimism and perhaps apprehension, India and Iran stand out as the best allies for the country.

Together, India and Iran can forge a long term partnership with Afghanistan which would not only ensure peace and security in the country, but also promote Indian and Iranian interests in the region. An India-Iran collaboration in Afghanistan could be a win-win situation for all.

THE CONFLICT WITHIN

Thumping their chests, hundreds of Shia mourners had crammed the narrow lane in the western Pakistani city of Quetta on the afternoon of 2 March 2004. The annual procession commemorating the martyrdom in the sixth century of Imam Hussein, the grandson of the Prophet Mohammed, moved at snail's pace. Suddenly, a huge explosion sent a massive shudder through the crowd. All hell broke loose as gunmen on the rooftop of surrounding buildings opened indiscriminate machine-gun fire and lobbed grenades into the procession. Meanwhile, two suicide bombers detonated themselves in the middle of the procession. Their bodies dangled from the balcony over the electricity wires.

The ghastly carnage left at least 44 people dead and scores of others wounded.

It was the third time in six months that the army garrison town bordering Afghanistan had been drenched in blood by Sunni militants. In July 2003 it had witnessed one of the deadliest acts of religious violence in the country's history, when attackers armed with machine guns and grenades stormed a Shia mosque. More than 2,000 worshippers were praying inside.

The three gunmen first opened fire with automatic weapons and then two of them removed the pins from the grenades they were carrying, causing terrifying explosions and killing 55 people, including themselves. It was the first time suicide bombing was used in such an attack, lending a new and dangerous dimension to sectarian terror. An earlier attack in June had killed 13 police trainees from the Shia Hazara community. The violence spread to Karachi and parts of Punjab province, leaving more than 350 people dead in the year 2004. The 2 March Quetta massacre coincided with the bomb attacks on Shia processions in the Iraqi cities of Baghdad and Karbala, which had left more than 200 people dead.

Although no direct link between the two incidents could be established, there appeared to be some familiar pattern among the different theatres of jihad across the globe. The perpetrators were driven by the same ideological world-view and the dynamics of their operation appeared similar. The objectives and the goals of Pakistani sectarian terrorists in the post-9/11 world appeared closer to those transnational jihadists. It was two-track jihad: they simultaneously fought internal sectarian jihads and external jihad against the West in general and, more specifically, against the USA. Religious sectarianism, the principal source of terrorist activity in Pakistan, presented the most serious threat to the country's internal security. Sectarian terrorism had been deeply intertwined with the Islamization of the state, as non-Sunni sects felt increasingly threatened by the Sunni orthodoxy propagated by the power of the state. The spate of killings in Quetta and other parts of the country had sent a grim reminder that the religious terrorist network was not only intact, but had also expanded. The surge in sectarian terrorism raised serious questions about Musharraf's efforts to combat Islamic extremism. It was all the more inexplicable given Pakistan's success in capturing key al-Qaeda leaders.

Heavily armed terrorist groups continued to operate despite the government's claim that it had rooted out Islamic extremism. While the administration silently watched the situation drift into anarchy, the armed marauders carried out their deadly operations with impunity. The pattern and scale of violence had indicated that the sectarian militants were armed and well organized. Pakistan's largest city and commercial capital, Karachi, and Punjab province had long been the main centres of sectarian violence; now the sphere of strife had extended to new areas, with a series of bloody attacks in the western border city of Quetta where such incidents were previously unknown.

The upsurge in Sunni militancy was linked to al-Qaeda and the Taliban insurgents using Pakistan as a base for their activities. The connection had emerged after an investigation showed that Dawood Badani, a close relative of Khalid Sheikh Mohammed and Ramzi Yousuf, was the prime suspect in the Quetta attacks which had been carried out by Lashkar-e-Jhangvi (LeJ), the Sunni group closely linked to al-Qaeda and to former Taliban rulers in Afghanistan. Claiming responsibility, the group said the attacks were a protest against the Musharraf government, Iran and the United States. A videotape distributed by the group showed that the two suicide bombers were madrasa students. LeJ and other Sunni extremist groups had a history of sectarian violence in Pakistan, but those tensions were inflamed by the US military intervention in Afghanistan and Pakistan's support for it.

Sectarian conflict in Pakistan took an organized militant form in the 1980s. It had its roots in the so-called Islamization process initiated by General Zia ul-Haq's military regime. The government's secular disposition gave way to a professed determination to Islamize the society. The Islamization of law, education and culture illustrated the Sunni sectarian bias of the Pakistani state. General Zia's Islamic penal code was derived entirely from classical Sunni-Hanafi orthodox sources. The official dissemination of a particular brand of Islamic ideology not only militated against Pakistan's sectarian diversity, but also bred discrimination against non-Muslim minorities. The political use of Islam by the state strengthened a clerical elite and created sectarian groups that aggressively pushed their militant ideas. The move towards the establishment of a Sunni-Hanafi state, reflecting the beliefs of the dominant sect, created a sense of insecurity among the Shia minority community. The dynamic of exclusion and minoritization, which had existed since the creation of the country in various forms, was sanctified by General Zia's Islamization. As a result, the more orthodox and militant version of Sunni Islam had grown in strength and public influence. The promotion of Deobandi orthodoxy intensified the sectarian conflict. The spread of jihadist literature from Afghan training camps to Pakistani madrasas in the 1980s fuelled radicalism among the students. Islamization of education created mass sectarian consciousness far beyond the confines of the madrasa, which resulted in a dramatic shift towards extremist Sunni orthodoxy and anti-Shia militancy. More extremist Sunni groups demanded a constitutional amendment to declare Shias a non-Muslim minority and excommunicate them from the realm of Islam.

The Shia community reacted strongly to the enforcement of the Hanafi laws by the military regime. Until 1979, Pakistani Shias were a politically moderate community and had supported secular political parties. But General Zia's Islamization and the Iranian revolution spurred them into political activism. The Islamic revolution in Iran had inspired Shias everywhere. Tens of thousands of Shias gathered in Islamabad in 1980 to protest their marginalization by the Sunni majority, the biggest show of strength by the Pakistani Shia community. It was also the period when a Shia political party known as Tehrik Nifaz-e-Fiqh Jafaria (TNFJ) (Movement for the Implementation of Shia Jurisprudence) was formed, a move reflecting the community's newfound assertiveness. As the only Shia Islamic state, Iran became the centre for spiritual guidance and political support for most Pakistani Shias. The military government and its Sunni allies perceived it as an Iranian conspiracy to export its revolution to Pakistan. The divide, deepened by the actions of the state, could never be bridged. The

Shia revolutionary idealism was followed by the emergence of militant Sunni sectarian organizations. Sipah-e-Sahaba Pakistan (SSP; Army of the Prophet's Companions) was formed in 1985 by the fiery Deobandi cleric Haq Nawaz Jhangvi with a one-point anti- Shia agenda. A prayer leader at a mosque in the central Punjab city of Jhang, he was reported to have close links with Pakistani intelligence agencies. An offshoot of JUI, SSP represented a state-sponsored and Saudi-backed movement against Pakistan's pro-Iran Shia minority. It sought to turn Pakistan into a Sunni state.

A market district in southern Punjab, Jhang was the birthplace of organized sectarian militancy in Pakistan, and the rise of SSP reflected its socio-economic division in the area. The bazaar and merchants supported the Sunni militant group in order to counter the Shia feudal aristocracy which had traditionally dominated local politics. With funding from Saudi Arabia and some other Arab countries and tacit support from the military regime, SSP extended its organization across the country. It had a student wing, a welfare trust and a vast network of local offices. The outfit also operated as a political party, regularly contesting elections in Punjab province. With almost a million card- holding members, SSP emerged as one of the most well-knit Islamist groups.

Initially the SSP cadres came from Deobandi and Ahle Hadith madrasas, which had proliferated during the anti-Soviet jihad. But later it established its own madrasas mostly in Punjab and Karachi. It also drew support from among the urban poor and middle classes and received funds from expatriates in the Middle East.

External factors contributed hugely to stoking sectarian conflict in Pakistan. The Iranian revolution evoked a strong reaction throughout the Muslim world. The spill-over effect of the Shia revolution worried many Arab rulers, as well as the Pakistani military regime, which was trying to establish an Islamic system of a different kind. The rivalry between Sunni Arab states and Shia Iran was further heightened during the Iran-Iraq war. Money poured in from Arab countries anxious to counter the radical Shia Islam sponsored by Iran's revolutionary regime. In the process, Pakistan became the battlefield in an intra Islam proxy war. Iran and Saudi Arabia supported their respected allies. The Saudi government had consistently backed and funded the Deobandi school of thought in Pakistan which had many similarities to the Wahabi version of Islam. Madrasas funded by Saudi Arabia, Kuwait and other Gulf countries, especially after the Soviet invasion of Afghanistan, became the centre of Sunni militancy, as well the recruiting ground for sectarian organizations.

Deobandi and Ahle Hadith mullahs whipped up anti-Shia sentiments. Some Sunni leaders were on the payroll of Iraq. Pakistani and Iranian intelligence agencies had also been actively involved in the proxy war being fought on Pakistani streets since the 1980s. The rise of foreign- backed sectarian militancy set in motion a seemingly unending cycle of violence. Afghanistan's war-hardened fanatics declared their own jihad at home against the Shia community. Armed with sophisticated weapons they started targeting rival mosques and Shia leaders. Although the Shia and Sunni conflict in Pakistan pre-dated the emergence of the SSP, there had been a major escalation in sectarian violence since the anti-Shia riots in Lahore in 1986. Two subsequent events were to change the dynamics of the sectarian violence. In 1987, Allama Ehsan Elahi Zaheer, a Saudi-backed Sunni cleric, was killed in a bomb blast in Lahore. The following year, a prominent Shia leader, Arif Hussaini, was murdered in Peshawar. He had spent time in Iran and was believed to have been closely associated with Iran's Islamic regime. The assassin was a serving army officer, Majid Raza Gillani, which raised suspicions of the ISI's involvement in the murder.

The violence spiralled with the murder of SSP founder Haq Nawaz Jhangvi in 1990, believed to have been carried out by Shia militants. Sectarian clashes broke out in Jhang and spread to other parts of the province. With some 5,000 to 6,000 well-trained militants, the SSP unleashed a reign of terror. The SSP supporters blamed Iran-backed Shia militants for the assassination of Jhangvi. In December that year, Sunni militants gunned down Sadiq Ganji, Iran's consul general in Lahore, in retribution. The incident drew international attention to the conflict, which reached a peak in 1994, one of the worst and the bloodiest years, with at least 74 people killed in sectarian attacks. Most of the deaths occurred in attacks on Shia religious gatherings. Many policemen were also killed in targeted attacks. Iranian interests were particularly targeted by the Sunni extremists. In January 1997, an Iranian cultural centre was set on fire in Lahore. A few days later a similar attack in the southern Punjab town of Multan killed seven people including an Iranian diplomat. In another attack five Iranian air force personnel were killed in Rawalpindi. Shia militants retaliated with a bomb attack at Lahore High Court, which killed the new SSP chief, Ziaur Rehman.

The sectarian conflict took a more violent turn with the formation in 1996 of LeJ. A breakway faction of SSP, the new sectarian outfit led by Riaz Basra, believed in using terror tactics to force the government to accept its demand of declaring the Shia community a non-Muslim minority and establishing an orthodox Sunni Islamic system in the country. Born to a poor farmer in the central Punjab district of Sargodha, Basra received his primary education at a madrasa in Lahore before joining the anti-Soviet jihad in Afghanistan. An injury forced him to return home and he joined SSP in 1986. A fiery orator, Basra quickly rose up in the hierarchy. In 1988, he became the chief of the party's propaganda department; the same year he stood in elections for a Punjab state assembly seat from Lahore.

Basra's notoriety as the most dangerous terrorist grew further after he was arrested for the murder of Sadiq Ganji in 1994. He made a daring escape from an anti-terrorism court in Lahore and later fled to Afghanistan, but he would often return to Pakistan to organize terrorist attacks. LeJ made its mark as the most feared terrorist outfit soon after its inception. Although the number of its hard-core cadres had never been more than five hundred, the group was responsible for most of the sectarian killings over the last decade. By 2001, LeJ had been involved in 350 incidents of terrorism.

Most of the LeJ militants came from among the rural unemployed and Deobandi madrasas, particularly those in southern Punjab, but its highly secretive and mobile organization made it more lethal. Unlike other Islamic militant groups, LeJ avoided media exposure and tried to operate as covertly as possible. Its only contact with the outside world was through occasional fax messages to newspaper offices claiming responsibility for attacks. Its other source of propaganda was its publication Inteqam-i-Haq. LeJ activists were divided into small cells that would dissolve after each action, making it more difficult for the police to break the network. The militants were taught to die rather than be captured by the security forces. 'To become a martyr is the dream of every Mujahid. It is a gift from God and will send a message to the enemy that a Mujahid would prefer to die in an interrogation cell rather than disclose any secret that could harm other Mujahids,' a guideline to party activists said.

Every LeJ activist would go through a tough regimen and ideological training before being sent on a terror mission. He was not supposed to maintain any links with family members during training or divulge any information to them about the group: 'Our relation is with God and whatever we are doing is for God. All other relationships are meaningless. Therefore try to avoid making friends and keeping in close touch with your relatives.' Police officials said it was never easy to interrogate people whose dream was to become martyrs. In Afghanistan, Basra became closely associated with the Taliban militia, which had by then extended its control over a large part of the strife-torn country. The rise of the Taliban in Afghanistan gave the Sunni sectarian groups a new impetus. The rising power of the armed, battle-hardened zealots became alarming and there was already talk about the Talibanization of Pakistan. 'Kabul ke baad Islamabad … Taliban, Taliban [After Kabul, Islamabad. Taliban, Taliban],' shouted a group of mullahs who had gathered at the Lahore High Court in May 1994 soon after Taliban forces had captured Kandahar. They were there for the hearing of a blasphemy case against two Christians. 'Come forward our Taliban to protect Islam in Pakistan.' The slogans were a manifestation of the heady sense of power generated among the religious zealots in Pakistan by the success of the Afghan Taliban. Some of the local militant groups sought to replicate the Taliban's sharia-based system in the border areas of the North West Frontier Province.

The Taliban also helped reinforce the old jihad ties between Pakistani sectarian groups and drug-smuggling cartels in Afghanistan. This mutually beneficial relationship resulted in the 'Islamization of criminal activities'. Afghanistan became a safe haven for Pakistani jihadist and Islamic extremist groups. Inspired by a Sunni revolution and anti-Shia jihad, hundreds of Islamic zealots joined the Talibanoperated terror training in Afghanistan. SSP and LeJ militants were also reportedly involved in the massacres of Shias and in the battle against the opposition Northern Alliance forces. The conservative Afghan regime gave protection to Basra and to some other terrorists wanted by Islamabad on murder charges. During their stay in Afghanistan, the fugitives developed close links with al-Qaeda. Basra was the chief of the Khalid bin Walid training camp in the Sarobi district near Kabul. Pakistani authorities, who backed the Afghan conservative regime, remained indifferent or sometimes consciously looked the other way to this dangerous nexus.

Most of the LeJ cadres were also involved in Pakistan's proxy war in Kashmir. The continuing state patronage of Islamic militancy in return produced an escalation in domestic sectarian conflict. The two were closely intertwined. Pakistan's elected civilian governments in the 1990s had to bear the brunt of sectarian violence and the resultant insecurity and alienation it generated. Both the Benazir Bhutto and Nawaz Sharif governments took steps to combat sectarianism but, given the military's backing for regional jihad, those efforts failed. The jihad connection made the sectarian militants more strident and with easy access to sophisticated weapons they turned more violent. By the mid 1990s, sectarian violence had spread from traditional arenas in Punjab and the northern region to urban heartlands. The nature of the attacks also changed. The initial pattern of targeting leaders, diplomats and other public figures extended to mosques and religious processions. Government functionaries, judges, police officers and doctors were assassinated because of their faith. In 1995, more than 250 people were killed in targeted attacks on Shia worshipping places in Karachi and other parts of the country. In 1997, celebrations of the 50th year of Pakistan's creation were accompanied by an unprecedented wave of sectarian killings.

More than 100 people, most of them Shias, were killed in ten days in the run up to the celebrations in August that year. Riaz Basra was blamed for the massacre. The widespread violence forced the government to take tougher action against sectarian organizations. Dozens of LeJ militants were killed by the police on orders of Shahbaz Sharif, the Chief Minister of Punjab, which had become the main centre of sectarian violence. For the government, extrajudicial killings appeared the only way to combat the highly motivated and well trained militants. Because of death threats, the judges of the lower judiciary – and even some of the superior judiciary – were reluctant to hear cases that involved leaders of LeJ and other powerful sectarian groups.

In 1997, the then Chief Justice of the Supreme Court of Pakistan, Sajjad Ali Shah, asked the authorities to send him a list of the judges who avoided such cases. LeJ retaliated by plotting to kill Prime Minister Nawaz Sharif, his brother Shahbaz and other senior members of his government. In January 1999, Nawaz Sharif escaped an attempt on his life when a bomb tied to a bridge close to his house in Lahore exploded just a few minutes before his cavalcade was to pass. Basra, who was at the top of the list of most wanted terrorists, remained elusive. The Taliban authorities ignored several requests from the Pakistani authorities to extradite him saying that he was a great 'mujahid'.

On 14 August 2001, General Musharraf outlawed LeJ and ordered a nationwide crackdown on the sectarian militants. The decision came in the wake of a series of attacks on Shia mosques and Christian churches. In a nationwide speech on the 55th anniversary of Pakistan's independence, the military ruler vowed to root out what he described as the 'most shameful and despicable examples of terrorism'. Five months later, on 12 January 2002, he banned another five militant and sectarian organizations, including the SSP. It was largely pressure from the international community in the aftermath of 9/11 that forced Musharraf to act against the Islamic extremists.

The fall of the Taliban regime came as a huge blow to LeJ and other militant groups, which had used Afghanistan as a base for ideological and military training for years. Basra fled to Pakistan with hundreds of his followers who had fought alongside the Taliban against the US forces. The militants returning home launched a new jihad against 'internal enemies'. In coordination with al-Qaeda and other groups, LeJ unleashed a series of terror attacks targeting western interests and Shia and Christian worshipping places. The footprints of LeJ could be found in the attacks on the US Consulate in Karachi in May 2002 and in a car-bomb attack outside the Sheraton Hotel, which killed some 12 French engineers.

On 30 January 2003, the US State Department added LeJ to its list of terrorist organizations and to those outfits covered under the executive order. Announcing the decision, a State Department spokesman said that LeJ activists had ties with al-Qaeda and the Taliban, in addition to LeJ involvement in the killing of American citizens. Investigations had shown that the group was responsible for the deaths of two American consulate officials who were killed when gunmen ambushed their vehicles on a busy road in Karachi in March 1995. Garry C. Durrell, aged 45, an undercover CIA official who was sitting on the back seat of a Hilux van died on the spot, while Jackie Van Landingham, 33, a consulate secretary, succumbed to her injuries on the way to hospital. A third employee, Mark McCloy, escaped with a shot to his ankle. The killing of the American officials came amidst a surge in sectarian and factional violence that had led to hundreds of deaths in Karachi, making it one of the most dangerous cities in the world. But it was the first time foreigners were targeted. Investigations indicated that the daring attack on the diplomatic vehicle was LeJ seeking revenge for the extradition to the USA of Ramzi Yousuf. The pattern of the attacks indicated that the same gang of terrorists involved in the attacks on Shia mosques weeks before could also be involved in the killing of American officials.

Pakistani authorities vigorously targeted LeJ following a series of attacks that jolted Pakistan in the aftermath of the US invasion of Afghanistan. During 2002, the security forces met with major success when they killed or captured a significant number of LeJ activists. Those who were killed also included two top LeJ leaders, Basra and Asif Ramzi. Basra and his three associates were killed in May that year in a shoot-out with police near Mailsi in Multan. Ramzi, believed to be the second-in-command to Basra, was killed in December in an explosion at a chemical warehouse on the outskirts of Karachi. One of the most wanted terrorists, he was involved in more than 80 cases of murder and was wanted for the attacks on the US Consulate and Sheraton Hotel. Ramzi was the key link between the local militants and al-Qaeda trying to regroup in Pakistan. Pakistani and US security officials suspected that Ramzi had manufactured the explosives used in the US Consulate attack.

On 17 June 2002, the security forces captured another notorious LeJ leader, Akram Lahori, wanted in more than two dozen murder cases. A deputy to Basra, he was a key planner of various sectarian-based terrorist attacks in Karachi and was believed to have trained many potential suicide bombers. Despite those setbacks, however, the group appeared to retain a substantial capacity to strike, and continued to provide logistical support and personnel to al-Qaeda and Taliban operating from their bases in Pakistan's tribal region. The death of senior LeJ leaders did not bring any respite to the violence. A new breed of well-trained and battle-hardened militants took over the charge.

The increasing use of suicide bombing in terror attacks gave a new and more dangerous dimension to the sectarian war. Both Shias and Sunnis started deploying suicide bombers to inflict maximum casualties. Mosques, religious processions and rallies became the prime targets of suicide attacks in the sectarian war. Unlike suicide bombers elsewhere who simply detonated their explosive-strapped bodies, Pakistani militants hurled grenades and fired on the crowd before blowing themselves up in order to cause maximum damage. Poverty, unemployment, romantic notions of jihad and the growing influence of radical Islamic groups were the main reasons for a young man to turn into a suicide bomber. Between March 2002 and May 2004 there had been 20 cases of suicide bombing, which had killed more than 200 people. The targets varied from western nationals to Christian and Shia worshipping places. The majority of the attackers were unemployed and came from poor families. The 22-year-old Kamran Mir, who blew himself up inside a Christian church in Taxila in

August 2002, killing several worshippers, was an unemployed school drop-out. He was trained by LeJ. The other two suicide bombers involved in the attack on a Shia religious procession in Quetta on 2 March 2004 were jobless former madrasa students. Abdul Nabi and Hidayatullah were made to believe that Shias were infidels and that they should be eliminated.

Despite their proscription, most of the militant groups continued their activities. Some of them resurfaced under new banners. Their leaders were temporarily detained, but none of them were tried in a court of law, even those against whom cases were pending. The example of Azam Tariq exposed the government's lack of sincerity in curbing religious extremism. While many politicians were prevented from fighting elections on patently frivolous grounds, the SSP leader, accused of sectarian killings, was allowed to contest from jail. He was freed after he agreed to join the pro-Musharraf alliance in the National Assembly. To retain Tariq's support the government ignored the non- bailable warrants of arrest issued against him by anti-terrorism courts. He was assassinated in 2003, apparently in a revenge attack by rival Shia militants.

The 42-year-old SSP leader was notorious for his virulent anti-Shia rhetoric. He was charged in several murder cases which had also earned him a two year jail sentence in the mid 1990s. Born to a poor farming family in the small town of Chichawatni in Punjab province, he graduated from a local madrasa before joining SSP. A firebrand cleric, Tariq went from being an ordinary activist to the head of the SSP in less than ten years. As the group's murder index shot up, so did Tariq's popularity among Sunni zealots. He was elected to the National Assembly no less than four times. He formed a new party, Millat-e-Islam, after the government proscribed the SSP. He escaped many attempts on his life before falling to an assassin's bullet outside Islamabad. His death led to a spate of revenge killings across the country. After Tariq's death his followers disintegrated into several splinter groups and many of them joined LeJ.

Though the government cracked down on those new groups which had replaced the outlawed outfits, the measures could not succeed in the absence of a coherent long-term strategy. It was easy enough for the militants to operate under new banners when their leaders moved around freely. Their hate literature was freely distributed across the country and pulpits of mosques were used by the mullahs to preach violence. The infrastructure of the banned sectarian groups and their capacity to carry out terrorist attacks remained unaffected, as was evident in the surge in sectarian violence during 2004. The pattern and scale of the violence demonstrated their extensive support network. The gruesome killings of 40 people in twin bomb blasts in Multan on 7 October 2004 highlighted the depth of the sectarian violence that continued to plague Pakistan. The attack occurred at a large SSP rally marking the first anniversary of the assassination of their leader. The bombing came a week after a suicide attack inside a crowded Shia mosque in the city of Sialkot in Punjab province, which had killed at least 30 worshippers.

The rising tide of sectarian violence was also linked to the inability of intelligence agencies and the police to pre-empt and investigate sectarian crimes. The inaction could partly be attributed to fear of sectarian retaliation. Terrorists had killed many police officers who were investigating sectarian killings in Punjab and Karachi. In 2002, a police officer, Mohammed Jamil, was killed in Jhang after he had arrested several LeJ activists. In July 2004, a Rawalpindi police inspector was assassinated on his way to court to give evidence against the terrorists involved in an attack on a Shia mosque. The penetration of law enforcing agencies by terrorist organizations was particularly perturbing. A suicide bomber responsible for the attack on a Shia mosque in Karachi in May 2004 turned out to be a police constable who was also a member of SSP. At least two policemen were involved in the attack on a Shia procession in Quetta on 2 March 2004. Notwithstanding Musharraf's promise to eradicate extremism, the issue had never been on the government's priority list. Without any legal mechanism or a long-term strategy in place, the administration was unable to prevent the flow of funds to unregulated madrasas and other religious groups involved in extremist activities. The government's failure to curb the jihadist madrasas had largely been responsible for fuelling Islamic extremism.

Most religious schools continued to preach hatred and intolerance. As a consequence, the ranks of sectarian extremists swelled. After the failed attempts on Musharraf's life, the administration launched raids on some radical madrasas, but such half-hearted and piecemeal measures could hardly improve the situation. Security agencies had raided sectarian seminaries only to back down under the pressure from Islamic parties. In August 2004, the police raided a mosque and a madrasa in Islamabad to arrest the prayer leader and his brother for their involvement in terrorist activities, including collaboration with al-Qaeda. The two were not only released and charges dropped, but they also retained their government jobs despite a long history of inciting sectarian hatred.

While Musharraf was praised by the international community for his role in the war on terror, the frequency and fierceness of sectarian terrorism continued to rise. The sectarian conflict in Pakistan was also a consequence of the military government's policy of marginalization of secular democratic forces. Despite his close alliance with the USA, Musharraf continued to rely on the religious right to counter the liberal opposition. The politics of expediency was also a major factor in his government's failure to curb religious extremism and sectarian forces.

6

Iran and the Future of Afghanistan

In crafting a new approach to the war in Afghanistan, U.S. military and political leaders say Iran—once dubbed a member of the "axis of evil" by former President George W. Bush—could play a key role. Despite ongoing concerns over Iran's nuclear program and allegations of arming militants in the region, Gen. David H. Petraeus, commander of U.S. forces in the region, says Washington and Iran could coalesce around stabilizing Afghanistan. Admiral Mike Mullen, chairman of the Joint Chiefs of Staff, echoed the sentiment (PDF) in late January 2009. NATO partners, too, have sought to include Iran in Afghan strategy decisions. German lawmakers have called for the creation of a "contact group" of nations to chart a new regional course. "Such an initiative, that would include Iran, would benefit if it came to direct talks between Washington and Tehran," Andreas Schockenhoff, vice chairman of Germany's Christian Democratic Party, said in a statement reported by German media.

These overtures have been followed by concrete steps to bring Iran into the discussion on Afghanistan. On March 20, President Barack Obama reached out to Iran through a televised address in which he offered a "new beginning" for U.S.-Iran ties. In his new strategy for the Afghan war unveiled a week later, the president repeated Germany's calls for a "contact group" and listed Iran as a key player. Iran is also expected to attend (Reuters) an international summit on Afghanistan on March 31 in The Hague, succeeding a March 27 Shanghai Cooperation Organization meeting on Afghanistan in Moscow, which Iran attended with SCO observer status. The SCO meeting marked the Obama administration's first high-level encounter with officials from Tehran.

Yet matching pledges for broader cooperation with action from Tehran is complicated by Iran's historic relationship to its eastern neighbor. For one, Iran has been accused of supplying weapons to Taliban rebels operating along the Afghanistan-Pakistan border. Allegations have been tempered in recent months, but experts nonetheless see a number of reasons why a strengthened Taliban could serve Iran's interests, particularly in keeping U.S. forces off balance. "It is true that Iran was helping the Taliban out," possibly by supplying weapons and training, says Elizabeth Rubin, an Afghan expert. But, she adds, "in the big picture the Iranians do not want the Taliban back."

CROSS-BORDER TIES

Iran has close linguistic and cultural ties to Afghanistan, particularly with Tajiks, Persian-speaking Afghans in Herat Province, and the Hazara, a Shiite minority residing in central and northern Afghanistan. Iranian influence in this region runs deep; the city of Herat served as the capital of the Persian empire in the early fifteenth century, and remained a center of Iranian power and culture until it was taken by Dost Mohammed Khan in 1863 and made a de facto Afghan border state. In modern times, Tehran's role has often aligned with U.S. interests. Iran opened its borders to millions of Afghan refugees during the war against the Soviet Union in the 1980s. Later in the 1990s it worked with various mujahadeen groups, including the Northern Alliance of Tajik, Uzbek, and Hazara militias, to undermine Soviet influence and later Taliban rule. After the Taliban took power in 1996, Iran's supreme leader denounced the group as an affront to Islam, and the killing of eleven Iranian diplomats and truck drivers in 1998 almost triggered a military conflict.

A regional contact group "that would include Iran would benefit if it came to direct talks between Washington and Tehran." — Andreas Schockenhoff, Vice Chairman, German Christian Democratic Party

Iran's influence, however, has not always been welcomed by some local Afghans. CFR Senior Fellow Ray Takeyh writes in his book, *Hidden Iran: Paradox and Power in the Islamic Republic,* that "fiercely independent Afghan tribes have historically resisted Persian encroachment and have jealously guarded their rights." But Iranian cultural and economic expansion continues apace. Iranian radio broadcasts fill the airwaves, Iran-funded road and building projects are under way, a new teacher training center is planned for Kabul, and a Herat-Khaf rail link (Pajhwok) is being constructed to connect Afghanistan and Iran by train. Iran has also offered humanitarian aid to Kabul in the form of fuel and transport—as much as $500 million since 2001, according to the U.S. Congressional Research Service. CFR's Rubin, who has spent years as a journalist in Afghanistan, says Shiite Afghans are better off financially than most of their counterparts because of aid from Tehran.

MUTUAL INTERESTS AND MISSED OPPORTUNITIES

Iran has important domestic interests in seeing a stable Afghanistan rise on its eastern flank. Four percent of Iran's total exports in 2006 (PDF), according to the most recent data available, went to Afghanistan, accounting for more than $503 million in revenue. Iran is also building roads and expanding its industrial base inside Afghanistan's western border. But arguably the most pressing concern for Iran is gaining the upper hand in Afghanistan's booming drug trade. Iran serves as the major transport hub for opiates produced by its neighbor, and the UN Office of Drugs and Crime estimates that Iran has as many as 1.7 million opiate addicts.

Following the terrorist attacks in New York and Washington on September 11, 2001, Iran showed a willingness to facilitate U.S. efforts in Afghanistan, including drug interdiction programs. Tehran worked with Western countries as part of the Six-Plus-Two framework on Afghanistan and also at the Bonn Conference to cobble together a post-Taliban system of government. Tehran also normalized relations with the Afghan government of President Hamid Karzai, and "deported hundreds" (*National Interest*) of al-Qaeda and Taliban leaders who had sought refuge in Iran, according to two senior U.S. officials involved in regional policy at the time.

One of them, Hillary Mann Leverett, who served as director for Iran and Persian Gulf affairs at the National Security Council in the George W. Bush administration, told Congress in November 2007 that Iran's cooperation with the United States on al-Qaeda, Iraq, and especially Afghanistan after 9/11 was largely positive (PDF). In each case, she said, "Iran hoped and anticipated that tactical cooperation with the United States would lead to a genuine strategic opening between our two countries." But by May 2003-sixteen months after Bush's "axis of evil" declaration during his January 2002 State of the Union speech-channels of communication with Iran had closed. Mann Leverett now believes failed talks over the years have increased the mistrust between Washington and Tehran to nearly unworkable levels. Discussing limited tactical issues like Afghanistan, she says, must be part of a broader comprehensive strategy where everything—from U.S. nuclear concerns to Iranian frustration with security and sanctions—is on the table.

A Change in Tactic

Soured diplomatic relations were followed by claims of Iranian support to Islamic militants, first in Iraq, and then in Afghanistan. Defense Secretary Robert Gates told reporters in June 2007 that "given the quantities that we're seeing, it is difficult to believe that it's associated with smuggling or the drug business or that it's taking place without the knowledge of the Iranian government." U.S. officials say that Iranian-made weapons, including Tehran's signature roadside bomb-the explosively formed penetrator (EFP)-as well as AK-47s, C-4 plastic explosives, and mortars have been found in Afghanistan and used by Taliban-led insurgents. They are concerned because Taliban forces increasingly use more sophisticated weaponry and mimic the style of suicide attacks popular among insurgents in Iraq. Iran also stands accused of offering sanctuary to opponents of the Afghan government and violating Afghan airspace. Iranian officials deny the charges.

Experts say a strengthened Taliban would benefit Tehran in a number of ways. Peter Tomsen, former U.S. ambassador to Afghanistan, told CFR.org in 2006 that a weakened Afghan state lessens the likelihood it can become a U.S. ally against Iran. By maintaining a certain level of instability, he said, "it keeps us tied down. After all, we have air bases in Afghanistan where we could mount attacks on Iran." Some analysts call it "managed chaos," a strategy they say is similar to the one Iran employs in Iraq. Others see abetting the Taliban as a means to boost Iran's leverage at a time when it is under pressure to end its uranium-enrichment program. Despite Iran's Shiite brand of Islam, Tehran has thrown its support behind majority Sunni groups in Iraq and elsewhere. As Takeyh writes in his book, "[F]or Tehran the issue in Afghanistan has not been ideological conformity but stability."

"If they can get to the moderates ... then there is a lot of room for cooperation, especially if it is not pitched as a U.S. plan but a regional one." — Elizabeth Rubin, CFR Press Fellow

But experts disagree on whether the Iranian government is directly involved. Some have refuted Gates' remarks and say the weapons could have been smuggled into Afghanistan via various third-party channels. Others suggest they are being supplied by hard-line components within the Iranian Revolutionary Guards (the Mashhad-based Fourth Corps is responsible for projecting Iranian power in Afghanistan (PDF)), which has a separate agenda from the Iranian foreign ministry, which in turn has a separate agenda from Iran's business community. "We're talking about rogue elements," Col. Christopher Langton, a senior fellow at the London-based International Institute for Strategic Studies, told CFR.org in 2006, "maybe even cross-border organizational criminal groupings." He said that arms factories in Pakistan's North West Frontier Province make copies of the weapons made in Iran.

THE UNITED STATES, IRAN, AND THE FUTURE OF AFGHANISTAN

Suggestions persist that Iran might have a positive role to play in stabilizing its war-ravaged neighbor, where in early 2009 violence was spiking and Taliban fighters were gaining strength. U.S., NATO, and UN officials have all noted Tehran's support of the government in Kabul. A number of experts stress that Iran wants stability and prosperity on its eastern doorstep for commercial and trade reasons. Yet Iranian actions continue to raise doubts about Tehran's intent. The January 2009 deportation of Afghan refugees by Iran was just the latest in what Afghan officials in Kabul see as a string of "broken promises" (RFE/RL). An estimated 1 million UN-registered refugees remain in Iran. A U.S. State Department spokesman, meanwhile, expressed "great concern" with Iran's February 2009 launch of a satellite that he said "could possibly lead to the development of a ballistic missile system."

More broadly, experts question whether the issue of Afghanistan can serve as a bridge to broader negotiations for Washington and Tehran. CFR's Rubin says there is a whole moderate wing of Iranian lawmakers that hope it can: "If they can get to the moderates, and I believe the Iranian ambassador in Afghanistan is one of the moderates, then there is a lot of room for cooperation, especially if it is not pitched as a U.S. plan but a regional one." Karim Sadjadpour, an Iran expert at the Carnegie Endowment for International Peace, notes in an October 2008 policy paper (PDF) that "Afghanistan presents even more fertile ground for U.S.-Iranian cooperation" than the issue of stability in Iraq. And writing in *The New York Review of Books*, a trio of Iran experts suggests the Obama administration should, unlike its predecessor, treat negotiations over Afghanistan and Iraq border security—vital concerns for Iran—as inseparable from the nuclear issue.

But cooperation over Afghanistan—not to mention the nuclear problem or even Iraq—is far from a foregone conclusion. Barnett R. Rubin, an Afghan expert and director of studies at New York University's Center for International Cooperation, writes that reaching a consensus on Afghanistan is colored by the historic "animus" between Washington and Tehran, which began with the 1953 CIA-led coup in Iran and was cemented by the Iranian revolution of 1979. Zalmay Khalilzad, the former U.S. ambassador to the United Nations and a former envoy to Kabul, says that Iran still sees Afghanistan as a "bargaining chip" (Bloomberg) against American aggression. Masood Aziz, a former Afghan diplomat in Washington, meanwhile, predicts that "Iran is going to be one of the key pillars of our strategy which is going to help resolve this issue. Iran has the potential to be extremely helpful." But he adds: "Discussions and talks are one thing; how to go about implementing cooperation [with Iran] is another."

THE PARADOXICAL AFGHAN/IRANIAN ALLIANCE

Many in the West associate Iran with religious fanaticism and an adventurous, confrontational foreign policy. By contrast, Iran is viewed as a force for moderation and stability in Afghanistan. From Kabul's perspective, the U.S. and Iran share much common ground vis-à-vis Afghanistan – both support the establishment of a viable government in Kabul, have a shared interest in stemming the flow of narcotics across the Afghani-Iranian border, and neither country wants al-Qaeda to re-establish a safe haven in Afghanistan. While U.S. officials weigh the pros and cons of a possible rapprochement with Iran and its implications for the U.S., little is being said about how the prospects for stability in Afghanistan could improve if a thaw does indeed occur.

On one hand, Iran's Afghanistan foreign policy is contradictory. In 2001, Iran aided the coalition forces that overthrew the Taliban. Iranian pressure on Afghanistan's Tajik minority to share power with Hamid Karzai (a Pashtun) later contributed to the Karzai government's successful establishment. Since then Tehran has maintained strong ties with Kabul. On the other hand, Iran has also sponsored the Taliban, which continues to wage an insurgency against the Iranian and U.S.-backed Karzai government. The Iran-Taliban alliance is particularly paradoxical given the Taliban's anti-Shi'ite ideology and the fact that the movement nearly brought Afghanistan and Iran to war in 1998, following the killing of nine Iranian diplomats in Mazar-e Sharif.

Ultimately, Iranian support for the Taliban sheds light on Tehran's geostrategic calculations vis-à-vis the U.S. (the perception that the U.S. presence in Afghanistan was a grave security threat) more than on Tehran's long-term interests in Afghanistan. Iran has historically supported Afghanistan's Tajik, Hazara, and Shi'ite currents that are anti-Taliban. Tehran's sponsorship of the Taliban is thus consistent with Iran's strategy of countering U.S./NATO influence through asymmetric proxy warfare. While Iran's measured support for the Taliban provided Tehran with greater leverage over the Karzai government, it was primarily motivated by its hostile relationship with the U.S. Sponsorship of the Taliban added to Iran's capacity to deter the U.S. from waging a military strike against Iran, while bogging the U.S. military down in Afghanistan at a time when the U.S. threatened a military strike on Iran's nuclear facilities. According to former U.S. Ambassador Zalmay Khalilzad, Tehran has viewed Afghanistan as a "bargaining chip" against Washington. The Taliban has not been subtle about its preference for a continuation of a hostile relationship between the U.S. and Iran, and is clearly a beneficiary of this animosity. However, once NATO forces have departed, and if relations between Washington and Tehran thaw, it is plausible that Iran would lose interest in maintaining its alliance with the Taliban.

The story of Iran's influence in Herat throughout the past decade underscores Iran's potential to promote stability and moderation throughout Afghanistan. Herat (Afghanistan's third largest city) is situated within 100 miles of the Iranian border. Until the Treaty of Paris was signed — which ended the Anglo-Persian War (1856-1857) — Herat was considered an integral part of Iran. Today, many Iranians view portions of western Afghanistan as within Iran's sphere of influence. Given the cultural, economic, historic, linguistic, political and religious bonds that connect the Afghanis and Iranians on both sides of the border, an extension of Iranian influence in Western Afghanistan seems natural.

Moreover, since the Taliban's fall in 2001, Tehran has invested hundreds of millions of dollars into reconstruction efforts throughout Herat and many private Iranian firms (subsidized by the Iranian government) operate in western Afghanistan. Isma'il Khan, a warlord who previously served as Herat's governor, earned several million dollars each month from taxes imposed on Iranian imports. Up to 500 cars and trucks reportedly cross Iran's border with Herat province on a daily basis, delivering products into Afghanistan and Pakistan from Iran and the United Arab Emirates. Within the context of Afghanistan's realities, Herat's development in recent years has been marked by relative economic prosperity, stability and security; observers note the growth of a vibrant civil society, reflective of more tolerant and progressive values.

Iran looks to Afghanistan as a gateway akin to the Silk Road, as a pathway toward Greater Central Asia. Stability in Afghanistan would bode well for Iran's interests in establishing future pipelines linking Iran to the Central Asian Republics and China. In the near-term, however, Iran's security and foreign policy dilemmas will continue to drive Tehran's policies vis-à-vis Afghanistan. The killing of 14 Iranian border guards near the Iranian-Pakistani border last month underscored the reality that southeastern Iran remains troublesome, and the Sunni Islamist group Jundullah remains active and hostile toward Tehran. In addition to the lingering Baluchi insurgency, other transnational issues — such as the Afghan refugee question, water disputes and the narcotics trafficking — will continue to play a major role in Iran's calculations vis-à-vis Afghanistan.

The Iranian government knows it does not have the luxury of leaving Afghanistan for others to address. Humanitarian crises, sectarian clashes, and terrorism in Afghanistan will inevitably impact Iran. The Iranian government holds no illusions about Afghanistan's myriad of problems, nor is there any expectation that these will soon be resolved. It is within this context that Iran is vested in economic development and political stability in Afghanistan, contrary to the variables that have fueled violent cycles throughout Afghanistan's history. Obviously, the U.S. and Iran will not always see eye to eye on the plethora of challenges in Afghanistan, but the important issues that align Washington and Tehran's long-term interests should be acknowledged as the two governments test the diplomatic waters and entertain a rapprochement. In the interim, Kabul and Tehran's complicated and paradoxical relationship will continue to confound conventional wisdom.

IRAN'S UNAVOIDABLE INFLUENCE OVER AFGHANISTAN'S FUTURE

As the U.S. troop withdrawal approaches, Washington should consider how improving U.S.-Iranian relations can further its long-term goals in Afghanistan and the region.

Iran has positioned itself as an important regional actor in Central Asia and is committed to playing a role in neighbouring Afghanistan. As U.S. troops draw down their numbers in Afghanistan, Washington should consider how improved U.S.-

Iranian relations could further long-term U.S. policy goals in Afghanistan and in the region.

While the future of U.S.-Iranian relations remains unclear, any improvement in the relationship would facilitate the success of U.S.-supported initiatives in Afghanistan: the "New Silk Road" strategy, which seeks to improve Afghanistan's economic ties with Central and South Asia, and the "Heart of Asia" confidence-building process, which fosters high-level dialogue on security, political, and economic cooperation among Afghanistan and its neighbours. Both are catchwords for Washington's policy of trying to shift more responsibility for Afghanistan's reconstruction to the states of the region. But the international sanctions against Iran and the state of U.S.-Iranian relations are making it difficult for policymakers in Washington to implement this regional approach.

IRAN'S CLOSE TIES TO CENTRAL ASIA

Iranian leaders pride themselves on being important actors in Central Asia, and they take advantage of all available international forums to make this case. For their part, the region's other countries maintain normal diplomatic and trade relations with Iran.

The respect accorded to Iran in Central Asia was underscored by the presence of the presidents of Kazakhstan, Tajikistan, and Turkmenistan at Iranian President Hassan Rouhani's inauguration. The presidents of Afghanistan and Pakistan attended as well. Uzbekistan, which has kept somewhat more distance from Iran, sent the head of its parliament, as did Russia.

The three Central Asian presidents used their presence to bring up the topics of greatest importance to them. For the Tajiks, who share a language and culture with the Iranians and call Iran a "strategic partner," this meant discussing Tajikistan's hydroelectric plans.

Kazakh President Nursultan Nazarbayev used his visit to reiterate his country's interest in continuing to host the P5+1 nuclear talks between Iran and the five permanent members of the UN Security Council plus Germany, which are under the chairmanship of EU High Representative for Foreign Affairs and Security Policy Catherine Ashton. Kazakhstan hosted P5+1 sessions in Almaty in

February and April 2013. Transport links were major themes for both the Kazakh and Turkmen leaders. With Iran, these countries are constructing a new railroad to link Uzen in Kazakhstan with Gyzylgaya, Bereket, and Etrek in Turkmenistan and end at Gorgan in the Iranian province of Golestan. The railroad will expand access for the Central Asian nations to Persian Gulf ports.

The Kazakh and Turkmen presidents jointly opened the first section of the railroad on May 11, 2013, during Turkmen President Gurbanguly Berdymukhamedov's official visit to Kazakhstan. The nearly 50-mile Iranian portion was inaugurated later that month.

But international sanctions against Iran have complicated Tehran's attempts to gain influence in Central Asia. Given Iran's participation in the project, for example, the new railroad could not secure international multilateral institution funding. Instead, it is being built with funds of the national railway companies of Iran, Kazakhstan, and Turkmenistan.

Furthermore, Iran is not part of the Asian Development Bank (ADB) or the Central Asian Regional Economic Coordination, the ADB's ten-country partnership that is sponsoring six new transport corridors to better link Afghanistan and Central Asia with Europe and Asia.

Sanctions against Iran have also limited international oil and gas export routes from the region by making it impossible to secure international financing for such projects. While the new rail link will create options for Kazakhstan to send oil by rail to the Persian Gulf, the Kazakhs have been frustrated in their desire to transport "big oil" or "big gas" through Iran. They do, however, supply northern Iran with oil and receive the export income from oil swapped by the Iranians in the south.

Turkmenistan has also had to fund its own projects in Iran. Years before the prospect of shipping large amounts of gas through China became possible, the Turkmen, angered by the terms of trade with Russia, agreed to build a gas pipeline from Korpezhe in Turkmenistan to Kurt Kui in Iran. Built in 1997 with a maximum capacity of 8 billion cubic meters per year (bcm/y), or 282 billion cubic feet per year (bcf/y), 35 percent of the gas went to pay for Turkmenistan's share of construction costs during the first years.

A second Turkmenistan–Iran line, the Dauletabad–Khangiran Pipeline, with a capacity of 12 bcm/y (424 bcf/y) was completed in 2010.

In addition to cooperation on transport, all of the Central Asian countries trade actively with Iran; in 2010 Iran was the fourth-largest exporter to Central Asia, with 4.8 percent of all exports, following distantly behind China, Russia, and the EU. Iran is a major buyer of Central Asian cotton, traditionally purchasing from Tajikistan, but it also became an important source of cotton sales for Uzbekistan after the EU introduced trade restrictions against Tashkent.

Rouhani has signaled the importance of the Central Asian region by deciding to make his first international trip a visit to Bishkek to attend the Shanghai Cooperation Organization (SCO) summit being held there on September 3, just days before the G20 meeting in St. Petersburg. This will also be Rouhani's first meeting as president with Vladimir Putin.

Iran, an observer in the SCO, has long sought full membership in that organization. But Russia has spoken out against Iran receiving full membership because of the difficulties that this might pose for the organization as a whole given the international sanctions in place against Iran. Afghanistan is also an observer of the SCO, and Turkey just took on this status in April, suggesting that the SCO might well be positioning itself to play a greater role in Afghanistan after the withdrawal of U.S. troops in 2014.

IRAN'S ENGAGEMENT IN AFGHANISTAN

Playing a greater role in Afghanistan seems a clear goal of Iran. The two states share a border that is more than 560 miles long, and senior Iranian officials have participated in virtually every major international meeting on Afghanistan that they have been eligible to attend.

Ambassador James Dobbins, who served as U.S. special envoy for Afghanistan in 2001 and was appointed special representative for Afghanistan and Pakistan in May 2013, notes that the suggestion that Hamid Karzai should lead Afghanistan was raised by the Iranian delegation to the international conference on Afghanistan in Bonn, Germany, in 2001. According to Dobbins, he and Javad Zarif, then Iran's delegate to the conference and today the newly appointed minister of foreign affairs, found informal settings in which to "accidently" meet and hold important substantive discussions. Dobbins noted that Iran pledged $540 million in assistance at the first Tokyo conference in 2002, the largest commitment made by any non-Organization for Economic Cooperation and Development nation. Most of this assistance, according to Dobbins, was actually provided.

The U.S.-Iranian relationship soured soon after, when Mohammad Khatami was still president, and deteriorated dramatically during Mahmoud Ahmadinejad's presidency.

This created a very awkward moment for the United States at the fifth Regional Economic Cooperation Conference on Afghanistan meeting in March 2012. U.S. officials played a major role in helping organize the conference but were left playing more of a backstage role at the event itself given the participation of Ahmadinejad.

The Iranian leader used the occasion to attack the U.S.-led NATO presence in Afghanistan, demanding that reparations be paid to the Afghan people. This prompted the U.S. delegation, led by Assistant Secretary of State Robert Blake, to leave the room. But this departure failed to have the desired effect—the room was so enormous that only those seated near the U.S. delegation noticed the delegates' exit. Because the U.S. delegation was headed by Assistant Secretary Blake, it ranked way down on the protocol lists for speakers, especially given that Tajikistan, Afghanistan, Iran, and Pakistan were all represented by their presidents. Tajik President Emomali Rahmon also convened a summit of these four presidents in the days before the conference opened, on the occasion of Nowruz, the traditional spring holiday in the region, creating an exclusive format for discussions of Afghanistan's future in which "outsiders," including the United States, were not included.

AFGHAN NATION-STATE

Mir Wais Hotak, seen as Afghanistan's George Washington, successfully rebelled against the Persian Safavids in 1709. He overthrew and killed Gurgin Khan, and made the Afghan region independent from Persia. By 1713, Mirwais had decisively defeated two larger Persian armies, one was led by Khusraw Khán (nephew of Gurgin) and the other by Rustam Khán. The armies were sent by Sultan Husayn, the Shah in Isfahan (now Iran), to re-take control of the Kandahar region.Mirwais died of a natural cause in 1715 and was succeeded by his brother Abdul Aziz followed by his son Mahmud. In 1722, Mahmud led an Afghan army to the Persian capital of Isfahan, sacked the city after the Battle of Gulnabad and proclaimed himself King of Persia. The Persians were disloyal to the Afghan rulers, and after the massacre of thousands of religious scholars, nobles, and members of the Safavid family, the Hotaki dynasty was ousted from Persia after the 1729 Battle of Damghan.

In 1738, Nader Shah and his Afsharid forces captured Kandahar from Shah Hussain Hotaki, at which point the incarcerated 16 year old Ahmad Shah Durrani was freed and made the commander of Nader Shah's four thousand Abdali Afghans. From Kandahar they set out to conquer India, passing through Ghazni, Kabul, Lahore and ultimately plundering Delhi after the Battle of Karnal. Nader Shah and his army abandoned Delhi but took with them huge treasure, which included the Koh-i-Noor andDarya-ye Noor diamonds. After the death of Nader Shah in 1747, the Afghans chose Ahmad Shah Durrani as their head of state. Regarded as the founder of modern Afghanistan, Durrani and his Afghan army conquered the entire present-day Afghanistan, Pakistan, Khorasan and Kohistanprovinces of Iran, along with Delhi in India. He defeated the Sikhs of the Maratha Empire in thePunjab region nine times, one of the biggest battles was the 1761 Battle of Panipat.

In October 1772, Ahmad Shah Durrani died of a natural cause and was buried at a site now adjacent to the Shrine of the Cloak in Kandahar. He was succeeded by his son, Timur Shah Durrani, who transferred the capital of Afghanistan from Kandahar to Kabul in 1776. After Timur Shah's death in 1793, the Durrani throne was passed down to his son Zaman Shah followed by Mahmud Shah, Shuja Shah and others.

The Afghan Empire was under threat in the early 19th century by the Sikhs in the east and the Persians in the west. The western provinces of Khorasan and Kohistan were taken by the Persians in 1800. The biggest blow to Afghans however came on 13th July 1813, when the Vizier of Afghanistan Fateh Khan and his brother Dost Mohammad Khan came face to face with Sikh armies atAttock(Battle of Attock). The Sikh armies as usual were led by their famous Hindu General Diwan Mokham Chand who was 70 years old at that time, the battle saw the gruesome massacre of Afghan armies, over 9,000 Afghan soldiers laid their lives in this battle, Dost Mohammad Khan save himself with great difficulty whereas Vizier Fateh Khan fled back even before the Afghans were defeated.. The defeat created a sensation in Kabul the capital of Durrani Empire, the defeat of the Wazir of Afghanistan by Mohkam Chand roused fear in Afghans that Sikhs may now march upon Kabul. However the grand victory of Sikh Armies coincided with the Holy Festival of Diwali which is celebrated by Hindu, Sikhs, Jains and Buddhists which resulted in the return of victorious Sikh armies and their Famous Hindu General Mohkam Chand back to Lahore(Now In Pakistan). This defeat ended the Afghans dream of regaining Panjab and instead push Afghans on more defensive approach. Post this defeat Afghans mostly fought defensive battles. Another Hindu General Diwan Misr Chand plundered Afghan general Jabbar Khan in Kashmir in 1819 which saw the end of Muslim rule over Kashmir(1339-1819).

The Sikhs of Punjab, under Ranjit Singh, invaded Afghanistan's Khyber Pakhtunkhwa region and in 1834 captured its second capital, Peshawar. The regions of Multan, Kashmir, Sindh and Balochistan were also lost. Fateh Khan, leader of the Barakzai tribe, had installed 21 of his brothers in positions of power throughout the Afghan Empire. After his death, they rebelled and divided up the provinces of the empire between themselves. During this turbulent period, Afghanistan had many temporary rulers until 1826 when Dost Mohammad Khan rose to power. In 1837, Akbar Khan and the Afghan army crossed the Khyber Pass to defeat the Sikhs at the Battle of Jamrud, killing Sikh Commander Hari Singh Nalwa.. However, the arrival of the Sikh army under Wazir Dhyan Singh Dogra and his elder brother Maharaja Gulab Singh in the vicinity of Jamrud didn't allow the Afghans to occupy the Jamrud fort. Akbar Khan and his Afghan army fled back to

Kabul. By this time the British were advancing to the area from the east and the First Anglo-Afghan War or better known as the Great Game was initiated.

Western influence

Following the 1842 Battle of Gandamak that was fought between Akbar Khan and William Elphinstone, the British established diplomatic relations with the Afghan government but withdrew all forces from the country. They returned during the Second Anglo-Afghan War in the late 1870s for about two year military operations, which was to defeat Ayub Khan and assist Abdur Rahman Khan establish authority. The United Kingdom began to exercise a great deal of influence after this and even controlled the state's foreign policy. In 1893,Mortimer Durand made Amir Abdur Rahman Khan sign a controversial agreement in which the ethnic Pashtun and Baloch territories were divided by the Durand Line. This was a standard divide and rule policy of the British and would lead to strained relations, especially with the later new state of Pakistan.

After the Third Anglo-Afghan War and the signing of the Treaty of Rawalpindi in 1919, KingAmanullah Khan declared Afghanistan a sovereignand fully independent state. He moved to end his country's traditional isolation by establishing diplomatic relations with the international community and, following a 1927–28 tour of Europe and Turkey, introduced several reforms intended to modernize his nation. A key force behind these reforms was Mahmud Tarzi, an ardent supporter of the education of women. He fought for Article 68 of Afghanistan's 1923 constitution (declared through a loya jirga), which made elementary education compulsory.

Some of the reforms that were actually put in place, such as the abolition of the traditionalburqa for women and the opening of a number of co-educational schools, quickly alienated many tribal and religious leaders. Faced with overwhelming armed opposition, Amanullah Khan was forced to abdicate in January 1929 after Kabul fell to rebel forces led by Habibullah Kalakani. Prince Mohammed Nadir Shah, Amanullah's cousin, in turn defeated and killed Kalakani in November 1929, and was declared

King Nadir Shah. He abandoned the reforms of Amanullah Khan in favor of a more gradual approach to modernisation but was assassinated in 1933 by Abdul Khaliq, a Hazara school student.

Mohammed Zahir Shah, Nadir Shah's 19-year-old son, succeeded to the throne and reigned from 1933 to 1973. Until 1946 Zahir Shah ruled with the assistance of his uncle, who held the post of Prime Minister and continued the policies of Nadir Shah. Another of Zahir Shah's uncles, Shah Mahmud Khan, became Prime Minister in 1946 and began an experiment allowing greater political freedom, but reversed the policy when it went further than he expected. He was replaced in 1953 by Mohammed Daoud Khan, the king's cousin and brother-in-law. Daoud Khan sought a closer relationship with the Soviet Union and a more distant one towards Pakistan. Afghanistan remained neutral and was neither a participant inWorld War II, nor aligned with either power bloc in the Cold War. However, it was a beneficiary of the latter rivalry as both the Soviet Union and the United States vied for influence by building Afghanistan's main highways, airports and other vital infrastructure. By the late 1960s, many Western travelers were using these as part of the hippie trail. In 1973, while King Zahir Shah was on an official overseas visit, Daoud Khan launched a bloodless coup and became the first President of Afghanistan.

MARXIST REVOLUTION AND SOVIET WAR

In April 1978, a prominent member of the People's Democratic Party of Afghanistan (PDPA),Mir Akbar Khyber, was mysteriously killed. Leaders of the PDPA feared that the government was planning to dismantle them because many were being arrested. Hafizullah Amin along with other PDPA members managed to remain at large and organised an uprising. The PDPA, led by Nur Mohammad Taraki, Babrak Karmal and Hafizullah Amin, overthrew the regime of Daoud by assassinating the President along with his family and relatives. Taraki quickly took over and moved to carry out an ill-conceived land reform, which was misunderstood by virtually all Afghans. The PDPA began imprisoning, torturing and murdering thousands of members of the traditional elite, the religious establishment, and the intelligentsia. On the other hand, they prohibited usury, made statements on women's rights by declaring equality of the sexes and introducing women to political life.Anahita Ratebzad was one of several female Marxist leaders and a member of the Revolutionary Council.

As part of its Cold War strategy, the United States strengthened political ties with Pakistan although Zbigniew Brzezinski, National Security Advisor to U.S. President Jimmy Carter, has warned that this might prompt a Soviet intervention. The Central Intelligence Agency (CIA) began using Pakistan's Inter-Services Intelligence (ISI) as a proxy network to recruit, finance and arm the multinational Mujahideen fighters inside Pakistan, which was aimed to prevent the Soviet Union from reaching the oil-rich Persian Gulf through Balochistan. In March 1979, Hafizullah Amin took over as Prime Minister of Afghanistan, retaining the position of field marshal and becoming Vice-President of the Supreme Defence Council. Taraki remained the president and in control of the army until he was killed in September 1979.

To bolster the Parcham faction and as part of its Cold War strategy to ultimately reach Gwadar in Balochistan, the Soviet Union decided to invade Afghanistan in December 1979 by sending 100,000 soldiers of the Red Army to its southern neighbor. In the meantime, Hafizullah Amin was killed and replaced by Babrak Karmal. In response to all these, theReagan administration in the U.S. increased arming and funding of the Mujahideen, thanks in large part to the efforts of Charlie Wilson and CIA officer Gust Avrakotos.

Early reports estimated $6–20 billion but more recent reports suggest that up to $40 billion were provided by the U.S. and Saudi Arabia to Pakistan. This was in the forms of cash and weapons, which included over two thousand FIM-92 Stinger surface-to-air missiles. The money and weapons were directly given to Pakistani Armed Forces, which was distributed by its ISI network to various Mujahideen groups although much of it was secretly kept for Pakistan's own defense and other purposes. Despite receiving only minor aid compared to leaders of other Mujahideen groups, Ahmad Shah Massoud was named "the Afghan who won the Cold War" by *The Wall Street Journal*.

The 10-year Soviet war resulted in the deaths of over 1 million Afghans, mostly civilians and due to land-mines. About 6 million fled to Pakistan and Iran, and from there tens of thousands began emigrating to the European Union, United States, Australiaand other parts of the world. Faced with mounting international pressure and great number of casualties, the Soviets withdrew in 1989 but continued to support Afghan President Mohammad Najibullah until 1992.

U.S.-IRAN RELATIONS AND THE FUTURE OF AFGHANISTAN

There is no reason to think that U.S. priorities on Afghanistan will be of anything other than marginal concern when the Obama administration considers how to deal with the new Rouhani administration.

The lifting of international sanctions against Iran depends on a breakthrough in the P5+1 talks on Iran's nuclear industry and on the international community being satisfied that Tehran is indeed only pursuing the peaceful use of nuclear energy.

But an improved U.S.-Iranian relationship would yield many other dividends to U.S. foreign policy goals, not the least of which is that it would make the regional solution to Afghanistan's economic recovery that Washington yearns for a much more realizable goal. Hopefully Javad Zarif and James Dobbins will have new opportunities to negotiate with each other and shape a more productive relationship for Iran, the United States, and Afghanistan.

NEW AFGHAN GOVERNMENT AND PROSPECTS FOR FUTURE IRAN-AFGHANISTAN COOPERATION

First of all, it should be noted that under its new president, Mohammad Ashraf Ghani, Afghanistan has signed the Bilateral Security Agreement with the United States, which makes it possible for Washington to keep its military presence in the West Asian country up to 2024 and station its troopers at five important military bases across Afghanistan. As a result, the country will most probably enter a new phase of the intensification of regional and international rivalries as a result of this development. At regional level, rivalries will take place between India and Pakistan, on the one hand, and the Islamic Republic of Iran and Saudi Arabia, on the other hand. At the same time, such regional states as Turkey, Qatar and the United Arab Emirates are also expected to get involved in regional rivalries over Afghanistan. At international level, the main rivalries will take place among the United States, China and Russia. Of course, European countries, especially three major European powers; that is, the UK, France and Germany, should not be overlooked. On the whole, regional and international rivalries over Afghanistan will become focused on four specific fields:

1. Cultural and religious field;
2. Economic field;
3. Political field; and
4. Military and security field.

It is evident that any one of the aforesaid countries has its own special advantages in every one of the above-mentioned fields and, naturally, should make the most of its advantages. At present the United States has consolidated its military presence in Afghanistan and the viewpoints of Mohammad Ashraf Ghani show that he has apparently accepted Western liberal concepts. Therefore, under present circumstances, culture and religion constitute the most fertile grounds for further cooperation between Iran and Afghanistan with economic cooperation following in the second place. Iran will be facing more obstacles in political as well as military and security fields in Afghanistan. Therefore, and for a variety of reasons, one can expect cooperation between Iran and Afghanistan to be promoted mostly in cultural fields under the rule of Mohammad Ashraf Ghani. The main reason is the existence of a multitude of language-related, cultural, civilizational and historical commonalities between Iran and Afghanistan as both countries are considered as parts of the Iranian and Islamic civilization. At the same time, no other country has the same amount of cultural commonalities with Afghanistan, which is a major advantage for the Islamic Republic of Iran.

In addition, it is a reality that the United States has currently the power that influences Afghanistan's general political orientation as a result of which the main field that will be open to Iran's activities is culture. The Persian language and its prevalence in both countries is a factor which can help promote cooperation between Tehran and Kabul. Of course, there are other cultural fields for collaboration between the two neighbouring countries, which include:

1. Education from elementary school to university;
2. Print and non-print media as well as audiovisual media;
3. Publication of textbooks for schools and universities and other kinds of publications;
4. Exchange of academics and students; as well as
5. Training an adequate number of teachers for Afghan schools due to serious need of Afghanistan to teachers and shortage of educational facilities.

It is a reality that Iran has no rival in Afghanistan in the above fields. Although the Islamic Republic has been already active in these fields, the full capacities that exist in this regard have not been taken advantage of. For example, Afghanistan's textbooks are currently being printed in Germany while it is possible for Iran to do that both because of its technical capacities in the area of printing and due to the existence of the Persian language in both countries as a common denominator. No other country enjoys the same position as Iran in this regard. It is only India that can be a serious competitor for Iran in the field of audiovisual media through its movie industry. However, when it comes to cultural activities with a religious orientation, it would be conceivable to assume that Iran and Saudi Arabia are possible to get involved in an intense ideological rivalry in Afghanistan because the government of Mohammad Ashraf Ghani is expected to give more maneuvering room to Saudi Arabia in comparison with Iran.

Saudi Arabia and Afghanistan have recently signed an agreement for the construction of an Islamic university in the Afghan capital city of Kabul. The cost of the project has been estimated at USD 100 million. It is also supposed to include the construction of the country's biggest mosque and an affiliated Islamic center, which would admit a total of 10,000 students on a round-the-clock basis. This is one of the most objective examples of the investment that Saudi Arabia is making in Afghanistan with an eye to securing its long-term ideological sway over the country. There is no doubt that such a great Islamic center will have great effects in the long run and if Iran does not increase its activities in cultural fields in Afghanistan, it is sure to lose the competition to Saudi Arabia.

At the same time, the Persian language in Afghanistan is facing certain challenges. This is due to efforts made by nationalist Pashtuns who are working hard to make Pashtun the official language and culture of Afghanistan. On the other hand, there is increasing tendency among Afghan youth to learn English. These factors are sure to wear off Iran's cultural influence in Afghanistan in the long run.

The second fertile ground for the promotion of future cooperation between Iran and Afghanistan under Mohammad Ashraf Ghani is the economic field in which Iran will be competing with China and India as its main rivals. Iranian companies can really get active in certain economic areas in Afghanistan, which include: trade, transportation, exploration and extraction of underground reserves; as well as development and reconstruction projects. The most important advantage of Iran in this field, includes Bandar Abbas and Chabahar port cities in southern Iran, which can be of great help to the landlocked Afghanistan by connecting it to the free waters of the Indian Ocean, thus, facilitating exports from and imports to India. The sole competition that Iran will be facing in this field is from Pakistan. Of course, there are currently political and territorial differences between Pakistan and Afghanistan. Therefore, if Iran succeeded to conclude a bilateral trade agreement with Afghanistan to boost Afghanistan's foreign trade through its southern ports, the future prospect for cooperation between Tehran and Kabul in all possible fields without serious competition would be totally bright.

Most analysts believe that the room for political as well as military and security cooperation between Iran and Afghanistan will be very limited. This is true as neither the United States will allow Iran to play a determining role in this regard, nor the liberal views of Mohammad Ashraf Ghani will allow Iran, with its dominantly Shia religious ideology, to gain great influence in his country. Although Mohammad Ashraf Ghani pretends to be a believing Muslim, his secular views do not let him establish strategic relations with Iran's specific brand of Islamic ideology. His first choice for such relations among the Islamic countries will be Saudi Arabia, in the first place, followed by Turkey in the second place. At present, Turks have already started important activities in various sectors in Afghanistan with a view to long-term cooperation. Naturally, Iran should bank on its own advantages in order to organize its strategic relations with Afghanistan with an eye to future collaboration. Therefore, under present circumstances, the field of Islamic and Iranian civilization offers the most fertile ground for cooperation between Iran and Afghanistan.

POWER SHARING, BEST SOLUTION TO AFGHAN CRISIS

The recent concession to a plan for accepting division of political power in Afghanistan by the country's presidential candidates, Dr. Abdullah Abdullah, and his rival, Dr. Ashraf Ghani Ahmadzai, following the controversial presidential polls in the country, has revived hopes about possible reduction in tensions and disputes. In his first public speech addressed to his supporters, Abdullah described the power sharing formula as the best option under the current sensitive conditions for his country and noted that it also conformed to the country's constitution as well as the good and expediency of Afghanistan and its people. Since Abdullah had already claimed that his election rival had rigged the vote by a margin of 2-2.5 million ballots, his felicitation to Ahmadzai as the new president of Afghanistan seemed somehow odd, but without a doubt, it was also realistic and rational.

However, without any premature judgment, we must first accept that equal division of power between Abdullah's Reform and Partnership Team and Ashraf Ghani Ahmadzai's Change and Continuity Team was the best possible option out of all available options. In fact, the election deadlock, which continued for a period of six months, offered limited options as the way out of the crisis, which if rejected, the country's election turmoil, would have simply worsened. Out of all options available to the two sides, the following three options were taken more seriously:

1. The first option was the establishment of a parallel government by Abdullah in case he failed to achieve an agreement with his rival;
2. The second option was the continuation of Hamid Karzai's government and arranging a reelection; and
3. The option of reconciliation.

In reality, the option of reconciliation was only option which was also recognized as the best option. It also gained domestic, regional and international support in the last steps of the dispute and through mediation of the US Secretary of State John Kerry. The other two options could have led Afghanistan into domestic war and possible disintegration along ethnic and regional lines. The option of forming a parallel government would have greatly increased the risk of violence and forceful transfer of power, which was not a favorite choice for any of the involved parties. Although the option of reconciliation is not totally free from problems and serious differences may surface in the course of its implementation, at least, it was advantageous in that it paved the way for the peaceful transfer of power from one president to his successor. Such a state of affairs has had no precedent in the tumultuous history of Afghanistan during the past four decades, at least since 1976 and the coup d'état against Sardar Mohammed Daoud Khan.

Of course, this peaceful transfer of power has been incomplete and incompatible with democratic norms and has also deprived the Afghan nation of a historical opportunity which would have allowed the nation for the first time after about 300 years to break the Pashtun people's monopoly on power and make way for transfer of power through the democratic mechanism of ballot boxes to a non-Pashtun ethnicity. However, even in its current state, such a reconciliation should be considered a step forward under special conditions that rein in Afghanistan. It is a step forward because the division of power has taken place between two rival political currents with ethnic roots. The acceptance of such a reconciliation was a civil move and its importance should be assessed apart from its main weakness, which was bypassing the ballot boxes as well as the expectations of the Afghan society. The power sharing formula is significant because in its totality, it is a clear demonstration of the ethnic equation of power in present-day Afghanistan. This means that one side of this equation is the Pashtun people with its monopolistic mentality according to which, it considers the control on power as its historical and natural right. However, this ethnic group has now conceded to accept other ethnicities as a partner in power. On the other hand, there are non-Pashtun ethnic groups that were not ready to give in to the monopolistic power of Pashtun people without a question. As a result, they were mentally ready to go ahead as far as the division of their country. However, now all of them have accepted the power sharing in spite of all signs that show they were actual winners of the election.

Now, there should be no doubt that implementation of the power sharing formula between Ashraf Ghani Ahmadzai, who has been announced as the winner of the election and the country's new president, and Abdullah Abdullah, the runner up who has been appointed as the chief executive of the country, will have its own difficulties. As a result, the government of Ashraf Ghani may face problems over the next five years and even fail. This would be especially true because the formula for establishing a national unity government has been developed in such a way that it prevents emergence of Afghanistan as an independent power from a strategic viewpoint and when national interests of Afghans are taken into consideration. Consequently, Afghanistan will always remain in need of the effective intervention by the United States. Signing of the security agreement between the United States and Afghanistan by the country's new president, while former president, Hamid Karzai had refrained from signing it due to his own concerns, clearly proves that the United States will have the upper hand in the country. As a result of the conclusion of the Bilateral Security Agreement between the two countries, the US Army will keep, at least, five permanent and a number of non-permanent military bases in Afghanistan and will, as such, maintain its influence on the future developments of the country.

Meanwhile, the power sharing formula between Abdullah and Ahmadzai can be considered important from another angle, which is paving the way for the progress of national reconciliation talks between the central government, on the one hand, and the Taliban group and other anti-government armed groups, on the other hand. It is very important that the power sharing formula has predicted for Loya Jirga to meet within the next two years to amend the country's constitution in such a way that it would meet the two main demands put forth by Abdullah. Possible amendments in the constitution of Afghanistan will take place along two major lines:

1. They will turn the country's political system from a centralized presidential system into a non-centralized parliamentary system while the chief executive will be promoted to prime minister.
2. The country's administrative system will be a federal one in which every ethnic group will have its own ethnic parliament and local government within its geographical boundaries and will be also given a fair share of power in Kabul.

This power structure and the federal system of government in Afghanistan will heed ethnic lines. It is also compatible with a plan previously proposed by the former head of foreign troops in Afghanistan, General David Petraeus. According to Petraeus' plan, the Pashtun ethnic group would be allowed to establish its own Islamic system of power in the eastern and western parts of the country where it sways majority and would have a share of central power in Kabul as well, provided that its people would lay down their arms.

The same formula would be extended to the other three major ethnic groups, which include Tajiks, Uzbeks, and Hazara people as a result of which, Afghanistan would turn into a federal country where the distribution of power would be more balanced. Of course, it should be noted that there is remarkable ethnic diversity in Afghanistan as 54 big and small ethnic groups live in the country each with its own specific culture, traditions, and ethnic demands. In addition, a federal system of government is actually special to more advanced societies and it would be very difficult to adapt it to a nomadic traditional society.

Despite all these facts, the power sharing formula should not be considered as a silver bullet and a final and lasting solution to all problems. There are unresolved conflicts in Afghanistan and as long as they exist, the power sharing formula will be prone to crisis and failure. The combined ethnic and ideological monopoly that Pashtun people have been seeking in various forms, including in the form of Taliban group, does not allow them to get along with division of power in the long run. On the other hand, since long years of war and Jihad have changed the attitude of non-Pashtun ethnicities and they are now familiar with weapons and resistance, they are not likely to give in to renewed monopoly of Pashtuns and the Taliban over the political power. As a consequence of this situation, Afghanistan will remain prone to violence and will constantly need foreign intervention.

In view of such facts regarding the future outlook of a national unity government, there can be two optimistic and pessimistic views in this regard. According to the optimistic view, the national unity government will become stronger and cooperation between Abdullah and Ahmadzai will continue during the entire five-year tenure of the new president. In this state, whenever a major problem pops up, the foreign power that is present in the country will intervene to impose a solution. In the pessimistic view, Afghanistan will return to the situation that has prevailed in the country during the past four decades. As a result, ethnic rivalries and various ideological readings of Islam – from the radical views of Deobandi school to the moderate Islam of the Muslim Brotherhood spearheaded by Tajiks and led by Abdullah – will be once again activated along ethnic lines. In addition, supporters of a monarchial system, liberal democrats, and even former Marxists will see their chance to come to the fore again. The combination of these centrifugal forces will prevent establishment of an efficient central government in the war-weary country. It seems that establishment of a national unity government and power sharing was the best option available. However, there is a long way to go before this option will be able to protect the country against such major threats as renewed crisis, civil war, and even total disintegration of Afghanistan into two major divisions of Greater Pashtunistan and Greater Khorasan.

7

Cultural Awareness and Counterinsurgency in Afghanistan

The current war in Afghanistan began on October 7th 2001 when the United States (U.S.) launched Operation Enduring Freedom (OEF) and overthrew the Taliban's Islamic Emirate of Afghanistan. Having been removed from power, the Taliban set about establishing themselves as an insurgent movement hidden within and outside the country. Since then, the International Security Assistance Force (ISAF), which currently constitutes troops from forty-seven nations, has struggled to establish nationwide security and defeat the Taliban insurgents. This apparent paradoxical reality poses a significant danger to international stability, and is therefore a puzzle that urgently needs solving.

The acclaimed U.S. Army and U.S. Marine Corps (USMC) counterinsurgency manual defines an insurgency as "an organized, protracted, politico-military struggle designed to weaken the control and legitimacy of an established government, occupying power, or other political authority while increasing insurgent control." Meanwhile, Paget has claimed that an insurgency can comprise of differing levels of guerrilla warfare, sabotage, subversion and terrorism. It can safely be said therefore, that the concept of insurgency has existed for hundreds, if not thousands of years, perhaps dating as far back as the Maccabbean Revolt of 167-160 BC. Therefore, how is it still so misunderstood? Has two thousand years of historical experience not been at all useful in contributing towards the development of an effective counter-strategy?

Without question, a great deal *has* been written and learnt proving definitively that counterinsurgency wars*can* by won. Nevertheless, one significant factor critical to a successful counterinsurgency has too often been the missing link to victory – cultural awareness. In the author's view, this is certainly the case in Afghanistan.

This chapter aims to explain why a lack of such awareness will condemn a counterinsurgency to almost certain defeat, and then to link this statement's accuracy to the current campaign in Afghanistan, and thereby suggest potential improvements. In order to do this, three distinct theoretical and analytical angles will be separately examined.

Succeeding this introduction, a theoretical framework will provide an overview of this paper's preeminent focus – cultural awareness – and will explicate its relationship to counterinsurgency theory and the campaign in Afghanistan. The succeeding section will seek to define the concept of counterinsurgency and establish why and how employing cultural awareness is so critical to attaining success. In order to demonstrate this, the author will establish how a widespread *lack* of cultural awareness in the campaign in Afghanistan has inherently disadvantaged its chances of success. This negative analysis of the Afghan campaign will be approached using two broad foundations – (1) the existence of ethnocentrism and (2) a lack of an attempt to positively influence local-level perceptions, both of which directly discredit any chance of attaining legitimacy in the eyes of the Afghan people. The analysis will therefore evaluate the Afghan counterinsurgency campaign with the intention of proving this paper's fundamental premise – that the primary objective of counterinsurgency is to gain the acquiescence of the local population, and therefore prevent the insurgent from gaining popular support. In such competition, it is only logical that culturally aware interaction is indispensable.

Following this, another section will employ three historical case studies – Malaya, Vietnam, and Dhofar – to demonstrate how the integration of cultural awareness into *all* levels of counterinsurgent operation can positively define their chances of success. Two of these military endeavors, Malaya and Dhofar, conducted by British forces, have become established cases of exemplary counterinsurgency success, whilst the third, Vietnam, has proven to be a model example of "the triumph of [an] institutional culture" that relied on "firepower and technological superiority" over the need to adapt to new forms of modern warfare. Subsequent analysis will show how innovative concepts that integrated local culture and its specific demands successfully persuaded the population to support the counterinsurgent and helped contribute towards combating the insurgency.

This chapter final focus will be upon how institutional military culture can pose significant obstacles to organizational adaptation to fighting counterinsurgency. As will be explained, this "COIN syndrome" affects some militaries more than others. The U.S., epitomized by its experience in Vietnam, has often struggled to adapt to counterinsurgency-type conflicts due to a military culture that has often remained loyal to Clausewitzian-Jominian conventional warfare, whilst the British military, with its colonial history, has found this institutional adjustment less challenging.

Having covered such substantial ground, it should become explicitly clear that cultural awareness and population engagement is critical to acquiring popular support and defeating the insurgent. By defining the actual concept and substance of counterinsurgency as a military strategy vis-à-vis cultural awareness, and by analyzing its theoretical and practical applications, this paper's question should find itself answered. The subsequent examination of the theory blaming stubborn military culture and insufficient organizational learning for the U.S.' failure to adapt to fighting counterinsurgencies will therefore allow for a concluding section that expounds the future of warfare and the place of conventional militaries within it.

SECURITY, DEVELOPMENT AND PERSPECTIVE

Security, an essential public good, is widely seen as a central issue for Afghanistan's reconstruction and development. Security impacts on the whole range of development issues faced by

Afghanistan, ranging from state building and capacity development to revenue collection, service delivery, and encouraging private sector-led growth. For the purpose of Afghanistan's National Development Strategy (ANDS), currently under preparation, the Government has added a Millennium Development Goal (MDG) on enhancing security to the internationally agreed list of MDGs. This demonstrates the importance assigned by the Government to security and rule of law as a critical development issue. Afghanistan's external partners (including the World Bank) have consistently highlighted the importance of security as a key enabling factor for Afghanistan's reconstruction and development And most important, the Afghan people themselves emphasize the importance of security and the protection of property rights in their daily lives and for building their livelihoods and communities. More specifically:

- Security and rule of law as public goods have been grossly underprovided in Afghanistan during the past quarter-century, with state functions in this regard usurped by factions, regional and local powerbrokers, and external actors. Remedying this situation is an urgent, high-priority task.
- Improving security is also a core component of the state-building agenda, seen by most Afghans as an essential function of an effective, accountable government.
- Moreover, an adequate level of security is a critical prerequisite for effective delivery of other public services.
- Politically, security improvements have been and will continue to be essential for the success of Afghanistan's transition toward political normalcy.
- Economically, security and law and order, along with the protection of property rights, are required for robust private sector development, which will be the only way to achieve sustained rapid economic growth over the medium term.
- Insecurity and narcotics are closely linked - insecurity is the environment in which Afghanistan's opium economy thrives, and the drug industry is a major source of instability and insecurity.

- And finally, from the individual, household, and community standpoints, security and rule of law are extremely important components and enabling factors in the quality of life, as is almost universally recognized by Afghans.

In addition to its importance as a central development issue for Afghanistan, the security sector accounts for a very high proportion of the country's total public expenditures as well as external assistance and raises major public expenditure management issues including risks to fiscal sustainability and possible crowding out of spending on other basic services. Therefore the security sector is also very important from a public finance management perspective. In view of these considerations, the Government of Afghanistan requested that the security sector be included in the World Bank's Public Finance Management (PFM) Review, and this volume is the result. There are in addition a number of specific rationales for the World Bank's engagement in analytical work on Afghanistan's security sector as part of the PFM Review and from a development perspective. First, as indicated above, security is of central importance for Afghanistan's development prospects, including in particular the state-building agenda. This means it has to be incorporated in the country's development strategy and planning (which the Government is doing), and that development partners need to be engaged in areas of their competence.

Second, given the great importance of security spending in the national budget (accounting for around 40% of total Core and External Budget expenditures), the security sector must be incorporated in the analysis of expenditure composition, budget prioritization and trade-offs, downstream expenditure implications of decisions and investments, fiscal sustainability, etc. These issues lie at the heart of the PFM Review.

Third, a weak PFM system in the security sector (and particularly if the security sector gets left behind while improvements in the PFM system are occurring elsewhere) would adversely affect the overall progress of PFM reform and institutional strengthening, distort choices made by the Government, reduce the effectiveness and efficiency of public spending, and increase vulnerability to corruption. All of these areas are of concern to the Bank.

And fourth, security sector expenditures are largely donor-financed, raising important issues of aid management, aid harmonization, and aid effectiveness, as well as capacity development and effectiveness of technical assistance. These issues comprise an important part of the overall PFM agenda and hence need in the context of the security sector to be included in the PFM Review.

The main objectives of this review of security sector expenditures in the context of the PFM Review and taking a development perspective are as follows:

- To gain as complete an understanding as possible of the current level and structure of security related expenditures, recent trends, and likely future expenditure requirements based on current plans.
- To assess the extent to which coherent strategies, for the security sector and the major parts of the security sector, guide public expenditure allocations.
- To review the processes for determining funding levels, expenditure allocations, budget execution, and post-execution functions, with a view to assessing the extent to which they follow sound PFM principles.
- To describe the institutional framework for the security sector and ascertain the extent to which it embeds or is conducive to sound public financial management.
- To assess the strategic coherence and consistency and the fiscal sustainability of security sector expenditures.

This chapter sets forth the conceptual framework for analysis of security sector expenditures from a development and public finance management perspective. It first provides a working definition of the security sector. The chapter goes on to outline key linkages between security and development (based on recent international thinking on this subject). It then discusses key public finance management principles and their application to the security sector. The final section briefly summarizes the service delivery perspective and its application to the security sector. Some background on the historical legacy from the long period of conflict in Afghanistan, and summarizes the progress made in building the security sector since 2001. It then overviews Afghanistan's security sector at present - its legal basis, size, institutions, salient characteristics, and coordination - and at the end outlines the key security issues faced by Afghanistan from a development perspective. PFM principles and their application to the security sector, the implications for Afghanistan including gaps and constraints, and the Afghan budget process for the security sector.

The crucial issue of the fiscal sustainability of security sector decisions and investments, which is an important driver of the fiscal sustainability of Afghanistan's public finances as a whole. Building on the analysis of fiscal sustainability, At strategic prioritization and sequencing issues in the security sector and how these can be managed in particular through the national budget process. The budget execution for effective and efficient use of funds provided to the security sector.

Meaning of the Security Sector

The security "system" is defined broadly in OECD (2005b) as including the following main components: core security actors, security management and oversight bodies, justice and law enforcement institutions, and non-statutory security bodies. A broad definition of the security sector along these lines makes the most sense from a development and PFM perspective, as all different parts of the security sector have significant development implications as well as varying budgetary implications (for both expenditures and revenues).

However, some components clearly do not apply to Afghanistan (e.g. coast guards), while other institutions like Parliaments have not been functioning and hence are not relevant for analysis of recent developments and the current situation (although the role of the legislature will be important starting in the very near future).

Moreover, non-statutory security bodies, although they have been major actors in Afghanistan (and mirror the breakdown of the formal security system during the protracted conflict), for the most part do not have direct budgetary implications and would require a very different mode of analysis. Therefore they are not looked at closely in this volume except in terms of their immediate budgetary implications - notably the Disarmament, Demobilization, and Reintegration (DDR) program - although their development implications and impact on the formal security sector will be kept in mind.

In sum, consistent with the overall objectives and approach of the PFM Review and in line with the increasingly recognized development implications of the security sector, this volume uses a broad definition of the security sector but focuses on those components which are of major importance from a PFM perspective. In terms of budget categories and programs, those that form part of the security sector and which are analyzed in the PFM Review include: defence, police and other internal security services, intelligence, counter-narcotics, the judiciary and penal system, mine clearance, and the DDR program.

The main security institutions in Afghanistan which will be looked at in the PFM Review include the following: (i) *government security management and oversight bodies:* National Security Council and National Security Advisor, Ministry of Defence, Ministry of Interior, Ministry of Counter Narcotics, Ministry of Border and Tribal Affairs, Ministry of Justice, Ministry of Finance, and the Auditor General's Office; (ii) *security services:* Afghan National Army (ANA), Afghan National Police (ANP), National Border Guards, Counter-Narcotics forces, National Directorate of Security (NDS - responsible for intelligence), Customs General Directorate under MoF, remnants of earlier military and police forces (the former subjected to DDR); and (iii) *justice and legal institutions:* Supreme Court, Judiciary, Attorney General's Office and prosecutorial offices *(saranwal).*

Excluded from detailed analysis in this volume are the non-statutory security bodies, including remaining unofficial militias and armed factional groups, private body-guards, and security companies. Foreign and international armed forces operating in Afghanistan also will not be analyzed in detail, except to some extent the Provincial Reconstruction Team (PRTs) which are intended to help strengthen governance and carry out reconstruction activities. However, the overall size and cost of these forces will be considered and their impact on the fiscal and PFM aspects of the formal security system will be taken into account. The absence of a Parliament means that its oversight role with respect to security can be incorporated in terms of future options and recommendations, but not in relation to the analysis of recent developments and the current situation. Independent and civil society institutions which play a monitoring and advocacy role with respect to security, such as the Afghanistan Independent Human Rights Commission (AIHRC) are extremely important but are not analyzed in detail in this volume.

THEORETICAL FRAMEWORK

Since 1945, there has been a considerable proliferation of small wars defined by insurgent movements employing guerrilla warfare strategies to defeat incumbent or occupying powers. In fact, Marston has calculated that only twelve percent of conflicts since 1945 could be categorized as conventional, with the remaining eighty-eight percent being irregular. According to Huntington, this shift has been the result "of rapid social change and the rapid mobilization of new groups into politics, coupled with the slow development of political institutions." Smith stresses that these "wars of the people" are now the dominant form of warfare, and due to globalization and the increased interconnectedness of the international system, are likely to remain prevalent for decades to come. Consequently, counterinsurgency theory has found itself under increasing focus, and many public figures have become synonymous with developing new tactics and strategies to defeat insurgencies.

Counterinsurgency is defined as composing of "military, paramilitary, political, economic, psychological, and civic actions taken by a government to defeat insurgency." From a simplistic perspective, ISAF in Afghanistan is broadly acting within all these spheres. However, in the author's view, one critical facet consistently highlighted as a prerequisite for a successful counterinsurgency is critically missing within the institutional culture of the Afghan operation – *cultural awareness*.

What Is Cultural Awareness?

For the sake of this chapter, cultural awareness shall be taken to represent a local-level understanding and appreciation of the foundational norms, values and expectations that govern and structure individual societies. More specifically, and perhaps more applicable to Afghanistan, one may apply what T.E. Lawrence identified as "tribal structure, religion, social customs, language, appetites [and] standards." Knowledge of this "human terrain" allows a counterinsurgent to "demonstrate a genuine engagement with the population" and aim towards winning legitimacy and "the hearts and minds of the people" – a key counterinsurgency objective. Integrating such knowledge requires counterinsurgents to become "3D operators" or "warrior diplomats" and, according to Galula, be "prepared to become a propagandist, a social worker, a civil engineer, a school teacher, a nurse, [and] a boy scout." Therefore, in line with local understanding, political sensitivity and local or tribal engagement, cultural awareness has become a critical "force multiplier" in counterinsurgency warfare.

CULTURAL AWARENESS AND COUNTERINSURGENCY THEORY

As Sun Tzu proclaimed over two thousand years ago, "if you know yourself but not the enemy, for every victory gained, you will also suffer defeat." In other words, "it is hard to defeat an enemy who you do not understand." Employing a counterinsurgency strategy suggests an active competition between the incumbent government (or representatives of it) and the insurgents for the loyalty and acquiescence of the local population. It is therefore, as Nagl emphasizes, a direct (military or coercive) and indirect (non-military and persuasive) battle for "hearts and minds" exercised 'on the ground' throughout a society. Whilst ensuring civilian security *will* require kinetic activity, gains made on that front can only be short-term. To sustain the security of "the human environment," and develop legitimacy through "the unconditional support of a population," it is principally the 'political, economic, psychological and civic actions' stated in the above definition of counterinsurgency that are most important. Showing "respect for local people [and] putting the well-being of noncombatant civilians ahead of any other consideration … especially ahead of killing the enemy," also becomes preeminent. Such a campaign consequently becomes an attempt "not to win – as if the emotions and aspirations of the local population can be co-opted to the counterinsurgent cause – but to understand and persuade." It is here that the importance of cultural awareness and understanding is truly underlined for "persuasion always is culturally sensitive. You cannot persuade someone if you do not understand his language, motivations, fears, and desires."

Henri Boré explains the complete operational utility of cultural awareness by stressing its three principle resulting advantages – (1) being able to anticipate how the enemy will act, (2) making it easier to win the trust and cooperation of the population, and (3) enhancing the ability to garner valuable human intelligence (HUMINT).

The relationship between cultural awareness and counterinsurgency is well established in traditional theory. The influential writing and conduct of T.E. Lawrence, Mao Tse-Tung, Che Guevara, Frank Kitson and David Galula all placed considerable attention upon culture. Moreover, the anthropological profession has, over much of the twentieth century, played a noteworthy role in integrating indigenous cultural knowledge into national security and foreign policy spheres – Ruth Benedict in Japan, Gregory Bateson in New Guinea, Tom Harrisson in Borneo and Gerald Hickey in Vietnam to name only a few.

In terms of this paper's case studies, all three, including Vietnam, which ended in defeat, developed innovative concepts that integrated local culture and its specific demands. The 'New Villages' and the *Iban*tribal force in Malaya; the cattle drives and *firqat* tribal forces in Dhofar; and the Strategic Hamlet Program, the Combined Action Platoons (CAP) and the Civilian Irregular Defense Corps (CIDG) in Vietnam, all successfully persuaded the local population to support the counterinsurgent and thus helped isolate and, except for Vietnam, defeat the insurgent.

CULTURAL AWARENESS & AFGHANISTAN

Cultural awareness is absolutely crucial in Afghanistan, where macro-oriented Western militaries are confronting an enemy which resembles "an influence, a thing invulnerable, intangible, without front or back, drifting about like a gas" within an alien society of an "intensely local nature." Afghanistan is a traditional society, dominated by ancient tribal practices, Islamic culture and a well-established suspicion of outsiders. A foreign force in such an environment cannot defeat the insurgency by itself – "only locals have the access to the population and deep understanding of a particular insurgency that is necessary" – and to secure sufficient legitimacy and trust from the population, one *must* appear sympathetic and receptive to it.

Unfortunately, instead of cultural awareness and local engagement, ISAF activities have helped develop a persona of disconnection from the population. This has primarily arisen from an extraneous employment of technology, which encourages an institutionalization of risk aversion and thus separation from the local population.

Instead, what is needed is a counterinsurgency that thoroughly integrates cultural awareness, so as to "work by, through, and with indigenous forces and populations" towards victory. Due to the local and tribal nature of the Taliban' and Afghan society, which is inherently rooted in the Pashtun concepts of*woleswali* (district) and *alaqadari* (subdistrict), a culturally aware bottom-up engagement with tribes is necessary in order to discern an acceptable solution to Afghan civilians. Therefore, in this context, there is a distinctly dual nature of cultural awareness in that its application is necessary within all tactical-level counterinsurgency activities, *and* on a strategic-level, to develop a solution acceptable to Afghan society.

AFGHANISTAN: A LACK OF CULTURAL AWARENESS

OEF was primarily an unconventional military operation conducted by companies of Afghan Northern Alliance and U.S.-British special forces. While the invasion was largely successful, conditions soon demanded the deployment of conventional forces to definitively defeat what remained of the Taliban and al-Qaeda. Unfortunately this failed to occur, and considerable numbers of the Taliban and al-Qaeda were able to flee to neighbouring Pakistan. As a result of this, and of the subsequent failure of ISAF and the newly-empowered Karzai government to conduct effective post-conflict reconstruction and political development, the Taliban soon filtered back to Afghanistan as an insurgent force. By 2006, ISAF faced a sizeable Taliban insurgency that had shifted from conducting occasional operations in rural heartlands, to frequent large-scale attacks against "more populated areas, urban centres, and main infrastructure"

A major factor in facilitating this Taliban regeneration was ISAF's failure to adequately appreciate counterinsurgency principles, especially that it is essentially a competition between two or more actors for legitimacy in the eyes of the host population. This chapter will seek to justify this paper's premise, that a fundamental lack of cultural awareness in strategy and tactics has been instrumental in ISAF's failure to gain the legitimacy required to discredit the Taliban as a viable political actor.

Ethnocentrism

Taken to mean 'evaluating other cultures according to preconceptions originating in one's own culture,' ethnocentrism is widely accepted as a fundamental problem in ISAF's ongoing counterinsurgency campaign in Afghanistan. As a multinational non-Afghan, and indeed non-Asian body, ISAF characterizes a foreign entity to Afghan people. Given that "the need to have one's culture acknowledged if not approved is a universal human desire," a foreign ethnocentric military force in an alien land is condemned to fail. An ideal counterinsurgent force should seek to ameliorate this impediment by integrating a thorough understanding and awareness of the culture within which it operates into its strategic- and tactical-level endeavours. 'Using preexisting indigenous political systems would create legitimacy for ISAF's actions, and avoiding the imposition of foreign norms and values would help generate public cooperation for ISAF's development programmes.' Unfortunately however, since OEF, ISAF has largely failed in this regard, and has instead generated policy and operated on the ground based on mirror-imaging Afghanistan with Western ideals and norms. This has sabotaged most of its initiatives aimed at garnering popular support and legitimacy.

The most prominent area where ISAF forces have displayed ethnocentrism is concerning the political nature of the state it wants to help build. While ISAF-contributing states have centralized political systems, Afghanistan has a well-established history of decentralized power, where local tribal authorities retained considerable influence vis-à-vis the central government. Unfortunately, ISAF states have focused on centralized nation-building, and consolidation through democratic elections, while traditional local power sources have been disregarded as illegitimate. To make matters worse, elections *have* been held and corruption has been consistently widespread, thus undermining the very foundation of legitimacy upholding ISAF's presence. Indeed, government misrule, corruption, and a consequent lack of legitimacy is emphasized by insurgency analysts as being "*the* root cause" of guerrilla recruitment and strategic success. Afghanistan is a predominantly rural society "where dynastic and religious authority has been unquestioned for over a thousand years" – "state-or nation-building, therefore, is a futile enterprise." To regain legitimacy, ISAF must strive to develop a solution acceptable to *Afghans*, which is inherently local in nature, comes from the bottom-up, and incorporates "a blend of central *and* local/ tribal power."

While local issues dominate Afghan popular concern, the Taliban is also distinctly local in nature. In fact, between forty and fifty percent of Taliban fighters are thought to be "local allies" fighting for personal, local or tribal reasons, such as individual pride, to protect one's tribe, or to exact revenge for the death of relatives. Unfortunately, without learning from these dynamics, an ISAF focus on acting conventionally within a more urban centre of gravity will continue to provide micro-oriented motives for Taliban foot-soldier recruitment. Neutralizing these 'accidental guerrillas' by ceasing such action, as well as through persuasive and culturally-aware information and psychological operations, and the provision of local-level security and employment, is arguably the key to critically weakening the Taliban as a credible threat.

Thus far, ISAF seems to have perceived Afghanistan's tribes as representing both a major threat to success, and an illegitimate form of political authority. Conversely, the Taliban directs much of its activity towards appealing directly to local cleavages, and to manipulating traditional tribal *Pashtunwali* codes like *nang* (honour) and *haya* (shame) against ISAF's presence. For Pashtuns, who make up a majority of the Taliban, tribal identity creates a fierce sense of loyalty through blood ties and obligations. Instead of isolating this potential and leaving them open to Taliban coercion, ISAF should embrace tribes by funding, organizing and training local tribal security forces to protect their respective locales against Taliban infiltration. Indeed, Afghanistan has an established history of successfully "pluralizing" its security, dating as far back as Abdul Rahman Khan's tribal levy forces in 1880. Reinvigorating tribal security in the form of *arbakai, laskhars, tsalweshtai and chalweshtai,* whilst simultaneously endorsing tribal bodies like the *jirga* and *shura* (that actually embody many democratic values) with jurisdiction over them would generate multiple benefits, including 'disincentivizing' 'accidental guerrilla' recruitment, lending ISAF essential local-level legitimacy, and connecting locals with their government whilst retaining some extent of mutually-acceptable autonomy.

Lack Of Focus on Positively Influencing Perceptions

The United States is losing the war in Afghanistan one Pashtun village at a time, bursting into schoolyards filled with children with guns bristling, kicking in village doors, searching women, speeding down city streets, and putting out cross-cultural gibberish in totally ineffectual campaigns – all of which are anathema to the Afghans.

While ISAF operations clearly *do* influence perceptions in Afghanistan, and while counterinsurgency doctrine *does* recognize the importance of doing so positively, there is, as the above quote implies, not a sufficient incorporation of cultural awareness in the actual performing of operations.

With regard to the military aspect of ISAF activities, counterinsurgent forces present an image of inherent disconnection and isolation from the population. As counterinsurgency success depends on acquiring the support of 'the people,' such separation is deeply damaging to ISAF's chances of defeating the Taliban and establishing nationwide stability. Deploying counterinsurgent forces in large isolated heavily-defended forward-operating bases, and employing them in sweeps and patrols shadowed by air support and shielded by heavily-armed armoured vehicles, prevents genuine engagement with those who matter most – the civilians. After all, how can a counterinsurgent become truly aware of "the community's real interests, attitudes and desires" in order to try to satisfy them, without walking, talking and *living* amongst them? By appearing superior, unapproachable and averse to risking themselves for unarmed civilians, ISAF forces appear apathetic to the interests of those they claim to be fighting for, and from whom they require legitimacy to succeed.

This introduces a major criticism of 'Western, especially American, forces – they are institutionally over-accustomed to fighting conventional attritional conflict, and organizationally slow to adapt to fighting asymmetrically. For example in June 2009, somewhat incredibly, the U.S. Army reintroduced the 'body count' as the metric for success in Afghanistan, and by the end of that year, less than five-percent of U.S. forces in Afghanistan had reconstruction and development as their primary mission. In general, ISAF forces have continued to favour kinetic-centric and intrusive operations where the chance of civilian casualties and the breaching of cultural customs is elevated. Given that Afghan culture has a deeply ingrained suspicion of 'outsiders,' and that many Afghans are still haunted by horrific memories of civilian casualties during the Soviet War, such culturally offensive and belligerent exploits serve to further delegitimize ISAF's presence in the country.

A more effective counterinsurgency strategy would involve giving the Afghan National Army (ANA) a more front-line role in fighting the Taliban, but more importantly, in providing local-level security. Given their inherent cultural awareness and linguistic fluency, "after years of watching from the back seat," the ANA could beneficially act as local intermediaries, help boost local-level counterinsurgent legitimacy and encourage HUMINT collection from those who have best access to 'the hidden enemy.' Rather than "falling in love with the guy who speaks English," the leveraging of ANA ties to the Afghan community could potentially open access to those more influential residents who may have previously been hesitant to approach foreign soldiers.

ISAF could capitalize on such extra stimuli and work towards acquiring a more developed local-level cultural understanding by deploying its troops *within* strategic villages and towns – or *tache d'huile* (oil spots), to use Lyautey's expression. Renting and operating out of a *qalat* (fortified family compound) would guarantee genuine population engagement and expose avenues for acquiring sincere mutual cultural understanding between ISAF and local Afghan residents. The counterinsurgents could therefore begin building relationships based on legitimacy, through communication and trust, and from which an impression of an acceptable solution to locals would be prompted. Rather than "throwing money" into building western-style motorways, it would soon become clear that local markets, and agricultural assistance are of far greater value. An idea of "good enough governance" would lead to an acceptance that self-styled Afghan 'warlords,' though distasteful to Western eyes, should be seen as potential major players and power-brokers in state building.

ISAF is predominantly composed of soldiers from the U.S., with further sizeable contributions from Britain, Italy, Germany and France, all of which are highly developed, internationalist states. It is surprising therefore, that on a matter of such importance, their counterinsurgency endeavours in Afghanistan reveal such low levels of cultural awareness. While the Iraqi insurgency helped initiate a doctrinal re-evaluation of counterinsurgency strategy (epitomized by Field Manual (FM) 3-24), and helped stimulate a considerable analytical focus on the subject, actual tactical-level behaviour and operations have, by and large, failed to sufficiently adapt themselves in order to make a concrete difference.

In Afghanistan "three decades of war, population displacement and social upheaval" have left the people both tired of, and used to conflict. The Taliban exploit their familiarity with the environment to conduct a Maoist strategy of transiently infiltrating and exerting influence in strategic localities, whilst also remaining predominantly hidden. ISAF forces meanwhile, too often locate themselves away from population centres, conduct themselves in a culturally offensive fashion and are too risk averse to attempt sincere or permanent local-level engagement. As a result, the Taliban corroborates the famous maxim that "control of local systems and structures inherently shapes collaboration" by exploiting the fact that they can spread their influence through coercion and control more easily than ISAF can. ISAF's only viable opportunity to counteract this is to adopt a culturally aware strategy based on local-level engagement that is in harmony with indigenous norms, values and expectations.

There is in fact a considerable historical precedent for such a strategy – if only one could learn to more effectually adopt useful lessons from history, and integrate them into military structures and thinking.

SOCIAL AND ECONOMIC WELL-BEING

While large-scale famine has been avoided in Afghanistan this winter due to major efforts led by the World Food Program (and principally supported by the United States), additional steps are needed to prevent humanitarian problems that could jeopardize political, social, and economic rejuvenation of the country. The Afghan people continue to be threatened by a lethal combination of conflict, starvation, and the harsh Afghan winter. 1.3 million internally displaced persons (IDPs) and 3.5 million refugees in Pakistan and Iran will continue to tax international capacity, and may threaten political stability if not handled properly. In addition to the need for immediate humanitarian assistance, numerous essential issues of economic and social well-being deserve the attention of the international community and the U.S. government. They include a revival of the agricultural sector and transportation networks, education, the role of the diaspora, revenue generation, human rights, and women.

Agricultural markets must be re-established. Despite the massive investment of international assistance over the past year, millions of Afghans remain at risk of severe malnutrition and starvation.

The UN Food and Agriculture Organization (FAO) warns that the current crisis of population displacement is coinciding with the current planting season and a multi-year drought, meaning that next year's crop yields will be even lower. Assistance is currently needed to restock seeds and livestock, develop irrigation systems, and jumpstart sustainable long-term food production. Refugee outflows from Afghanistan place undue burdens on surrounding countries' infrastructures already at or beyond maximum operating capacity. The agriculture sector in Afghanistan contributes 53 percent of the GDP and employs 67 percent of labor. Regenerating a viable agricultural sector will improve the availability of food, and will provide temporary and permanent employment.

A partial reason for the difficulty in generating food supplies is the fact that Afghanistan has been a major source country for the cultivation, processing, and trafficking of opiate and cannabis products. In 2000, it produced more than 70 percent of the world's supply of opium. The new government in Afghanistan will need to make a serious effort to help eradicate opium poppy fields. The agricultural reconstruction plan must integrate reconstruction of irrigation systems, absorptive labor capacity of the sector, a balance between external provision of immediate relief and incentives to increase domestic production, and crop substitution.

The establishment of local food and commodity markets will also require the repair and construction of transportation networks, especially those linking the northern and southern parts of the country. Afghanistan has just over 15 miles of railway and 13,125 miles of highway, with only 1,745 of those paved. Furthermore, the country's telecommunications network has been largely destroyed over the last 20 years, including over 80 percent of the telecommunications in Kabul. The United States should work with the multilateral development banks to rebuild both transportation and telecommunications infrastructure.

Education must be made a top priority, with focus on several key areas. First, educational opportunities need to be provided as an option to help demobilize and reintegrate young combatants. Second, schools must be made available to women and girls to reestablish their role in Afghan society. Afghanistan is faced with nine illiterate women out of every ten, and only 3 percent of girls are receiving primary education.

Third, special attention should be paid to the university in Kabul. The Taliban closed this once proud center of learning and social dynamism.

Reopening the university might help to attract some Afghans back, and provide a locus for the Afghan intelligentsia to help address the many reconstruction needs of the country. The U.S. can help provide means for the large, and highly trained Afghan diaspora to have access and immigration rights to return to support its reconstruction.

Afghanistan, for many years the heart of trade throughout Central Asia, desperately needs foreign investments to revive that role. To date, companies have invested $30 billion in developing oil and gas fields in Kazakhstan, Turkmenistan, Uzbekistan, and Azerbaijan, but exportation of this resource to markets in the West involves expensive and lengthy pipelines. Recently, Washington has proposed a $3 billion pipeline from Azerbaijan, on the Caspian Sea, through Georgia, to Turkey's Mediterranean coast, with a section running through Afghanistan. This shorter pipeline would be much less costly, and if the next government in Afghanistan is able to guarantee internal security, the country could reap enormous economic benefits.

Any new government, with the staunch help of the international community must reverse the Taliban's extreme subjugation of half of the Afghan population. The emancipation of women should not be viewed as a culturally insensitive imposition from the outside.

Afghanistan has a strong history of women's involvement in society at all levels. Prior to the civil war and Taliban control, 70 percent of the schoolteachers, 50 percent of the government civilian workers, and 40 percent of the doctors in Kabul were women. Between 1963 and 1973, there were women continuously in the cabinet. This history may help to reestablish rights and central roles for women. At the same time, programs targeting education for women and girls will be necessary to restore this proud history to new generations of Afghans.

The potential of Afghanistan's professional diaspora living all over the world must be tapped to contribute to a strengthening of the socio-economic sector. The positive effects of the return of a committed educated and skilled diaspora, such as increased investment and the opening of trade channels, are needed to reverse the substantial "brain drain" Afghanistan has suffered due to two decades of violent conflict.

It is reasonable to expect negative consequences of diaspora returns, including reprisals and loss of remittances. These problems must be taken seriously and mitigated through their integration into the local communities.

Recommendations for U.S. Involvement

1. Humanitarian Assistance and Repatriation: The U.S. should continue to respond in a generous and timely manner to appeals from UN humanitarian agencies, such as WFP, UNHCR, UNICEF, UNOCHA, UNDP, IOM, and FAO. The U.S. has already dispersed over $110 million to international and local NGOs to support the distribution of food and medical supplies. To date, the U.S. has pledged $320 million. U.S. military on the ground should help to secure key routes to enable a rapid expansion of emergency aid to the most needy parts of the country.
2. Employment Generation and Absorptive Capacity: USAID, through the Office of Foreign Disaster Assistance and the Office of Transition Initiatives, should develop and fund high-impact and visible employment generation projects to jumpstart the economy, restore social tranquility, and build political momentum. Drawing on recent experience in East Timor and other places, a similarly structured program in Afghanistan should utilize U.S. resource capacity and UN managerial oversight while encouraging strong local participation in the decision making process.
3. Agriculture and Food Security: The United States should provide significant support for multilateral initiatives that address both short-term and long-term food production and rural development needs of Afghanistan and its neighbours. This support should be both financial and technical. The activities of international organizations, NGOs, regional actors, private donors, and indigenous

entities should be coordinated to ensure that local needs are met.

4. Education: Emergency education needs must not be delayed. The United States should strongly support a World Bank lead in rebuilding the educational system of Afghanistan. This should include support for building at least 15,000 new village schools. Based on previous experience, this would cost only $150 million to build, and approximately $90 million to run annually. The U.S. should also support a multi-donor effort to revive Kabul University.
5. Diaspora Engagement: The U.S. government should facilitate investment from, and possible return of, the Afghan diaspora living in the United States. This can be accomplished through supporting existing programs such as UNDP's TOKTEN initiative, and IOM programs, as well as through offering a variety of protections and guarantees for would-be returnees. Key among these would be offering visa guarantees for those who may go to Afghanistan, but who may wish to return to the United States. Opening a coordination office to legally channel diaspora funds and investments would also facilitate diaspora involvement in the rebuilding process.
6. Private Investment: The international community could provide (as was done for East Timor) a high-ranking diplomat to represent and advise the Afghan government in negotiations with potential international investors regarding a natural gas pipeline deal, which could reap benefits of $100 million revenue a year.
7. Social Development: The U.S. should be prepared to provide assistance to long-term social development issues such as health, food security, social safety nets, HIV/AIDS, gender equity, and the environment, through various international organizations (i.e. the World Bank, WHO, UNDP, UNIFEM, UNEP).
8. Economic Development: Similarly, the U.S. should be prepared to provide technical and expert assistance in economic development issues such as infrastructure, micro

enterprise loan programs, narcotics control, investment, trade, banking, regulatory reform, and finance through the World Bank's Economic Recovery Strategy. The U.S. Treasury should help facilitate the clearing of arrears so that Afghanistan can once again be eligible for loans through the World Bank.

HISTORICAL COUNTERINSURGENCY EXPERIENCE

Having covered the Afghanistan campaign's lack of cultural and local awareness, this ensuing section will seek, via reference to three case studies, to demonstrate that ISAF's two preeminent contributing states, the U.S. and especially Britain, have a considerable historical precedent for successfully integrating cultural awareness into counterinsurgency conflicts. While two cases, Dhofar and Malaya, ended in counterinsurgent victory, and the third, Vietnam, ended in defeat, they all developed tactics and strategies that understood and exploited cultural awareness in order to neutralize and combat the insurgent enemy.

The Malayan Emergency (1948-60) was "one of the largest and bloodiest conflicts waged by British Commonwealth forces after World War II." Initially armed and funded by the British government to counter Japanese occupation, the Malayan Communist Party (MCP) organized an insurgency to combat British rule through a Mao-inspired peoples' war. Having begun ominously with large-scale "jungle bashing" operations, the British, under an inspired leadership aware of the indigenous culture and social dynamics, initiated an effective bottom-up counterinsurgency strategy that gradually destroyed the insurgency.

The Vietnam War (1959-72) was fought between the U.S. (fighting with, and on behalf of the South Vietnamese government) and the Vietcong – a military front of the North Vietnamese Communist government. Although the conflict's historical narrative is dominated by the U.S.' "bureaucratic inability to adapt to unconventional situations," America did in fact develop countless innovative programmes that successfully harnessed indigenous culture and capabilities. While only speculation, it is possible that had many of these programmes been implemented on a national scale, and been given more time to develop, the end result of the conflict may well have been different. The Dhofar Rebellion (1965-75) was initiated in 1965 by the Popular Front for the Liberation of the Occupied Arabian Gulf (PFLOAG). Although a relatively small conflict, a successful rebellion in British-backed Oman would have had severe Cold War strategic consequences for the West, especially given its proximity to the Strait of Hormuz, a key oil transit route. Initially, as a result of Omani Sultan Said bin Taimur's repressive policies, PFLOAG enjoyed considerable initial success. However, after a British-assisted coup in 1970 by the Sultan's son, Qaboos bin Said, the counterinsurgency strategy, buttressed by two squadrons of the British Special Air Service (SAS) and four hundred and fifty British officers, acquired a higher focus on civil development and indigenous responses, resulting in "the best conducted counterinsurgency campaign ever fought."

A fundamental aspect in developing a counterinsurgency strategy is discerning the local-level dynamics driving the insurgency. While a simple inquiry will indicate the drivers as being primarily political, there are often more elementary motivations stimulating an insurgency, especially the human desire for security and survival. If the counterinsurgent threatens human security, such as by employing excessive firepower, the insurgent cause is only strengthened and the counterinsurgent becomes more isolated from the indigenous people and culture, and success drifts further from its grasp.

It is for this reason that the British Army in Malaya adopted the principles of minimum force and small decentralized military units. This explicitly restrained the use of heavy weaponry or airpower, and reduced the foreign force 'footprint,' both of which substantially aided General Templar's foundational effort to win the Malayan people's "hearts and minds." In Vietnam, initial strategy actually emphasized the use of heavy weaponry in tandem with employing the body count as a metric of success. However, when General Abrams took command of the campaign in 1968, he emphasized the provision of "meaningful continuing security" for the Vietnamese population and an immediate end to the "often irrelevant 'body count' preoccupation," which, despite some U.S. institutional resistance, helped to improve perceptions in some areas of Vietnam. Furthermore, in regions where USMC were deployed, the use of airpower was largely prohibited so as to constrain perceived risk aversion and to intimate an equality with the locals.

In addition to attempts to limit the foreign footprint and prevent civilian casualties, a counterinsurgent can also establish indigenous irregular militias as the predominant counterinsurgent 'face.' By developing self-defence militias, like the Home Guard in Malaya, or the People's Self Defence Force in Vietnam, the counterinsurgent can exploit a naturally superior knowledge of local terrain, people and indeed the enemy itself. Furthermore, by ensuring that indigenous forces are locally seen to "bear the brunt" of the conflict, the danger of backlash against an 'interfering foreign power' is limited. Consequently, indigenous militias and tribal forces can serve as exceptional force multipliers. For example, the Dhofari *firqat* tribal forces, who trained and fought with the SAS, 'functioned not only as scouts and guides ... but also as 'home guards,' consolidating and defending areas [recently] ... swept clear by the Sultan's Armed Forces.' The *firqats* also acted as reliable sources of intelligence that "could not have been obtained in any other way," while their knowledge of the local terrain and impressive speed of manoeuvre, neutralized*adoo* advantages. In Malaya, the British exploited tribal antipathies towards the ethnic-Chinese guerrillas in order to develop militias with invaluable jungle knowledge – the *Dyak* and *Iban*tribes featured most prominently. Given the ethnic-Chinese nature of the Malayan insurgency, the British also established ethnic-Chinese Special Constables, Auxiliary Police and Home Guard to protect villages and man local police posts. Similarly, in Vietnam, U.S. special forces and the Central Intelligence Agency (CIA) focused considerably on developing local indigenous forces that "associated and intermingled with the people on a long-term basis" and that could lend cultural expertise towards combating the Vietcong. As well as more orthodox militia, like the Popular Forces (PF) and the CIDG, the U.S. also established unique cells. For example, under South Vietnamese leadership, the Phoenix Program created Provincial Reconnaisance Units, composed of former-Vietcong militants who, as 'counter-guerrillas,' targeted the Vietcong infrastructure in order to sever its links with the population.

Moreover, the Rural Development Cadre, created to imitate the Vietcong's social organization, was established as a paramilitary group of "highly trained and motivated men were sent to work in villages to ameliorate conditions for villages and establish rapport between the governors and the governed." In other words, they were doing what counterinsurgents often try, and fail to do as a result of their cultural and local ignorance.

Another important aspect relating to exploiting cultural and local dynamics is treatment of the enemy. Given that many insurgents are 'accidental' and fight for personal or local motivations, the WHOLESALE killing of insurgents can in fact be detrimental to acquiring popular support. In Dhofar, Sultan Qaboos introduced an amnesty promising a "cash grant and full immunity" for surrendering insurgents. Many of those who did surrender actually ended up joining the SAS-trained tribal *firqat* forces. Not only is 'persuading a man to join you cheaper than killing him,' but capturing enemy personnel provides an invaluable source of HUMINT on the enemy. Similarly, the Vietnamese *Chieu Hoi* amnesty programme aimed to procure informants and recruits for the pro-South irregular militias. Reminiscent of Frank Kitson's 'counter-gangs' employed during the Kenyan Mau Mau uprising, the British frequently employed captured Malayan guerrillas "to track down their former comrades in the jungle."

With a more thorough understanding of local culture and social dynamics as they relate to the insurgency, culturally aware psychological operations can be designed and employed towards specific target audiences. In Malaya, a nearly entirely ethnic-Chinese insurgency stimulated the inauguration of organized Chinese language courses, as well as the appropriation of Chinese-speaking British officials from all government departments for strategic 'oil spots' where insurgent influence was high. Combined with a village development programme, these culturally and linguistically fluent counterinsurgents helped ease "the transition from rural squatter to village dweller," thus removing the principle incentive (economic deprivation) for insurgent support. In addition, the 'Psywar' section of the Malayan Information Services, manned predominantly by former-insurgents, developed a culturally aware programme – via

Radio Malaya, Chinese language newspapers, air-dropped leaflets, government films and 'voice aircraft' – aimed at persuading the Chinese population to turn against the insurgents, and at converting current guerrillas. The use of these ex-militants has since been deemed fundamental "in the success of the counterinsurgency effort." In Dhofar, highly trained Arabic-speaking SAS intelligence troops situated themselves living*amongst* the population, which not only established a culturally sensitive counterinsurgent presence, but helped develop valuable relationships that, within a few months, produced "an enemy order of battle showing unit names, boundaries, personalities and re-supply routes in unprecedented detail" – something the Omani military had failed to generate in six years.

Given that insurgents appear "invisible, fluid and uncatchable," collecting local-level intelligence on them is crucial, but, to gather such information requires the acquiescence of local populations. In Vietnam, the USMC recognized this and deployed CAPs to live and operate within strategic villages, where they interacted every day with the local population, learning their fundamental desires and cultural norms. A CAP would then help develop a village militia, whose valuable indigenous knowledge would further augment the collection of HUMINT and help generate an air of counterinsurgent legitimacy. In Dhofar, British Army officers were seconded directly to the Sultan's Armed Forces (SAF), and thus, rather than being external advisors, gained culturally aware intelligence and helped convey to the population that "the government in Muscat ... was calling the shots," something crucial in earning incumbent legitimacy. Like Afghanistan today, Dhofar commonly disseminated information by hearsay and rumour, and having SAS forces operating at the village level helped acquire and propagate valuable and judicious intelligence. Meanwhile, in Malaya, while they provided effective and legitimate local-level security, the ethnic-Chinese village forces and police were invaluable in collecting intelligence on the enemy, especially regarding its dependence on local populations for food supplies. Having security forces cohabiting with the population also helps reveal societal concerns for local future security and wellbeing, which can, if understood, be resolved to the inherent advantage of counterinsurgent legitimacy.

In fact, cohabitation with the population was a central theme throughout much of the campaigns in Malaya, Dhofar and some of Vietnam. In Dhofar, the SAS lived and operated with the *firqat* tribal forces they had developed, which inevitably led them to inhabit populated areas where contact with civilians was beneficial for gaining legitimacy and trust. Similarly, in Vietnam, U.S. special forces, the CIA and the USMC lived and operated with irregular counterinsurgent units – such as the Montagnard tribal forces, the PFs and the Apache Force – and in Malaya, the British Army and SAS did much the same with the Ferret Force, the Malayan Scouts and the Sarawak Rangers. Such operational posture prevents a perception of risk aversion, and conveys a willingness for the foreign counterinsurgent to assume equal status with the local population, which is surely more constructive than locating oneself within large, isolated, and heavily guarded bases.

Being locally situated also allows the counterinsurgent to pursue culturally and locally aware civil development programmes, which help to prove that the incumbent offers a better alternative to the insurgent. In Dhofar, SAS commander, Lieutenant Colonel Watts recognized this and accordingly attributed more value to civil assistance tasks than to military operations. Four-man SAS Civil Aid Teams (CATs) traveled extensively and provided countless services to locals, including basic medical, dental, veterinary and agricultural assistance. After realizing what was truly needed at a local level, a CAT established a model farm where Dhofaris could learn how to increase crop and livestock yields, and the SAS even undertook a "Texan-style cattle drive supported by jet fighter cover and 5.5-inch artillery" to market at the Dhofari capital, Salalah. As Major General Jeapes claims, "there was no doubt that [the cattle drive's] demonstration of government power did more to impress the people than all the broadcasts and leaflets put together." There was a comparable focus on culturally aware development and aid in Vietnam and Malaya. For example, in Malaya, Lieutenant General Briggs established civilian control over the counterinsurgency, and placed attention upon a culturally sensitive 'New Village' programme, where ethnic-Chinese citizens were paid to relocate from their squatter homes into newly built, Chinese-guarded villages. A similar scheme in Vietnam, the Strategic Hamlet Program, aimed to separate the insurgents from the population upon which they depended for food, supplies and recruitment. Although the programme was stopped due to its perceived failure, subsequent evidence has shown that the hamlets brought "good [counterinsurgent] control to the countryside" and the Vietcong considered them "to be a genuine threat to their control." As part of the 'pacification' program, the South Vietnamese government also passed the Land to Tiller Act, which redistributed land to peasants and thus "addressed ... the rural population's grievances with the government" and undercut a major Vietcong recruitment theme.

While counterinsurgency is indeed a military strategy designed to combat an armed insurgent threat, this chapter has shown that it is still wholly possible to design culturally aware tactics and strategies for countering such a threat that encourage positive engagement with local populations. Moreover, it has shown that the U.S. and Britain, the two most prominent actors in the current Afghanistan campaign, have a valuable historical precedent for integrating and exploiting cultural awareness and local dynamics into successful counterinsurgency strategies. While conducted in different contexts and against unique adversaries, the crucial importance of acquiring and maintaining popular legitimacy, whilst simultaneously conducting a military campaign, was apparent in much of the strategic-and tactical-level thinking and activity in Malaya, Dhofar and Vietnam. So why has the current Afghanistan campaign not been able to sufficiently apply it on a practical level?

MILITARY CULTURE AND ORGANIZATIONAL LEARNING

Now that it has been established that the Afghan campaign's lack of cultural awareness is undermining its chances of success, and that the primary counterinsurgent actors there have a strong historical precedent for effectively integrating cultural awareness into combating foreign insurgencies, this chapter will seek to give possible explanations for why this seeming paradox exists. Three prominent theories will be expounded: Lyall and Wilson's thesis blaming the modern mechanized military culture of the modern counterinsurgent; Taber's notion of the versatile 'flea-like' military culture of the insurgent; and Nagl's eminent theory that fuses military culture and organizational learning within the counterinsurgent structure.

Mechanization & Modern Militaries

Lyall and Wilson famously claim that the increasing mechanization of militaries after World War One is the principle reason behind a forty-one percent decline in great power success in counterinsurgency conflicts. With regards to cultural awareness and its application to counterinsurgency, they convincingly associate the interrelation between a mechanized military and the level of cultural engagement, and thus awareness, that it acquires.

"Nineteenth century militaries were organized around 'foraging' principles in which soldiers extensively interacted with local populations to acquire supplies in the conflict zone." Inevitably therefore, "foraging armies had excellent awareness of local-level power relations, cleavages and languages" – things this chapter has deemed fundamental for a successful counterinsurgency. Furthermore, regarding the necessary acquisition of popular legitimacy, constant engagement with the population, and the learning of its dynamics and languages, will generate a counterinsurgency presence that appears more "credible in the eyes of locals."

Conversely, the late-nineteenth century's introduction of the railway into national infrastructures, and its subsequent association with improving military efficiency, reduced counterinsurgent engagement with the host populations, and thus eroded their cultural awareness and "information-gathering capabilities." The ensuing mechanization of military structures definitively broke this link with the population, and "machine war" was institutionally adopted as the norm. Given their inherent reliance on technology, modern militaries apportion more manpower to maintenance, are ill-suited to operating in inhospitable terrain, and, while 'machines' may afford considerable force protection and reduced casualty rates, this only encourages risk aversion and a consequent separation from the centre of gravity, the population. As Lyall and Wilson accurately indicate, the U.S. CAPs in Vietnam were "routinely judged more politically reliable" than other forces in the country "because the Marines were constantly present.

Lyall and Wilson conclude that the shift from 'foraging' to 'machine war' has resulted in an eighty-nine percent decline in the probability of counterinsurgent victory. They also valuably include other contributing factors, such as counterinsurgent fluency in the indigenous language, which is deemed "significant," and can be reinforced by the foreign nature of a counterinsurgency – a fifty-nine percent reduction in chance of success. Finally, to demonstrate that culturally aware and locally-based counterinsurgency can still occur in the twenty-first century, Lyall and Wilson compare the activities of the U.S. Fourth Infantry and the 101st Air Assault Divisions in Iraq. They conclude that the 101st, which prioritized joint Iraqi-U.S. "daily patrols by dismounted soldiers" that resembled "police-style … 'walking beats'" were by far, the more successful – they perpetually collected reliable HUMINT, built up local relationships of trust, and "convinced locals that U.S. forces were willing to share the same risks," thus improving their legitimacy.

The Insurgent 'War of the Flea'

The guerrilla fights the war of the flea. The flea bites, hops, bites again, nimbly avoiding the foot that would crush him. He does not seek to kill his enemy at a blow, simply to bleed him and feed on him, to plague and bedevil him, to keep him from resting and to destroy his nerve and morale.

Robert Taber's notorious exposition of guerrilla (or insurgent) warfare, and his metaphorical use of the flea to represent the insurgent, explains effectively why ISAF struggles in Afghanistan. When an insurgency adopts a "disciplined strategic mindset that seeks to avoid enemy strength while attacking enemy weaknesses through countless attacks by dispersed guerrillas," the counterinsurgent is forced to counterintuitively "spread himself as thin as possible," which presents the insurgent with more, weaker targets. In a Maoist manner, "the enemy advances, we retreat; the enemy camps, we harass; the enemy tires, we attack;

the enemy retreats, we pursue," the Taliban in Afghanistan have forced ISAF into a costly and politically-unsustainable protracted war of attrition. When the insurgent poses such a perpetually unpredictable threat, the counterinsurgent will be hesitant to base itself within population centres, or to regularly engage with the population. The subsequent lack of counterinsurgent cultural awareness and local contact provides the insurgent with the opportunity to exercise its second crucial function – being a political actor. As Taber emphasizes, "the guerrilla is a political insurgent, the conscious agent of revolution; his military role, while vital, is only incidental to his political mission."

So while the counterinsurgent constantly aims to acquire the legitimacy needed to qualitatively neutralize the insurgency, the flea-like insurgent proactively operates in ways that ensure its own survival *and* negate sustained counterinsurgent cultural contact. Moreover, the exasperating nature of the flea-like strategy tends to provoke counterinsurgents into becoming "their own worst enemies ... [and reacting] with indiscriminate violence against innocent people," or by favouring the "substitution of machines for manpower" in order to avoid casualties, which often cause illegitimate damage and death.

Taber stresses the Maoist exploitation of time, space and will against the counterinsurgent. As the Taliban has repeatedly proclaimed, "NATO has all the watches, but we have all the time." So long as the insurgent maintains its flea-like advantage, it will lack a military centre of gravity, thus making itself difficult to defeat by force of arms alone. The longer it survives, the more pressure will build within the counterinsurgent's domestic audiences calling for withdrawal, and thus defeat.

Military Organizational Culture & Learning

John Nagl's well-known treatise, *'Learning to Eat Soup With a Knife'* famously claims that "military organizations [especially the U.S.] are essentially conservative and reflexively opposed to change." This statement implies that national militaries tend to favour traditional Clausewitzian or Jominian warfare strategies that "fight purely military battles with high-technology weaponry and overwhelming firepower." It also indicates that military organizations that choose to fight unconventional adversaries will struggle to adapt to counterinsurgency strategy and tactics. While Nagl claims that the British military has, as a result of "its comparatively small size and its organizational culture," been better at adapting to 'small wars,' he stresses that adapting large military organizations, like that of the U.S., "is a task of an entirely different scale." It is not surprising therefore, that the multinational ISAF has struggled to sufficiently adapt throughout its strategic, operational and tactical levels.

Given that cultural awareness and local engagement has been deemed a critical facet of a successful counterinsurgency strategy, employing a military that institutionally favours 'Powell-esque' "decisive force," or simply a "massing [of] a large number of men and machines [combined with] the predilection for violent and direct assault," is deleterious to any chance of success. Nagl analyses the U.S.' role in Vietnam to show how the World War Two "good war" concept of warfare remained even when it was clear that an unconventional strategy was required. It is evident from his analysis that the "find 'em, fix 'em and finish 'em philosophy" does not correlate with a culturally aware engagement with indigenous communities aimed at acquiring intelligence and developing the state from the bottom-up.

Since Vietnam, rather than organizationally learning from its failure, the U.S. military implemented "no significant conceptual change." Concurrently, the 'Never Again School's' prominence, and General William Depuy's restructuring of U.S. Army doctrine eventually inaugurated the notoriously conventional Weinberger Doctrine. Counterinsurgency thus became "something of an affront to the organizational culture of America's military," hence the difficulties in Afghanistan (and Iraq) today. Although recent U.S. experience has coerced its institutional memory to codify itself within military doctrine – especially FM 3-24 – "field manuals say less about how a given military force *actually* behaves than about how it *wants* to behave." Consequently, the ideal-type counterinsurgency campaign for Afghanistan, encompassing culturally aware tribal engagement aiming towards solutions acceptable to Afghans, will require a "complete paradigm shift at the highest levels of [U.S.] military organization."

While other theories exist that seek to explain why 'big states' struggle to win counterinsurgency conflicts, the three discussed above relate most closely to the place of cultural awareness in counterinsurgency.

While Lyall and Wilson and Taber provide valuable theories regarding the military cultures and strategies of counterinsurgents and insurgents respectively, Nagl employs a framework that incorporates parts of both, *plus* the organizational difficulties states face when fighting unconventional enemies. When incorporated into an analysis of ISAF's Afghanistan campaign, all three theories are wholly relevant. The Taliban can certainly be perceived to be successfully employing a 'flea-like' strategy, while ISAF has undoubtedly struggled to adapt its mechanized structure to an unconventional conflict on inhospitable terrain and surrounded by warily cynical locals.

Nevertheless, as covered, ISAF, and most specifically the U.S., *has* made remarkable strides in terms of formulating progressive counterinsurgency doctrine and implementing less-conventional operational postures more in keeping with culturally aware counterinsurgency engagement. The Human Terrain System is an excellent innovation, as is increased pre-deployment training in Afghan culture and language, and the increased deployment of special forces as tribal engagement units. Nevertheless, despite these strategic-level improvements, "a military organization's structure, philosophy and preferences have a much greater influence on the conduct of operations than written doctrine."

Conclusion

The purpose of this chapter has been to substantiate the fundamental importance of cultural awareness and all its derivations to a successful counterinsurgency campaign by using Afghanistan as a contextual example. While a great deal of recent thought has been devoted to *military* counterinsurgency strategy and new ways of integrating twenty-first century weaponry and force structures, the most elemental foundation of this form of warfare – cultural awareness – has too often been dismissed as insignificant. While events in Afghanistan and Iraq have served to corroborate this paper's premise, and significant improvements *have*been made in doctrine and strategy, tactical-level activities reveal little constructive change.

Besides its horrific human rights record, Taliban-ruled Afghanistan was the safe-haven from where al-Qaeda grew and sanctioned the arguably world-changing September 11th 2001 attacks. It is crucial therefore, that Afghanistan is prevented from becoming such a state ever again. As has been explained, not only does counterinsurgency require a local, bottom-up culturally aware focus, but the "intensely local" nature of Afghanistan inherently necessitates such an approach. "Culture-centric warfare" is the future, and the great powers of the world *must* learn to adapt their impersonal conventional military customs to what is intrinsically a personal form of warfare. Malaya, Vietnam and Dhofar have served as three invaluable examples of what can be done, but the U.S., Britain, and indeed many other states, have an extensive historical record of experience in counterinsurgent warfare from which to draw upon. Rather than 'adopting a policy of abstention from small wars,' military organizations must embrace the increasingly globalized nature of the international system within which they operate, and structurally integrate cultural understanding into their operational existence. It seems apt therefore, to end with a statement made by the current Commander of the NATO Training Mission in Afghanistan, Lieutenant General Caldwell, someone on whose shoulders, the future of Afghanistan's national security largely lies:

> *The future is not one of major battles and engagements fought by armies on battlefields devoid of population; instead, the course of conflict will be decided by forces operating among the people of the world. Here, the margin of victory will be measured in far different terms than the wars of our past. The allegiance, trust, and confidence of populations will be the final arbiters of success.*

DEVELOPMENT THEORY AND CONFLICT: A CHANGING PARADIGM

The theory of economic development has evolved significantly over the past fifty years. In the immediate post-war period, development was seen in strongly mechanistic terms. In this conception, the state invariably was understood to play the catalyst in fostering economic growth and social and institutional development. In the 1980s, however, a liberal revival denied the exceptional character of developing states and placed markets rather than states at the centre of the development process. Over the course of the last decade, however, an economic crisis throughout much of the developing world has introduced a range of caveats to this liberal model including a reappraisal of the role played by states, as well as the vital contributions to development made by civil society, cultural factors, women, markets and macro-economic policy.

Unfortunately, today the development community confronts another set of intellectual and policy dilemmas in conflict-ridden societies. Since the end of the Cold War, Western governments, international development and lending institutions, the United Nations and NGOs are increasingly compelled to help countries torn asunder by war to move from dependence on humanitarian relief to a reconstruction process and ultimately into a long-term development phase. Triggering sustainable development in the wake of war itself obviously poses a daunting range of intellectual, political, economic, social and cultural challenges. Violent conflict inflicts appalling visible and invisible damage on developing societies.

Vital economic infrastructure is ruined, state institutions often collapse, mistrust of the state soars, schooling is disrupted, refugees flood into cities, fear replaces confidence, skilled workers flee, and war profiteers with a vested interest in conflict lurk in the shadows prepared to resurrect the very tensions that allowed them to flourish economically and politically at the expense of the society as a whole.

The World Bank notes that post-conflict societies often labour under a dominating narrow elite, a fragile peace, a lack of confidence among political and economic actors and weak judicial, financial, fiscal, administrative and regulatory institutions. (Barnet, Eggleston, Webber).

The damage inflicted by war can be the equivalent of several years of the country's peacetime GDP. Normal economic activity is utterly hampered by the fall in productivity capacity, physical destruction, a dearth of investment, and internal market fragmentation. Moreover, war rarely resolves underlying conflict. For societies already living under precarious economic conditions, mass violence is a disaster, and the longer conflict rages the more destructive are its consequences.

Much of this violence, moreover, does not fit the classic definition of inter-state conventional war. Sometimes armed sub-state groups simply seek to seize resources and other economic assets and do not hesitate to target civilians in the process. These wars can literally destroy formal economies and create enormously daunting problems for those charged with reconstruction and development (Bojicic-Dzelilovic). Not coincidentally, fifteen of the world's 20 poorest countries have experienced conflict over the past 15 years.

It is one of the paradoxes of international relations that the daunting costs of conflict fail to inspire more pre-conflict preventive initiatives, which, invariably, are far less costly than post-conflict interventions. In a world that still accords the notion of national sovereignty pride of place, such cost-benefit analysis is hardly sufficient to inspire a proactive approach to conflict (Schnabel). That said, in recent years, Western forces have intervened to halt a conflict in Kosovo, deployed forces in the midst of an ongoing Afghan civil conflict and waged a war in Iraq where internal conflict had long been suppressed but has subsequently boiled over. (Chesterman).

Moreover, for some analysts, the attacks of September 11 demonstrated that disengagement from the developing world was far more perilous and costly than engagement. Indeed, Afghanistan, a failed and highly impoverished country shattered by Soviet invasion and civil war, had hosted training centres for thousands of Jihadists, who received detailed instruction in the modalities of employing terrorist violence to achieve their millenarian vision.

The nexus between security and development has also been made apparent in the borderless nature of other development-related challenges including refugee flows, the spread of disease, and environmental catastrophe, to name just a few. The attacks on New York and Washington stimulated serious rethinking of the

Western approach to development issues. In the broad reassessment that ensued, US officials identified post-conflict societies as a challenge of particular importance.

The change in mindset was somewhat startling as one of the major campaign themes of the Bush team in 2000, for example, had been the promise that no more would the United States entangle itself in dubious nation building projects. Although the term "nation building" is now studiously avoided for obvious reasons, the reality is that the United States has become an active proponent of nation building, most notably, although not exclusively in Afghanistan and Iraq. A newfound appreciation of how dangerous failed states are to global stability made this change of heart inevitable, (Carothers) and President Bush's subsequent National Security Strategy noted that, "America is now threatened less by conquering states than we are by failing ones." (Hamre)

Perhaps the most significant difference between the development challenge faced by a poor country and a poor post-conflict society lies in the hidden effects of conflict. Institutional breakdown, limited or absent government legitimacy, the existence of power vacuums, a traumatized society lacking confidence in the future, a pervasive lack of trust, fear in the revival of conflict and the presence of armed irregular forces in urban and rural areas reinforcing those concerns and willing to use those arms for plunder and political blackmail.

As long as these forces remain armed, the risk of renewed fighting is real and will be seen as such by the population and the international lending community.

Concerns about managing post-conflict development are obviously not uniquely American. OECD (Organisation for Economic Co-operation and Development) member countries, the World Bank, the UN and a broad range of increasingly active NGO's have all engaged in considered reflection on reconstruction and development challenges in post-conflict settings (Bojicic-Dzelilovic). Yet, Western governments are still not properly structured to conduct coherent post-conflict policies. This is particularly ironic given the number of post-conflict situations in which American and Allied troops have been engaged over the past decade. More worrisome is the fact that the trend line has moved from small countries with relatively manageable problems to large countries consumed by grave difficulties. (Secretariat Report, 145 EC 04 E) Governments have been very slow to internalize the lessons of the past decade. In many Western governments there is a critical need for greater inter-agency co-operation, standing start deployability of assets, and additional funding. Vastly improved multinational coordination is also in order.

An entire new body of academic literature on the subject has also come to the fore, and this work reflects both the importance of the topic and the daunting and controversial intellectual and policy challenges it poses. (Duffield) From this literature, a clearer picture is emerging of what one study has identified as the four pillars of post-conflict reconstruction.

These are: security or the establishment of a safe and secure environment through the establishment of legitimate and stable security institutions; justice and reconciliation which incorporates an impartial and accountable legal system, a means to deal with past and current crimes, and a humane prison system; Social and economic well being achieved through the provision of emergency relief, restoration of basic services, laying the foundation for a viable economy and sustainable development; and finally Governance and Participation, by building viable constitutional structures, capacity building in state institutions and public administration and the nurturing of an articulated civil society capable of participating in governance and relieving the state of some of its myriad burdens. (Association of U.S. Army and CSIS)

A reasonable degree of peace and security is the absolute sine qua non for economic, political and cultural reconstruction to commence. Few economic actors, for example, will consider assuming investment risks without assurances of a minimum degree of security.

Increasingly, international peacekeeping forces are asked to provide that security. NATO itself has deployed troops in recent years to Bosnia, Kosovo, the former Yugoslav Republic of Macedonia*, and Afghanistan, and several NATO member states have sent forces to Iraq with some NATO support. NATO is also soon to begin training Iraqi security forces. Western militaries are also being asked to perform vital development tasks. US forces in Iraq were not only deployed to confront rebel spoilers but also rebuild key infrastructure-a visceral manifestation of growing security-development links. In Afghanistan, NATO member countries have deployed Provincial Reconstruction Teams (PRTs) with a range of reconstruction responsibilities from bridge repair to political support. Deployed forces are asked to ensure that basic humanitarian needs are met with great dispatch, and oftentimes, by default, they are compelled to manage these operations. Simply clothing, housing and feeding an often-traumatized population poses enormous difficulties, particularly when forces are not trained for such operations. The problem can be made all the more difficult when the end of conflict prompts a massive return of refugees and internally displaced persons (IDPs).

Oftentimes the international community lacks both the local knowledge and the resources to establish law and order, build public administration, provide social and humanitarian services, launch the process of long-term economic development and engage in capacity building for longer-term self-government. (Schnabel) Finding resources for post-conflict reconstruction and development obviously poses a critical challenge.

There is little doubt, however, that the strategic interests of large Western donor countries ultimately determine the level of aid. This is apparent if one looks at how the West has responded to conflict in Africa where the level of forces and resources dispatched into conflict and post-conflict settings are far less than, for example, in the Balkans.

Building security also demands effective reconciliation strategies and eventually the disarmament of warring factions. This is particularly difficult in the wake of bitter civil war. As is evident in both Afghanistan and Iraq, internal reconciliation can prove enormously challenging. Furthermore if the peace operation itself inadvertently unleashes long-suppressed conflict, the development task becomes onerous. In such cases, the occupying force risks becoming a kind of scapegoat for a bleak security and economic outlook. Effective pre-deployment planning, conducted in close consultation with regional experts, is therefore critical.

Only after active hostilities have ceased can shift attention from humanitarian relief operations to longer-term reconstruction efforts and the return of basic government services. In these areas, there is greater scope for the institutions of the recipient country, provided, of course, that those institutions have been properly reconstituted. When the state apparatus is reasonably operational and the country stabilised militarily, the government and the international community are positioned to initiate longer-term development strategies.

One very important difference between normal development and post-conflict situations is that the international community is more than likely to assume a degree of authority within the war-ravaged societies in which international forces have intervened. This has potential advantages but a myriad of drawbacks. It confers representatives of the international community a higher degree of leverage in the implementation of reconstruction and initial development strategies.

Some would argue that it thus presents an opportunity to implement best practices. But whether this authority can be put to effective use hinges on whether the international community is ready to accept this burden, whether the local population sees the occupying authority as legitimate and is fully consulted, and ultimately whether the international community actually understands what best practices are in local conditions. In any case, the beneficiaries of any large-scale aid project must be systematically engaged in decision-making. Whoever controls the purse strings for development assistance will need to undertake a policy of wide and deep consultation with the recipient society. The US occupying authorities initial efforts to impose a market revolution in Iraq's nearly anarchic conditions provides a case study of what not to do. (ICG Report) There is a paradox at the core of this issue and one is forced to ask whether it is even possible to establish conditions for legitimate and sustainable national governance through a period of benevolent foreign autocracy. (Urqhart)

Development theory itself is increasingly focused on the need for community driven development strategies, and this is all the more important in post-conflict settings. One approach that has had some success is premised on setting up local and broadly representative councils charged with deciding how development funds will be spent. When properly implemented, such Community Development Strategies (CDRs) can help empower local communities, reinforce democratic practice and nourish a fruitful dialogue between the centre and the periphery. They can help ensure that development funds are spent on projects that communities feel are most needed - something that can spark to genuine empowerment. CDR's also increase transparency and reduce corruption by eliminating many of the middlemen who are positioned to skim away aid and budget resources. (Cliffe, Guggenheim, Koster)

Establishing proper levels of aid over time poses another set of dilemmas. Paul Collier and Anke Hoeffler of the World Bank have found that while the absorptive capacity for aid in post-conflict societies is roughly the same as for other developing countries over the first three years after a conflict, for the rest of that first decade, it is double that of non-conflict developing countries. Absorptive capacity is a measurement of the increments of aid that triggers economically productive activity and demonstrates the point at which further aid will only trigger economically unproductive and even parasitic activity.

Generally in post-conflict societies there is a brief phase of very rapid growth related to the sudden influx of aid funds and the restoration of infrastructure. This means that this initial aid is unusually productive, although high levels of corruption, ongoing violence, and poor administration can have countervailing effects. The post-conflict countries that Paul Collier studied initially grew on average 1.13% more rapidly than other developing countries. Growth tended to peak between the 4th and 7th year after a conflict, although even in the early post-conflict period it can be as much as 2% higher than normal long range growth.

The need for foreign assistance and the recipient country's capacity to put it to good use generally increases significantly after three years. This suggests that foreign development assistance should rise significantly at that juncture. But in practice, aid is almost never disbursed in this way. The largest inflows tend to occur in the immediate wake of a conflict and decline from that point over time (Collier and Hoeffler). Once the television cameras have gone away, sustaining a high level of political interest in donor countries can prove problematic.

In the past, there has been a tendency to advise countries emerging from conflict to employ policies that, while effective in normal conditions, are hardly optimal after a conflict. This happened in the early months of the Iraq occupation when some officials of the Coalition Provisional Authority (CPA) aspired to create a laboratory to neo-liberal ideas in a post-conflict setting. There are certainly many instances in which a developing country might be well counselled to push for rapid macro-and micro-economic reform, particularly when that society's institutions are sufficiently robust to sustain a difficult fiscal, monetary or other structural adjustment as well as micro-economic reforms like privatisation. Rarely, however, are societies emerging from conflict in a position to sustain such difficult transitions, at least over the short term. For this reason, Collier comes to a tentative conclusion that for post-conflict societies, priority should be accorded first to social policies, secondly to sectoral policies and only lastly to macro-economic measures (Collier and Hoeffler). While monetary reform can clearly be helpful in the early period, mass privatisation of state assets is not.

8

Missed Opportunities: Iran Negotiations 2003–Today

In a comparative study of Iran and North Korea, it is natural to assume that Iran presents the greater challenge. Iran is a major petroleum producer and a rising regional power capable of threatening U.S. interests in the Middle East and Southwest Asia, with or without its nuclear pro-gram. Iran is important in its own right, as are the two regions it inhabits. However, North Korea is equally important because its neighborhood, Northeast Asia (China, Russia, Japan, and South Korea), is a region with a concentration of wealth and military power that may be unrivalled in the world. This region is critical to global peace, stability, and prosperity. In reality, therefore, North Korea and Iran both pose geopolitical challenges of great magnitude and complexity.

Tat different U.S. policies to address the nuclear challenges posed by Iran and North Korea have yielded similar results is striking. The United States has pursued largely incentive-based policies toward North Korea, including limited engagement through bilateral and multilateral talks. Washington has not had bilateral nuclear talks with Iran since the late 1970s and only joined the multilateral process initiated by the Europeans 3 years after it had begun, entering talks in 2006. U.S. constraint-based policies toward Iran have aimed at preventing Tehran from developing civilian nuclear infrastructure on the assumption that it would not remain purely civilian in nature. This objective motivated what appeared to be contradictory U.S. policies: the

United States promised North Korea advanced civilian nuclear reactors in exchange for its 1994 nuclear freeze, but urged Russia in 1995 not to sell Iran the same technology. In fact, Moscow went even further, agreeing to limit military and nuclear cooperation with Iran in exchange for U.S. support for the Russian space program. This agreement was subsequently renounced in 2000 by then-President Vladimir Putin.

These very different policy approaches to Iran and North Korea were also based on the U.S. assessment that the Iranian nuclear program posed no immediate military threat but that the North Korean program did. As a result, the United States pursued incentive-based policies including limited engagement toward North Korea, but constraint-based policies centering on "technology denial" toward Iran. Washington's effort to stop the Iranian program did not succeed. Iran has a nuclear program today that is behind where North Korea was in 1993: Iran has about one or two bombs' worth of fissile material, but this fissile material is not weapons-grade, as North Korea's was in 1993. Iran continues its nuclear program in defence of UN Security Council resolutions calling for a halt to domestic uranium enrichment.

NUCLEAR ELITISM: THE KHATAMI GOVERNMENT AND THE EU-3 NEGOTIATIONS, 2003–2005

The Iran nuclear crisis erupted in the summer of 2002 during the presidency of Mohammed Khatami. Iran had completed a uranium enrichment plant and a heavy water plant without informing the IAEA, which implied the existence of a covert nuclear program. From the mid-1980s on, Iran had failed to report acquisition of and experiments with nuclear materials, as required by its Safeguards Agreement. However, Tehran relied on a loophole—that it had not adopted a revised clause in its Safeguards Agreement—to justify its failure to disclose the new facilities. Revelation of these facilities triggered unsuccessful IAEA efforts to clarify the nature and intent of Iran's program. A September 2003 IAEA resolution called on Tehran to cooperate or face a report to the UN Security Council. Concerned by the precedent of the war with Iraq, the EU-3 (the United Kingdom, France, and Germany) launched talks with Iran.

Nuclear negotiations during the Khatami government offered promising conditions to reach a nuclear deal. Fear of facing Iraq's fate was Iran's key vulnerability, and Tehran focused on avoiding a report to the UN Security Council, which would set an uncomfortable parallel with Iraq. Also, grievances unrelated to the nuclear issue could be introduced at the UN, such as Iran's support for terrorism and, as negotiations continued into 2005, its destabilizing activities in Iraq. While the EU-3 negotiated with Iran, the United States pushed the IAEA to report Iran to the UN Security Council. This dual-track approach placed effective diplomatic pressure on Iran.

At the same time, changes in the region presented Iran with new opportunities. The prospect of a Shia-led post-Saddam Iraq and the overthrow of the Taliban in Afghanistan eliminated the most serious threats to Tehran and suggested a convergence of interests with the United States—a view Washington did not share. Iranian compromise marked this early phase of the negotiations, which yielded three major achievements: Iran agreed to a temporary suspension of domestic enrichment; signed the voluntary IAEA Additional Protocol allowing intrusive and surprise inspections of nuclear sites; and adopted a revised clause in its Safeguards Agreements regarding disclosure of information on new facilities, closing the loophole that had precipitated the crisis.

Why did these negotiations fail to clinch a comprehensive and enduring deal with Iran? A review of the European diplomatic effort suggests four reasons it did not succeed. First, the

United States and the EU-3 were not aligned on goals and tactics. Although Washington was not at the negotiating table, it played a powerful consultative role, and the EU-3 were unwill-ing to stake out an independent course. Second, the negotiations never addressed whether Iran could retain some domestic uranium enrichment—the issue at the core of the dispute between Iran and the international community. The failure to address whether Iran could resume domestic enrichment at some point removed any stake Iran's leadership might have had to engage in serious negotiations toward a nuclear deal. Third, this European ambiguity on domestic enrichment ended up helping Tehran manipulate the nuclear debate among Iranian political elites and constrain it to the narrow tactical question of whether to accommodate or defy the international community. Controversial strategic questions, such as whether Iran's nuclear program is civilian or military, were excluded from Iranian debate as a result. The fourth reason the EU-3 process failed was that Iranian elites favouring accommodation of international concerns over defence were set back when promised incentives to Iran never materialized (due to U.S. opposition), and when changes in the policy context led Iran to believe it had a stronger hand to play.

It is important to appreciate the difficulty the EU-3 faced in providing Iran incentives, and therefore in negotiating successfully with Iran. The EU-3 led the negotiations with Iran in close consultation with the United States but consistently failed to gain Washington's support for compromises and incentives. In effect, the EU-3 process was an EU-3+1 process, with the United States as the very powerful plus one. Lack of consensus between the United States and the EU-3 on tactics mirrored the problems in the North Korean case: the lack of bipartisan U.S. support for the 1994 Agreed Framework adversely affected that nuclear deal, and China's reluctance to isolate North Korea in the Six Party Talks process continues to hinder efforts to pressure North Korea. The EU-3 were united in seeking to prevent another Iraq and committed to finding a diplomatic solution with Iran. Why the EU-3 did not proceed without U.S. support is a lingering question. While European analysts argue that incentives were hostage to U.S. sanctions, it is hard to find this linkage. In fact, Europe had strayed from the United States before; some in the G-8 broke ranks in 2000 to support World Bank lending to Iran as a way to help Iranian reformers. In nuclear talks, however, the EU-3 stayed close to the United States except on the issue of reporting Iran to the UN Security Council.

Iranian Media and Elite Debate

Among the most significant and overlooked aspects of the EU-3's nuclear negotiations with Iran were how important this engagement with the outside was to Iran's leadership; how the leadership feared negotiations would be used by rival factions to advance their partisan political agendas; and how media and public discussion of the negotiations informed (in limited ways) average Iranians of the state's nuclear program. Until the revelations of Iran's undeclared nuclear facilities in 2002, Iranians had almost a total lack of knowledge about the state's nuclear program. As Iran moved into negotiations with the Europeans, the negotiations became a topic of political conversation in the country covered by journalists and political commentators, and discussed in the media by Iranian government officials and politicians in parliament. Public opinion was not a constraint on the regime's actions, but public dissatisfaction with the consequences of Tehran's decisions could also not be ignored without the risk of rival factions capitalizing on the opportunity to undermine the regime.

It is important for U.S. policymakers to understand the way in which the nuclear standoff played in Iran's domestic politics in order to appreciate the motivations driving Iranian negotiating positions. One of the peculiarities of Iran's political process is that foreign and security policy provides a major arena for domestic political competition. This is both a result of Iran's estrangement from the international community since 1979 and because Tehran regards foreign policy as a symbol of Iran's continued influence. For these reasons alone, then, the nuclear negotiations with the EU-3 were destined to become a serious battleground among competing Iranian factions. However, they became exponentially more important because they were Iran's first significant engagement with the international community after a long hiatus. The government equated them with U.S.-Iran negotiations to end the 1979 U.S. Embassy hostage crisis and Iran-Iraq negotiations in 1988 following their 8-year war.

A glimpse of the government's political considerations has been provided by President Khatami's chief nuclear negotiator, Hassan Rowhani, a political heavyweight who concurrently served as Secretary of Iran's Supreme National Security Council (equivalent to National Security Advisor). Rowhani has contended that Tehran was so concerned about managing negative public reaction to the possible consequences of the negotiations that complex questions of nuclear policy were addressed to the Iranian public. This was seen as a way to prepare citizens for what was thought would be an inevitable report of Iran to the UN Security Council, and to gain their understanding and support for the government's negotiating stance. According to Rowhani, issues such as whether to sign the voluntary IAEA Additional Protocol, or whether that would be an "act of treason," were put to the public.

It is important to keep in mind that the political process in Iran is an insider's game in which average Iranians are spectators whose views do not count. However, the significance of the nuclear negotiations and the potential for the Khatami government's factional rivals to use them as a weapon against the government created a unique political environment in the country. Political insiders—the power centers, personalities, and factions who populate and define Iran's unusual political landscape—capitalized on the national spotlight on Iran's nuclear negotiations with the EU-3 to enhance their standing and weaken their rivals. During the Khatami government, therefore, Iranian political elites engaged in a public debate on the nuclear issue.

This debate was limited and constrained by the regime, manipulated to fit a familiar Iranian framework grounded in two longstanding and competing views of how Iran should interact with the rest of the world: accommodate it or defy it. Controversial strategic questions —whether Iran's nuclear program is military or civilian, and whether further isolation is an acceptable price to pay for pursuing a nuclear program—were conspicuously absent from the public conversation. However, as the nuclear negotiations became a promising field for competition among political factions, and as the Iranian public's appetite for information about the negotiations grew, government officials were forced to explain the decisions and moves they made in the negotiations. In essence, the more the Khatami government manipulated the media debate to deny its rivals a political weapon, the more the government became a captive of public opinion.

Elite debate over accommodation versus defence of international concerns gained its own momentum, as a result, with wide media coverage and debate in parliament that forced

Iranian officials to convey and defend the government's point of view to the public in news conferences and interviews to the media. In her study of Iranian media reporting on the nuclear issue during this period, Farideh Farhi describes how it encompassed virtually every key aspect of the negotiations, including whether to reject the NPT; enter negotiations with the EU-3; enter expanded talks with the United States; continue the enrichment suspension; and even whether to tone down Iranian rhetoric.

Undertaking a fairly sophisticated public affairs strategy, the regime portrayed the nuclear standoff in different ways, depending on the political faction it was addressing. In the reformist media, Iranian officials described the standoff as a "genuine disagreement" with the Europeans, in which Iran needed to offer "objective guarantees" while not giving up its rights. To forestall criticism from the right, Tehran emphasized a "whole-of-government" decisionmaking process that implied both ends of the political spectrum had been consulted and that consensus decisions were achieved.

What helped the regime frame the nuclear debate in simple, tactical terms of accommodation versus defence, however, was the European negotiators' refusal to answer the question of whether Iran's suspension of domestic enrichment was to be permanent or temporary. Tat allowed the regime to perpetuate the "denial of Iranian rights" narrative—rights the regime argued were based on the NPT's essential bargain between *Nuclear Weapons States* and *Nonnuclear Weapons States*: that the former will assist the latter in acquiring peaceful, civilian nuclear technology. Because the Khatami regime had succeeded in eliminating the question of whether Iran's program was indeed peaceful, and because it was a moderate government that did so— one potentially politically inclined to press the question of civilian versus military intent—there was no concomitant elite discussion of Iranian responsibilities under the NPT or to the IAEA. The EU-3 stance on domestic enrichment, thus, reinforced the focus of elite debate on negotiating tactics versus intent of Iran's nuclear program and was easily caricatured as a policy of singling Iran out for special treatment.

TRYING OUT NEW INITIATIVES ON ISOLATED REGIMES

The European position on domestic uranium enrichment was rooted in U.S. constraint-based policies of the 1990s aimed at denying Iran the capacity to build a nuclear infrastructure. In 2004, President Bush unveiled a proposal to limit domestic enrichment worldwide to those states that already have that capacity—with Iran in mind. However, intensive U.S. efforts to gain broad support among NPT member states for this initiative, which Washington characterized as a way to close loopholes in the NPT that permit leakage between civilian and military nuclear programs, was and remains a hard sell.

Nuclear "have-nots" challenged the effort to create what amounts to a nuclear fuel sup-pliers' cartel, raising questions about the juridical and economic implications, as well as the basic political question of who should control the nuclear fuel cycle and related technologies. If Washington had succeeded in making this proposal a widely accepted practice or a new feature of a revised NPT, "no domestic enrichment" might have become a viable deal with Iran. There is an instructive parallel with the 1993 IAEA special inspections procedure that triggered the North Korea crisis. Pyongyang's refusal to submit to these surprise and intrusive inspections was one of two reasons North Korea was reported to the UN Security Council in 1993, just as Iran was reported to the Security Council in 2006 for refusing to suspend domestic enrichment.

What the two situations have in common is that neither the special inspections nor the U.S. initiative on uranium enrichment were widely accepted practice or policy, but new initiatives applied to North Korea and Iran, respectively. North Korea was the first state asked to submit to special inspections; Iran was the first test case of the U.S. proposal on domestic enrichment. The demand for special inspections was abandoned in order to reach a nuclear deal with North Korea, the 1994 Agreed Framework. However, intrusive and surprise inspection procedures are now enshrined in the IAEA Additional Protocol. Many states have adopted this voluntary protocol to provide the international community additional assurances that their nuclear programs are civilian in nature. Iran, as a result of the EU-3 negotiations, is among the states that signed (but never ratified) the protocol. This example suggests the risks of applying new initiatives to international outliers before such initiatives become widely accepted practice or policy.

IRAN–EU-3 AGREEMENTS BEGIN TO FRAY

The Iranian domestic context was ripe for reacting negatively to EU-3 ambiguity on whether Iran could resume domestic enrichment after a suspension. In an attempt to break the deadlock with the EU-3 in March 2005, Iran offered to produce only low enriched uranium.

However, with Iran's presidential election just 3 months away, the EU-3 did not respond, banking on the victory of former President Rafsanjani, a pragmatic conservative, to close a deal with Iran.

The electoral upset by Mahmoud Ahmadinejad left the EU-3 adrif, with no Plan B, while facing U.S. infexibility and a hardening Iranian stance. European failure to respond to the Iranian overture to limit domestic enrichment affected Iranian elite debate, giving the upper hand to those favouring defence. Nearly 2 years of diplomatic efforts to resolve the nuclear standoff with Iran came to a screeching halt.

Accusing the Europeans of prolonging the suspension of enrichment and of failing to deliver promised incentives, Iran began undoing the agreements reached with the EU-3. At an August 2005 IAEA emergency meeting, Iran stated it would remain a Nonnuclear Weapons State party to the NPT but also declared that Iran and members of the Non-Aligned Movement were being denied the NPT right to peaceful uses of nuclear technology. Tehran threatened to suspend adherence to the voluntary IAEA Additional Protocol, which was signed but not ratified, if reported to the UN Security Council. Iran's leader-ship also began preparing for sanctions. In a warning to the international community, the head of the Iranian Revolutionary Guard Corps suggested that sanctions could send oil prices to $100 a barrel.

NUCLEAR POPULISM: THE AHMADINEJAD REGIME, 2005–2009

A new phase of nuclear negotiations opened in August 2005 as the new Iranian government under President Ahmadinejad took offence. This marked the start of Iranian defence of the international community, often attributed to the hardline politics of the regime and the new chief nuclear negotiators, Ali Larijani, replaced by Saeed Jalili in 2007. Iran's posture, however, had less to do with the more conservative leadership than with changed Iranian perceptions of opportunity and vulnerability. While Israel continued to warn of a military strike, this did not create the sense of threat posed by the 2003 U.S.-led invasion of Iraq. By 2005, the policy con-text had changed: Iran believed it held important cards in the face of unabated U.S. difficulties in Iraq and Afghanistan. Iran's leaders had even concluded, according to former EU-3 negotiator and German Foreign Minister Joschka Fischer, that the United States had been "weakened to the point that it [was] dependent on Iran's goodwill and that high oil prices [had] made the West all the more wary of a serious confrontation."

Thus, a confident Iranian leadership confronted the EU-3 in 2005 and was about to signal that if an acceptable deal was not forthcoming, the conversion plant at Isfahan would be re-started. An illuminating aspect of this decision was the leadership's concern that Ahmadinejad's election would be seen as the cause of Iran's tougher line. To discourage that view, an emergency meeting was convened while President Khatami was still in power, attended by leaders representing the Iranian political spectrum—Supreme Leader Ayatollah Khamenei, President Khatami, Ali Akbar Hashemi-Rafsanjani, Mir Hossein Moussavi, and President-elect Ahma-dinejad. This photo opportunity was designed to underscore Iran's internal consensus for both domestic and foreign audiences.

It was also a sign of evolution in the domestic policy context. The nuclear issue was, by 2005, a key factor shaping Iranian elite competition and factional politics. Nuclear politics had also become a matter of state legitimacy with the international spotlight on Iran's more defant tone. President Ahmadinejad decided to take the domestic debate among elites about the nuclear standoff into a new and uncharted direction, turning it into a populist issue. He began raising the standoff in his public appearances outside Tehran. In more than 30 trips to the provinces, President Ahmadinejad repeatedly described the nuclear standoff as a Western attempt to deny Iran its rights. He mobilized an otherwise neglected rural populace to get behind the slogan of defence, chasing away supporters of accommodation and drowning moderates in a sea of nuclear populism. Tehran now sought to pocket Iran's nuclear advances and avoid any major costs or consequences for having walked away from the EU-3 agreements.

P5+1 Negotiations and the Obama Administration

A new chapter in the nuclear standoff opened in 2006 with the expansion of the EU-3 to the P5+1 (the permanent five members of the UN Security Council plus Germany). The P5+1 offered Iran a new deal that included such carrots as cooperation with the United States, but still did not address what mattered most to Iran: retaining some domestic enrichment capacity.

Instead, the United States continued to focus on the international community, finally securing sufficient IAEA support to report Iran to the UN Security Council in February 2006. U.S. strategy since has succeeded in making the Iran standoff all about Iran's compliance with UN Security Council resolutions calling for a cessation of Iranian domestic enrichment, denying Iran the ability to sue for the rights it claims under the NPT to peaceful nuclear technology. This was a crucial U.S. diplomatic victory because it closed of any potential support for Iran from other states opposed to the new U.S. approach to domestic uranium enrichment. However, it was only a tactical win, and a Pyrrhic one at that. Since Iran was reported to the Security Council, it has become even harder for Iranian moderates to justify accommodating the international community. During the period that the UN Security Council passed Resolutions 1737, 1747, and 1803, imposing sanctions on Iran, Iran's uranium enrichment capability has improved substantially.

These Security Council resolutions, coupled with the failure of the EU-3 negotiations, and the absence of rewards for Iran's suspension of enrichment allowed President Ahma-dinejad to expand Iranian support—or at least the appearance of public support—for defiance of the international community over accommodation. In the process, proponents of moderation—not only those on the nuclear question but moderates in general—have been forced into the political wilderness. Thus, not only were opportunities for a negotiated settlement with Iran during the Khatami government squandered, but the potential for serious Iranian compromises has been lost without altering the basic terms of the deal. In the course of negotiations, moreover, like North Korea, Iran has also come to see its nuclear program as a way to achieve political credibility with the United States and to improve bar-gaining leverage. As an Iranian political scientist has argued, Iran's nuclear program makes Tehran "strategically worthy" of talks with the United States and has brought Washington to the negotiating table.

Why Negotiations with Iran Might Succeed

A modified version of the original P5+1 deal remains on the table. It includes the new element of a fuel swap to build confidence. There may be a hint of U.S. flexibility on domestic enrichment, with the caveat that Iran's rights to peaceful nuclear energy are predicated on its compliance with obligations under the NPT. However, this is not an explicit offer. It is conceivable that a deal involving limited domestic enrichment under conditions of strict oversight of Iran's nuclear program may be acceptable to Iran judging from the proposals it dribbled out in 2005 as the EU-3 process ended, and again in 2006 after being reported to the UN Security Council.

First, such a deal would allow the government to declare victory on domestic enrichment, which two very different Iranian administrations—the moderate (Khatami) and hardline (Ahmadinejad) administrations—identifed as a "right" worth defending. Second, an internationally monitored nuclear program is more in Iran's interest than Tehran may calculate. There is a fundamental conflict between Tehran's regional leadership aspirations and the distrust and opposition to Iranian ambitions and the exercise of Iranian power among the majority of states in the Middle East and Southwest Asia. Despite Iran's soft power among segments of the population in these regions, the leadership in most of these states resents Iran's destabilizing support for subnational surrogates that threaten their regimes. Iran's suspected nuclear weapons program only exacerbates these fears and antagonisms. While South Korea, Japan, China, and Russia have established a strategic modus vivendi with a nuclear weapons–capable North Korea, helped by the Six Party Talks process, Iran will not have that luxury. Tehran can never erase its neighbours' anxieties over its regional power ambitions, which are only heightened by Iran's nuclear drive. Stringent international oversight over Iran's nuclear program could reduce these anxieties.

The third factor favouring a deal is that Iran has not decided whether to build a nuclear weapon or pursue latency. Latency affords an opportunity for international oversight, while Iran's possession of a bomb, which would be a sign of further hardening in Iran's posture, would likely eliminate prospects for international oversight. A bomb carries significant liabilities for Iran: the more force Iran shows it has, the more it will be targeted and hedged against. However, continuing to insist that Iran eschew domestic enrichment could drive Iran to take the risk. Keeping Iran on the path of latency with strict international access and oversight is, therefore, in Washington's and Iran's interests.

At the moment, however, Washington seems to see no opportunity for a deal, calculating that the regime has been shaken by the aftermath of the June 2009 presidential election, and that the fallout from that has not yet settled. Certainly, there is substantial jockeying among political elites that was highlighted in October 2009 when, facing serious domestic opposition, President Ahmadinejad tried to accept the P5+1 fuel swap proposal. Invigorated by his weakness, politicians across the political spectrum opposed the deal. However, this fuel swap did not include limited domestic enrichment in Iran. Such a deal, properly packaged, would be harder for Tehran to reject since governments representing both ends of the political spectrum—moderate (Khatami) and hardline (Ahmadinejad)—went to great lengths to defend domestic enrichment.

Not attempting a realistic deal carries substantial risks. First, Iranian nuclear capacity can expand, and since Iran has greatly loosened cooperation with the IAEA, transparency over its program is limited. Second, the more the government rallies Iranians around unifying nationalist rhetoric, a certain momentum is generated that crowds out political moderation across-the-board, and not just on the nuclear issue. This could result in Iran's taking an even harder line and becoming harder to deal with—especially if the ascendance of Iranian hardliners is also backed by strengthened nuclear capability.

Washington has not been able to coerce Iran's acceptance of the current P5+1 offer so far. Neither existing sanctions nor threats of an Israeli strike have dampened Iran's nuclear drive. Iran has the ability to retaliate against an Israeli strike, and both U.S. and Israeli assets would be at risk. While some experts judge that strikes could delay the program, they also assess that strikes would not stop it. The Israeli strike on Iraq's Osirak reactor in 1981 was made with the expectation that it would delay, not stop, Iraq's nuclear weapons program. In fact, the strike only whetted Iraq's appetite for nuclear weapons and its commitment to the nuclear program substantially increased after the attack. Iran's nuclear facilities are dispersed and near population centers, making the international political costs of a strike for Israel and the United States potentially enormous. It is significant, moreover, that, although Iran is distrusted by a majority of states in the Middle East and Southwest Asia, none supports a military solution because that could lead to a wider war. Saudi Arabia, a bitter enemy of Iran, has publicly opposed a military strike because the consequences would be devastating to the region. French diplomats stationed in the Middle East believe average Syrians oppose Iran's nuclear program because it risks a military strike on Iran that would turn Syrians into collateral damage—and Syria has been a staunch ally of Iran for three decades.

Since sanctions have not yet been effective, and military strikes would create more problems than they would solve, that leaves diplomacy combined with incentives and pressures. For talks to be viable, however, the deal must be altered. Further delay of serious negotiations with Iran is risky. While U.S. experts contend that Iran is running out of uranium feedstock, which limits its nuclear advancement, Iranian public views over whether to accommodate or defy the international community can only harden—especially as the promise of the extended hand in President Obama's 2009 inaugural speech turns up as empty as President Bush's 1989 inaugural offer of "goodwill begets goodwill." Long intervals between negotiations, as the North Korean case shows, also aford time for expanding nuclear capability.

Iran Policy Recommendations

Nuclear Pause. The P5+1 should table a nuclear deal allowing limited domestic enrichment in Iran (limited by quantity produced, the number of centrifuges in place, and/or the level of enrichment). Such a deal would have two parts. The first part would be the basic bargain of allowing limited domestic enrichment under conditions of strict Iranian compliance with its IAEA Safeguards Agreement and the terms of the Additional Protocol (which Iran must ratify), to secure international oversight, access, monitoring, and transparency over the Iranian program, and the ability to secure dangerous fissile material produced in facilities dispersed around the country. Possible additional measures for the assurance of the international community could be considered, such as supplementary monitors in addition to IAEA monitors at certain sites. Verifcation procedures that could quickly detect any modification to the program or production of highly enriched uranium would need to be worked out with the IAEA.

The second part of the deal would entail nuclear-related environmental and public safety cooperation that serves the interests of the Iranian public and the region at large, and would introduce a regional element to the deal. These measures would include both dialogue and cooperation on ways to enhance the safety of Iranian nuclear facilities to reduce the risk of environmental damage arising from an earthquake or a man-made disaster. Gulf states are already concerned that a nuclear disaster at the Bushehr nuclear power plant could contaminate the waters of the Gulf, desalinated supplies of which provide 80 percent of the water consumed by the United Arab Emirates. This type of cooperation would address an important technical gap (safety) and produce a modest political dividend by improving "public safety" for Iranians and their neighbours. It would also build cooperation between the United States and Iran—potentially providing a basis for an expanded diplomatic agenda with Iran in the future. Nuclear safety talks and initiatives would include regional participation. Two important byproducts of such a deal could be a shifting of the political balance back to accommodation on the nuclear issue and an expansion of the political space for Iranian moderates.

Pragmatic Containment. This proposal draws on ideas submitted nearly 15 years ago by Zbigniew Brzezinski, Brent Scowcrof, and Richard Murphy, who suggested the possibility of convincing Iran to limit its nuclear program "enough to give outsiders reasonable confidence that further military progress is not being made." The authors suggested that the United States consult friends and allies to determine interests and policies, how to protect those interests, and how disagreements should be handled. These ideas remain sound today. This paper proposes situating such a nuclear deal in a broader policy framework of pragmatic containment: a departure from the anachronistic U.S. doctrine of hard containment, which produced rigid and formulaic policies that offered no prospects for engendering improved Iranian behaviour. Pragmatic containment would not offer any immediate prospect for improved U.S. relations with Iran. Rather, it would link U.S. Iran policy, conceptually and publicly, to Washington's efforts to stabilize Iraq and Afghanistan, and establish a strategic partnership with Pakistan. Constraining Iran's room for manoeuvre in its immediate neighborhood by surrounding it with states tilted toward the United States would be one pillar of pragmatic containment, aimed at keeping Iran's ambitions in check. This would also extend the focus of U.S. Iran policy to Southwest Asia, which is Washington's top foreign policy concern together with Iraq. The second pillar of this policy (and the basis for Iran's responsible coexistence with its immediate neighbours) would be the nuclear deal.

Over time, if the situation in Iraq, Afghanistan, and Pakistan becomes more stable, and Iran finds ways to support and encourage the maintenance of stability, coupled with successful implementation of the nuclear deal, improvements in U.S.-Iran relations could be explored. However, the United States would explicitly exclude immediate prospects for improved relations.

Washington and Tehran have such disparate visions and aspirations it would be impossible to reconcile them over the near term. (The Iranian leadership is also wary of improved relations with the United States.) Without significant improvement in Iranian behaviour, there is no U.S. domestic rationale for improved relations with Iran, let alone a justification acceptable to Israel and the Arab states. Tat said, Washington would need to carefully lay out the terms under which improvements in relations might be possible.

Pros and Cons

There are four potential drawbacks to this approach. First, friends and allies in the region would insist on constraining Iran's weapons delivery capability. A nuclear accord would need to be followed by a missile deal. In the case of North Korea, the 1994 nuclear deal fa-cilitated missile talks and an eventual missile test moratorium. Because Tehran is constrained by the U.S. and coalition presence in the Middle East and Southwest Asia, there is time to reach a missile deal with Iran. The second drawback is the risk of a nuclear domino effect— because Iran is perceived (by Israel and the smaller Gulf states) as a direct threat, or as a threat to the regional balance of power. Already, many states in the Middle East are exploring civilian nuclear energy programs presumably as a hedge against Iran. However, it could take another 10–15 years before "nuclear power becomes a national reality" in these states.

The third drawback is that a deal could legitimize and even empower the current regime, setting back the opposition. This is a real dilemma for U.S. policymakers and for the inter-national community. However, Iran's nuclear clock is ticking considerably faster than regime transformation. The more Iran's nuclear program advances, the harder it will be to contain it later. It should also be assumed that moderates are no less intent on pursuing the nuclear program than hardliners. Negotiating a nuclear deal, however, could have a moderating influences on Tehran and help those who support accommodating international concerns. Getting the Iranian political pendulum to swing back to this position would be an important achievement of negotiations, although not the main goal. There is a fourth drawback to this proposal: it would afford Iran nuclear latency, a nuclear breakout capacity.

First, it should be noted that Iran could achieve break-out with or without a deal. Latency at least affords the prospect of international oversight and possible additional measures for the assurance of the international community. Even with these safeguards, however, fears of cheating would persist. In fact, break-out is more likely at undeclared, rather than declared and monitored facilities, suggesting that deal or not, the international community would have to remain vigilant. However, a deal contains the immediate Iranian threat and could be a moderating influences.

TACTICS: IMPLEMENTING PRAGMATIC CONTAINMENT

Holding out the threat of UN Security Council action would be an integral part of the negotiating strategy; this put effective pressure on Iran during negotiations with the EU-3. A related incentive for Iran would be the prospect of removal of UN Security Council resolutions (those resolutions demanding Iranian compliance with enrichment suspension) in the event of a nuclear deal. Existing sanctions, military exercises, as well as the recent stationing of Patriot antimissile batteries in the region (reminiscent of steps taken to create a coercive dynamic during the 1993–1994 negotiations with North Korea) can be useful additional sources of pressure. However, as was the case with North Korea, if not carefully calibrated, such measures could also encourage the regime to harden its position.

Negotiations will inevitably be long and arduous. Decisionmaking in Iran is a complex process, especially on international issues. It may be easier for Iran to pursue a nuclear program than to interrupt it. Compromise is required among a multi-tiered structure of personalities, power centers, and political factions that at any given time can either be competing or cooperating with one another. The balance among these forces seems to have been disrupted by the growing role of the Iranian Revolutionary Guard Corps in the economic and political life of the country. However, a nuclear deal would undermine the "denial of Iranian rights" narrative underpinning the regime's rationale for defying the international community.

9

Taliban, Pakistan and Afghanistan

TIMELINE FOR HUMANITARIAN ACTION IN POST-TALIBAN AFGHANISTAN

This chapter presents a plausible timelinefor the returnto their homes in Afghanistanof displaced persons and refugees after the Talibanhas lost the capacity togovern, andhas been supplanted by a different political arrangement. The question of return implicates many aspects of humanitarian action, and Afghanistan's dislocated persons will clearly need considerable short-term humanitarian relief and longer-term relief and development assistance. This chapter recommends specific international and US government policies to enhance the effectiveness of humanitarian action.

The paper begins with a statement of assumptions, and then addresses three components: 1) immediate concerns (six months), 2) medium-term issues (12 to 18 months), and 3) longer-term prospects. In each part, the paper discusses the decisions that will have to be made, who will make them, what the obstacles will be, and how they can be overcome.

Prior to the horrific terrorist attacks in the US on September 11, 2001, Afghanistan was already in the midst of a humanitarian crisis. Over four million refugees were being aided by the United Nations High Commissioner for Refugees, mainly in Iran and Pakistan. Approximately one million internally displaced persons had been uprooted by conflict and hunger, and some six million persons were dependent upon external humanitarian aid from the World Food Programme for subsistence. A well-established aid effort was slowly beingeroded by a difficult operational environment for humanitarian agencies imposed by the Taliban, which inhibited donor support.

After September 11, foreign humanitarian workers were evacuated in the face of military action by the US and its allies; information today about current conditions on the ground in Afghanistan is fragmentary at best. Much of what little infrastructure there was will have been pulverized by a prolonged bombing campaign, although roads and smaller-scale infrastructure such as irrigation canals and wells are likely to remain intact to some degree. Nevertheless, there will be daunting challenges to the continuation and expansion of relief efforts and the prospect of sustainable return in a recovering Afghanistan.

Assumptions

The US-led military campaign will continue, but the Taliban will not collapse all at once. Rather, there will be a piecemeal process of disintegration over a period of weeks or months. A fragile coalition government couldbe assembled shortly. But the post-Taliban coalition of political factions will not be able to establish a centralized government and authority will remain largely decentralized and localized. At the same time, the humanitarian needs of the Afghan people, already great, will continue to grow.

International aid will continue to be deployedby governmental donors on both a multilateral and bi-lateral basis to assist the people of Afghanistan, not only through this immediate emergency period, but also through a period of recovery and reconstruction. However, the level of funding may fall as the emergency eases, even though there may be political pressure to keep funding levels higher than would normally be the case in post-emergency recovery operations. This will place a premium on achieving a high degree of effectiveness in humanitarian action, an outcomethat will be crucial to shaping a future Afghanistan conducive to the return of refugees and displaced persons.

TIMELINE

Immediate Concerns (the first six months)

The overriding immediate concern will be to avoid further unnecessary displacement by providing basic humanitarian reliefto the Afghan people during the first six months, especially food, shelter, clothing and medical services. The logistics of delivering aid and relief operations will be more difficult than before, and will grow increasingly difficult. The Afghan winter is now in its early stages. Temperatures will plunge, and snow falls will make already difficult delivery efforts nearly impossible in some remote locales. The logistical capacity of military forces may have to be used to meet this objective.

Depending on local conditions, the means of delivering aid will vary from cross-border programs based in surrounding countries and land transport, to deliveries by air. In particularly remote areas, airdrops may be required if it can be ensured that these airdrops actually reach needy people.

Nevertheless, things are likely to get worse before they get better. Even a partial collapse of the Taliban could precipitate large-scale internal and cross border movements if widespread anarchy ensues, particularly if there is fighting for the control of cities. This would again raise concerns about border closures and access by Afghans to the territories of Pakistan and Iran, and sharing the humanitarian burdens of the front line states.

While emergency relief operations will need to continue during the period of immediate concern, post-relief planning should begin and include programs to encourage Afghans to return to their homes and strive for self-sufficiency. The precise timeline for action relative to repatriation will be dictated by a variety of factors having to do with the security situation, the seasons, and the capacities of both returnees and the society to which they will return to absorb them.

Clearly the authorities in Pakistan and Iran will put pressure on Afghan refugees to return once the Taliban has been substantially supplanted. But it is highly unlikely that four million refugees and one million internally displaced persons will be able to return swiftly to their homes. Afghanistan has limited absorptive capacity and is likely to remain dependent upon external assistance and migrant remittances for the foreseeable future. Donor governments, including the United States and European Union, should ensure that aid to refugees is coordinated with, and supplemented by, development assistance to host governments.

The return of refugees and displaced persons is likely to be piecemeal. Refugee families are not likely to return on a wholesale basis during this period. Past experience has shown that it is more likely that young men will venture back to visit their former homes, and, if conditions permit, to plant crops, and repair or rebuild housing. Women, children and the elderly may remain in the relative safety of whatever refugee camp or internal refuge they have found. Only when the men are convinced that it is safe are whole families likely to relocate.

Agriculture will be a key determinant of repatriation. The exact period of the Spring planting season in Afghanistan varies from place to place. A variety of other factors will affect the prospects of cultivation, including whether the seed available is appropriate for the land parcels in question, depending on whether they are rain-fed or irrigated. Nor will the infrastructure likely to be adequate to support the distribution of large quantities of seeds, poultry, livestock and farming equipment. In addition, there will be an urgent need to rebuild agricultural irrigation systems and to repair roads in order to give farmers access to markets. But it would be necessary to work on the rehabilitation of irrigation systems when river levels are low. Work would be difficult in the Spring when rivers become flooded.

A premium will thus be placed on small-scale projects from the very outset. Similar projects were utilized in the past decade in places like Cambodia and Central America, where the United Nations High Commissioner for Refugees (UNHCR) and United Nations Development Programme (UNDP) undertook joint efforts.

The quality of public security will have particularly profound consequences for the delivery and distribution of humanitarian aid as well as refugee return. The history of Afghanistan shows that no external force is likely to be able to provide a sufficient degree of protection if the presence of that force is contested. An international protection force, whether based on paramilitary police or the military, could be needed to guard against banditry - but not as an occupation force. This would require UN Security Council authorization, and such an initiative would have to overcome a clear reluctance by many countries which are capable of contributing police or troops. But there may be little real choice if a minimal level of public security is to be established and maintained. Contingency planning on this issue should continue. The deployment of forces in Somalia in 1992 to protect the delivery of food assistance may be instructive. This is particularly so before the mission there evolved into a political objective and ended badly.

Afghanistan is afflicted with tens of thousands of land mines, a circumstance that clearly will inhibit the return of refugees and displaced persons.

Nor is this a new problem. A landmine clearance effort has been underway in Afghanistan for more than seven years, which has resulted in the clearing of 240 square kilometers. Another 350 square kilometres have been identified for clearing. One new feature is the new types of ordinance that have been dropped in the current campaign - namely, unexploded cluster bombs - which will necessitate new training for awareness and clearance. Also, a major focus in the future will be around the areas of the present front lines in northeast Afghanistan and in the Shomali plain north of Kabul. Planning for this should begin now. Problems associated with landmines in Afghanistan must be addressed early in any humanitarian action plan, with sufficient resources to undertake the task.

Cross-border relief and post-relief efforts will have to be launched, not just from Pakistan, but from all of the surrounding countries, including Iran and Uzbekistan. Diplomatic efforts should be undertaken now to strengthen the access of international organizations and NGOs to necessary facilities in these countries, including visas, travel permits, customs waivers, etc. The objective should be to secure a variety of routes for the delivery of humanitarian aid.

The importance of close coordination between the efforts to prepare and encourage refugees to return and the efforts to rehabilitate and reconstruct infrastructure in Afghanistan cannot be over-emphasized. Past Afghan refugee repatriation efforts show the utility of appointing a UN special envoy with authority and responsibility for planning the return of refugees in both the host countries and the country of return. This official should be associated with a broader UN recovery effort.

A consolidated humanitarian needs assessment will have to be undertaken as soon as access inside Afghanistan has been re-established. In order to promote accountability, the United Nations Office for the Coordination of Humanitarian Affairs (OCHA) should, as is normal, oversee this effort with a view to preparing a revised consolidated funding appeal. Governments and humanitarian NGOs should cooperate with this effort, but this outcome will depend ona closely coordinated group of donor governments, notably the US and European Union, to make this a disciplined strategic process.

In addition, US bilateral approaches will support particular foreign policy objectives. US objectives to eliminate terrorist networks with a global reach and to promote a stable post-Taliban Afghanistan which does not harbour and support them in the futurecould be served by particular assistance strategies. The design of these strategies will be informed by the ways in which the political and security situation evolves in Afghanistan. In order to achieve this goal, the US would have to play a serious role in the recovery of Afghanistan and the neighbouring countries. Nevertheless, coordination with other donors and international institutions will be necessary.

An inclusive coordination structure for humanitarian work already exists in the region. Building on past experiences and existing structures, arecovery office should be established under the auspices of the United Nations, led by the UN humanitarian and development agencies under the overall coordination of OCHA. A broad assemblage of agencies would be needed to address not only issues associated with refugee return, but also internally displaced persons and civilians who were never displaced but were trapped during the winter in remote locales. The leadership of the UN Secretary General with the concerted support of donor governments will be needed to overcome the policy coordination cacophony that typically characterizes the UN system in the midst and immediate aftermath of a humanitarian emergency. This is particularly so in relation tothe problem of linking together the work of agencies involved in relief and development assistance activities. An early endeavor of this recovery office would be to prepare and revise on a continuing basis a consolidated assessment and appeal process for recovery activities. A process is needed, not a static document, in order to ensure a sufficiently strategic element in the planning, implementation and evaluation of projects.

This has implications for the United Nations. The current integrated mission task force dealing with Afghanistan is limited to the UN system. Lakhdar Brahimi, the UN Secretary-General's special representative on Afghanistan, has assembled a small cadre of advisors. There is need for a broader process which systematically draws upon governments and the independent sector to think and pre-position ideas for the difficult policy formation and implementation tasks ahead with respect to the return of refugees and displaced persons.

Such an arrangementalso has implications for the US government. The merger of US AID over the past decade into the State Department and the erosion of the State Department's budget, including its planning functions, have weakened the capacity for development assistance policy coordination. Development "strategy" has given way to the necessity of handling immediate crises and managing food aid along with other humanitarian assistance. The thinking on the development-related aspects of refugee return must be strengthened on an urgent basis, including by establishing appropriate liaison relationships between those in government who are formulating and implementing policy with think tanks, NGOs, and scholars.

Besides designing and implementing recovery programs, a consolidated UN recovery effort would facilitate communication and consensus-building between local leaders, NGOs and donors.

One of the tools that could be very useful in Afghanistan is" quick impact projects". These are small projects which could be focused on improvements in things such as irrigation canals, seed distribution, income generation, education, and health infrastructure, etc. Such programs should pay particular attention to Afghan women because they have suffered systematic discrimination in their access to employment and social services.

While small projects do not address structural problems such as weak governance institutions or an undeveloped economy in Afghanistan, they will not only be of genuine help, but they will also be a means towards confidence building for returning refugees and displaced persons as well as the surrounding local community. Such an approach would be particularly apt in Afghanistan which is likely to be without significant national-level infrastructure for the foreseeable future.

Medium-term Issues (12 to 18 months)

Depending on local conditions, especially security, it may be possible to set in motion a large-scale voluntary repatriation program for Afghan refugees in Pakistan and Iran. To be successful, any such effort should include material incentives (seeds, oil, edibles, grain, farm implements, and money) to be given to refugee families as they return.

In this regard, it should be recalled that in the period 1992-93, some 2.9 million Afghan refugees returned from Pakistan and Iran. In 1992 alone, approximately 1.6 million Afghan refugees returned home, approximately 1.4 million of whom from Pakistan. In 1993, approximately 1.3 million returned to Afghanistan, more than one million of whom from Iran. UNHCR provided each returning family with 300 kilograms of wheat and $130 in cash.

This earlier repatriation effort was compromised by civil war that broke out between factions competing for political supremacy. Many Afghans who had returned once again went into exile where they remain to this day. In addition to an encashment program, well-crafted small-scale reintegration programs will also be needed to help sustain return.

A major new complication in the present Afghan displacement is the number of refugees and displaced persons who have fled their homes in urban areas in the wake of the bombing campaign. A significant commitment of funding as well as technical assistance and material aid will be essential if Afghan urban life is to be re-constituted. Not only homes but also hospitals, schools, public administration facilities and houses of worship will need to be re-constructedif the basic urban infrastructure is to be restored.

Once again, the recurrence of winter will highlight the most urgent needs of this recovering society; medical and food aid will be needed, depending on the drought. These medium-term recovery issues in Afghanistan should be addressed as well in the development of a strategic framework process administered by the UN.

Longer-term Prospects (18 months on)

A substantial, multi-year program of reconstruction, rehabilitation, economic development and institution building will be critical to any effort to make refugee return in Afghanistan sustainable. In this connection, particular attention should be paid to the indigenous human resources that have emerged by reason of past international action. This would include men and women from the Afghan Diaspora as well as refugees educated whilethey were in Pakistan or Iran, or introduced to organizational or business methods as members of the local staff of international humanitarian organizations. A highly participatory approach will be needed in Afghanistan in order to move from relief to recovery. This cohort of several thousand persons is likely to be a key resource for achieving a peaceful and stable future for Afghanistan. An inventory of the leadership and skills of these persons should be undertaken immediately. Special attention should be given to women in this exercise as they have been systematically excluded from public life in the past. The experience of the UN transitional mission in encouraging refugee repatriation and the growth of indigenous NGOs in Cambodia in the early 1990s could be instructive.

Afghanistan is one of the poorest nations in the world and has suffered through modern times as one of the last battlefields of the cold war. The largely subsistence agricultural sector has been depressed and increasingly devoted to drug production; men and boys have been recruited for war; health care and education for women and girls has been limited by the Taliban. Afghanistan's people have the lowest annual incomes anywhere. Millions of displaced persons and refugees have been exiles for over a decade.

Afghanistan and its people have been virtually ignored by development agencies (e.g., the World Bank does not include Afghanistan in the Tables of World Development Indicators that it provides for 130 economies because available data for Afghanistan is too sparse). A limited number of UN agencies and a handful of humanitarian NGOs have worked inside Afghanistan as well as with Afghan refugees, especially in Pakistan, and assisted with clearing landmines left by the Russians.

Development assistance and continuing humanitarian aid in post-Taliban Afghanistan will be difficult and daunting. US bilateral initiatives will be needed. Also, the World Bank, which is preparing a far-reaching reconstruction plan, and a variety of international organizations in the United Nations system (Office for the Coordination of Humanitarian Affairs, World Food Programme, United Nations High Commissioner for Refugees, United Nations Children's Fund, World Health Organization, United Nations Development Programme), as well as the International Committee of the Red Cross and a variety of NGOs, will be involved in the effort to re-build Afghanistan. Policy coordination will be a key determinant of effectiveness. United States leadership will be essential.

The international efforts for the recovery of Afghanistan are likely to be undertaken in a predominantly humanitarian mode. Humanitarian assistance will likely be accompanied by relatively light political, security and economic development deployment. These efforts would be assisted by re-animating an established international humanitarian policy coordination structure, the Afghan Support Group (ASG), a collection of donor governments, international organizations and NGOs supported by the UN (OCHA in particular). This would contribute to the enhancement of the effectiveness of longer-term relief and development assistance. The ASG is scheduled to meet shortly in Berlin. Again, leadership by the UN Secretary General and disciplined action by donor governments, particularly the United States and European

Union, would be required to strengthen the ASG. A consolidated longer-term needs assessment should be conducted under the auspices of the ASG in standard sectors for development activities, such as economic management, agriculture, infrastructure, social services, health, education, housing, water and sanitation, etc. This assessment should provide the baseline for longer-term strategic recovery efforts undertaken by the UN and World Bank.

To successfully create conditions conductive to the voluntary return of Afghan refugees and displaced persons, the international community will have to be willing to make long-term commitments. The people of Afghanistan have been brutalized by war, civil strife, oppression and draught for over 20 years. Past experience has shown that half-way measures of relief and rehabilitation do not sustain return.

The United States, which is taking the lead role effort to bring down the Taliban, has an equal lead role to take in creating the conditions for return and recovery. This will require a sustained commitment of financial and material aid, and support for the United Nations in coordinating, planning, and implementing the overall endeavor. There is no guarantee of success, but a determined and sustained effort by all parties will maximize the prospects for a satisfactory outcome.

RISE OF THE TALIBAN

The Taliban was formed in the early 1990s by an Afghan faction of mujahideen, Islamic fighters who had resisted the Soviet occupation of Afghanistan (1979–89) with the covert backing of the U.S. Central Intelligence Agency and its Pakistani counterpart, the Inter-Services Intelligence directorate (ISI). They were joined by younger Pashtun tribesmen who studied in Pakistani madrassas, or seminaries; *taliban* is Pashto for "students." Pashtuns comprise a plurality in Afghanistan and are the predominant ethnic group in much of the country's south and east.

The movement attracted popular support in the initial post-Soviet era by promising to impose stability and rule of law after four years of conflict (1992–1996) among rival mujahideen groups. Talibs entered Kandahar in November 1994 to pacify the crime-ridden southern city, and by September 1996 seized the capital, Kabul, from President Burhanuddin Rabbani, an ethnic Tajik whom they viewed as anti-Pashtun and corrupt. The Taliban regime controlled some 90 percent of the country before its 2001 overthrow, analysts say.

The Taliban imposed its brand of justice as it consolidated territorial control. Taliban jurisprudence was drawn from the Pashtuns' pre-Islamic tribal code and interpretations of sharia colored by the austere Wahhabi doctrines of the madrassas' Saudi benefactors. The regime neglected social services and other basic state functions even as its Ministry for the Promotion of Virtue and Prevention of Vice enforced prohibitions on behaviour the Taliban deemed un-Islamic, requiring women to wear the head-to-toe *burqa,* or *chadri;* banning music and television; and jailing men whose beards it deemed too short.

The regime was internationally isolated from its inception. Two UN Security Council resolutions passed in 1998 urged the Taliban to end its abusive treatment of women. The following year the council imposed sanctions on the regime for harboring al-Qaeda. Only Saudi Arabia, the United Arab Emirates, and Pakistan recognized the government. Many analysts say Islamabad supported the Taliban as a force that could unify and stabilize Afghanistan while staving off Indian, Iranian, and Russian influence.

LEADERSHIP AND SUPPORT

Mullah Omar, a cleric and veteran of the anti-Soviet resistance, led Taliban-ruled Afghanistan from 1996 to 2001 as *amir al-mu'minin,* or "commander of the faithful." He granted al-Qaeda sanctuary on the condition that it not antagonize the United States, but bin Laden reneged on their agreement in 1998 when he orchestrated bombings of U.S. embassies in East Africa. The episode was indicative of tensions that emerged between the two groups, analysts say. The Taliban was fundamentally parochial while al-Qaeda had its sights set on global jihad—yet after 9/11, Omar rejected U.S. demands that he give up bin Laden. Ethnic minority Tajiks, Uzbeks, and Hazaras in northern Afghanistan opposed to

Taliban rule formed the Northern Alliance, which assisted U.S.-led forces in routing the Taliban after 9/11. Though the regime was dismantled during the occupation, Mullah Omar and many of his top aides escaped to the frontier territories of Pakistan, where they reconstituted the Taliban's central leadership.

Dubbed the "Quetta Shura" for the capital of Balochistan province, where they are believed to have taken refuge, they maintain a degree of operational authority over Afghan Taliban fighters, but appear "unwilling or unable to monopolize anti-state violence," a UN Security Council monitoring team foundin September 2013.

Many experts suspect the Pakistani security establishment continues to provide Taliban militants sanctuary in the country's western tribal areas in an effort to counter India's influence in Afghanistan. Islamabad dismisses these charges. (Tehrik-i-Taliban Pakistan, commonly known as the Pakistani Taliban, is an insurgent group distinct from its Afghan namesake; it coalesced in response to the Pakistani military's incursions into that country's tribal areas. The Afghan Taliban, by contrast, views Pakistan as a benefactor.)

The Taliban's post-2001 resurgence has partially been financed by narcotics production and trafficking, though Mullah Omar issued injunctions against opium production, and the Taliban eradicated much of the poppy crop during its rule. Insurgents and other strongmen extort *ushr*, an agricultural tithe, from farmers and levies at roadside checkpoints. Revenues from illicit mining also contribute to Taliban coffers, whichnet some $400 million a year, the UN estimated in 2012.

Public Opinion of the Taliban

More than a decade since its fall from power, the Taliban enjoys continued, if declining, support. The Asia Foundation found that in 2013, a third of Afghans—mostly Pashtuns and rural Afghans—had sympathy for armed opposition groups (AOGs), primarily the Taliban. Nearly two-thirds of Afghans, the survey found, believed that reconciliation between the government and AOGs would stabilize the country.

Afghan support for the Taliban and allied groups stems in part from grievances directed at public institutions. While the Asia Foundation survey found the Afghan National Army and Afghan National Police garner high public confidence, many civilians see government institutions such as the militia-like Afghan Local Police as predatory. Likewise, international forces' support for warlords and strongmen, an expedient in securing territory, likely also alienated many rural Afghans from Kabul, analysts say.

Many rural Afghans have come to trust the Taliban's extensive judicial network over government courts to "solve disputes in a fair war, without tribal or ethnic bias, or more commonly, without having to pay bribes," says Graeme Smith, a Kabul-based senior analyst at the International Crisis Group.

A Resilient Insurgency

As the Obama administration wound down the war in Iraq, it recommitted the United States to counterinsurgency operations against the Taliban and allied groups in Afghanistan, authorizing a surge that brought peak troop levels to about one hundred thousand in June 2011 and redoubled civilian efforts. Pakistani safe havens stymied U.S. counterinsurgency efforts, though the CIA's targeted-killing program there has sought, in part, to fulfil a "force protection" mission where the U.S. military cannot operate.

But as the Pentagon withdrew the surge troops in 2012, further drew down its military footprint in 2013, and handed lead security authority over to Afghan forces in June of that year, the Taliban-led insurgency escalated.

The United Nations Assistance Mission in Afghanistan (UNAMA) documented 8,615 civilian deaths and injuries in 2013, a 14 percent increase over the previous year and the highest toll since it began keeping these records in 2009. UNAMA attributed the vast majority of these casualties to insurgents who deliberately targeted civilians or used such indiscriminate tactics as improvised explosive devices; other civilians were caught in the crossfire between insurgents and government forces.

In some outlying districts, Afghan forces and local insurgents have reached informal ceasefires that effectively cede a degree of authority to the Taliban. The UN reported in 2014 that the Taliban maintained outright control of four districts, out of 373 nationwide, but the insurgency's reach extends much further: Afghan security forces judged in late 2013 that some 40 percent of districts had a "raised" or "high" threat level.

AFGHAN TALIBAN

The Taliban were largely founded by Pakistan's Interior Ministry under Nasrullah Barbar and the Inter-Services Intelligence (ISI) in 1994. In 1999, Nasrullah Baber who was the minister of the interior under Bhutto during the Taliban's ascent to power admitted, "we created the Taliban".

William Maley, Professor at the Australian National University and Director of the Asia-Pacific College, writes on the emergence of the Taliban in Afghanistan: "In 1994, with the failure of [Gulbuddin Hekmatyar's alliance] attempt to oust [the Afghan] Rabbani [administration], Pakistan found itself in an awkward position. Hekmatyar had proved incapable of seizing and controlling defended territory: in this respect he was a bitter disappointment to his patrons.... In October 1994, [Pakistani interior minister] Babar [took] a group of Western ambassadors (including the US Ambassador to Pakistan John C. Monjo) to Kandahar, without even bothering to inform the Kabul government, even though it manned an embassy in Islamabad.... On 29 October 1994, a convoy of trucks, including a notorious ISI officer, Sultan Amir... and two figures who were later to become prominent Taliban leaders, entered Afghanistan."

The ISI used the Taliban to establish a regime in Afghanistan which would be favourable to Pakistan, as they were trying to gain strategic depth. Since the creation of the Taliban, the ISI and the Pakistani military have given financial, logistical, military including direct combat support.

According to Pakistani Afghanistan expert Ahmed Rashid, "between 1994 and 1999, an estimated 80,000 to 100,000 Pakistanis trained and fought in Afghanistan" on the side of the Taliban. Peter Tomsen also stated that up until 9/11 Pakistani military and ISI officers along with thousands of regular Pakistani armed forces personnel had been involved in the fighting in Afghanistan.

Human Rights Watch wrote in 2000: "Of all the foreign powers involved in efforts to sustain and manipulate the ongoing fighting [in Afghanistan], Pakistan is distinguished both by the sweep of its objectives and the scale of its efforts, which include soliciting funding for the Taliban, bankrolling Taliban operations, providing diplomatic support as the Taliban's virtual emissaries abroad, arranging training for Taliban fighters, recruiting skilled and unskilled manpower to serve in Taliban armies, planning and directing offensives, providing and facilitating shipments of ammunition and fuel, and... directly providing combat support."

In 1998, Iran accused Pakistani commandos of "war crimes at Bamiyan". The same year Russia said, Pakistan was responsible for the "military expansion" of the Taliban in northern Afghanistan by sending large numbers of Pakistani troops including ISI personnel some of whom had subsequently been taken as prisoners by the anti-Taliban United Front (Northern Alliance).

In 2000, the UN Security Council imposed an arms embargo against military support to the Taliban, with UN officials explicitly singling out Pakistan. The UN secretary-general criticized Pakistan for its military support and the Security Council stated it was "deeply distress[ed] over reports of involvement in the fighting, on the Taliban side, of thousands of non-Afghan nationals." In July 2001, several countries including the United States, accused Pakistan of being "in violation of U.N. sanctions because of its military aid to the Taliban." The Taliban also obtained financial resources from Pakistan. In 1997 alone, after the capture of Kabul by the Taliban, Pakistan gave $30 million in aid and a further $10 million for government wages.

"The Taliban are not Islam - the Taliban areIslamabad. " After the 9/11 attacks, Pakistan claimed to have ended its support to the Taliban. But with the fall of Kabul to anti-Taliban forces in November 2001, ISI forces worked with and helped Taliban militias who were in full retreat. In November 2001, Taliban and Al-Qaeda combatants as well as Pakistani ISI and other military operatives were safely evacuated from the Afghan city of Kunduz on Pakistan Armycargo aircraft to Pakistan Air Force bases in Chitral and Gilgit in Pakistan's Northern Areas in what has been dubbed the

"Airlift of Evil" A range of officials inside and outside Pakistan have stepped up suggestions of links between the ISI and terrorist groups in recent years.

In fall 2006, a leaked report by a British Defense Ministry think tank charged, "Indirectly Pakistan (through the ISI) has been supporting terrorism and extremism—whether in London on 7/7 [the July 2005 attacks on London's transit system], or in Afghanistan, or Iraq." In June 2008, Afghan officials accused Pakistan's intelligence service of plotting a failed assassination attempt on President Hamid Karzai; shortly thereafter, they implied the ISI's involvement in a July 2008 Taliban attack on the Indian embassy. Indian officials also blamed the ISI for the bombing of the Indian embassy. Numerous U.S. officials have also accused the ISI of supporting terrorist groups including the Afghan Taliban. U.S. Defense Secretary Robert Gates said "to a certain extent, they play both sides." Gates and others suggest the ISI maintains links with groups like the Afghan Taliban as a "strategic hedge" to help Islamabad gain influence in Kabul once U.S. troops exit the region. U.S. Chairman of the Joint Chiefs of Staff Admiral Mike Mullen in 2011 called the Haqqani network (the Afghan Taliban's most destructive element) a "veritable arm of Pakistan's ISI". He further stated, "Extremist organizations serving as proxies of the government of Pakistan are attacking Afghan troops and civilians as well as US soldiers."

From 2010, a report by a leading British institution also claimed that Pakistan's intelligence service still today has a strong link with the Taliban in Afghanistan. Published by the London School of Economics, the report said that Pakistan's ISI has an "official policy" of support for the Taliban. It said the ISI provides funding and training for the Taliban, and that the agency has representatives on the so-called Quetta Shura, the Taliban's leadership council. The report, based on interviews with Taliban commanders in Afghanistan, was written by Matt Waldman, a fellow at Harvard University. "Pakistan appears to be playing a double-game of astonishing magnitude," the report said. The report also linked high-level members of the Pakistani government with the Taliban. It said Asif Ali Zardari, the Pakistani president, met with senior

Taliban prisoners in 2010 and promised to release them. Zardari reportedly told the detainees they were only arrested because of American pressure. "The Pakistan government's apparent duplicity – and awareness of it among the American public and political establishment – could have enormous geopolitical implications," Waldman said. "Without a change in Pakistani behaviour it will be difficult if not impossible for international forces and the Afghan government to make progress against the insurgency." Amrullah Saleh, director of Afghanistan's intelligence service until June 2010, told Reuters in 2010 that the ISI was "part of a landscape of destruction in this country".

In March 2012, the Commander of NATO forces in Afghanistan, General John Allen, told the United States Senate that as of 2012 there was still no change in Pakistan's policy of support for the Afghan Taliban and its Haqqani network. When asked by U.S. Senator John McCain whether the ISI had severed its links with the Afghan Taliban, General Allen testified: "No."

Recruitment

The Pakistani army through ISI have been accused of recruiting fighters and suicide bombers for the Afghan Taliban among the 1.7 million registered and 1-2 million unregistered Pashtun Afghan refugees living in refugee camps and settlements along the Afghan-Pakistan border in Pakistan many of whom have lived there since the Soviet war in Afghanistan.

Abdel Qadir, an Afghan refugee who returned to Afghanistan, says Pakistan's Inter-Services Intelligence had asked him to either receive training to join the Afghan Taliban or for him and his family to leave the country. He explains: "It is a step by step process. First they come, they talk to you. They ask you for the information.... Then gradually they ask you for people they can train and send [to Afghanistan].... They say, 'Either you do what we say, or you leave the country.'"

Janat Gul, another former refugee who returned to Afghanistan, told the UN Office for the Coordination of Humanitarian Affairs, that Afghan refugees which had been successfully recruited by the ISI were taken to Pakistani training camps which had previously been used during the times of the Soviet war in Afghanistan. According to an investigative report among Afghan refugees inside Pakistan by the *New York Times*, people testified that "dozens of families had lost sons in Afghanistan as suicide bombers and fighters" and "families whose sons had died as suicide bombers in Afghanistan said they were afraid to talk about the deaths because of pressure from Pakistani intelligence agents, the ISI."

Pakistani and Afghan tribal elders also testified that the ISI was arresting or even killing Taliban members which wanted to quit fighting and refused to re-enlist to fight in Afghanistan or to die as suicide bombers. One former Taliban commander told the *New York Times* that such arrests were then sold to the Westerners and others as part of a supposed Pakistani collaboration effort in the War against Terror.

Provision of Safe Haven

Gen. James L. Jones, then NATO's supreme commander, in September 2007 testified in front of the U.S. Senate Foreign Relations Committee that the Afghan Taliban movement uses the Pakistani city of Quetta as their main headquarters. Pakistan's minister for information and broadcasting, Tariq Azim Khan, mocked the statement by saying, if there were any Taliban in Quetta, "you can count them on your fingers."

Training

From 2002 until 2004, without major Taliban activities, Afghanistan witnessed relative calm with Afghan civilians and foreigners being able to freely and peacefully walk the streets of major cities and reconstruction being initiated. The 2010 testimonies of former Taliban commanders show that Pakistan through its Inter-Services Intelligence was however "actively encouraging a Taliban revival" from 2004-2006.

The effort to reintroduce the Afghan Taliban militarily in Afghanistan was preceded by a two-year, large-scale training campaign of Taliban fighters and leaders conducted by the ISI in several training camps in Quetta and other places in Pakistan. From 2004-2006 the Afghan Taliban consequently started a deadly insurgency campaign in Afghanistan killing thousands of civilians and combatants and thereby renewing and escalating the War in Afghanistan (2001-present). One Taliban commander involved in the Taliban resurgence said that 80 percent of his fighters had been trained in an ISI camp.

ISLAMIC EMIRATE OF AFGHANISTAN

The Islamic Emirate of Afghanistan, was founded in 1996 when the Taliban began their rule of Afghanistan and ended with their fall from power in 2001. Even at the peak of their influence, the Taliban never controlled the entire area of Afghanistan, as about 10% of the country in the northeast was held by the United Islamic Front for the Salvation of Afghanistan.

History

The Taliban and its rule arose from the chaos of post-Soviet Afghanistan. It began as an Islamic fundamentalist politico-religious movement composed of students in the Helmand and Kandaharregion of Afghanistan. Overwhelmingly local ethnic Pashtuns, the Taliban blended Pashtunwalitribal code with elements of Deobandi Islamic teaching to form an anti-Western, anti-modern, and highly restrictive Islamic fundamentalist ideology with which it ruled. Spreading from Kandahar, the Taliban eventually seized Kabul in 1996. By the end of 2000, the Taliban were able to capture 90% of the country, aside from the opposition (Afghan Northern Alliance) strongholds primarily found in the northeast corner of Badakhshan Province. The Taliban sought to impose a strict interpretation of Islamic *Sharia law* and were later implicated as supporters of mujahideen, most notably by harbouring Osama bin Laden's Al-Qaeda network.

During the five-year history of the Islamic Emirate, much of the population experienced restrictions on their freedom and violations of their human rights. Women were banned from jobs, girls forbidden to attend schools or universities. Those who resisted were punished instantly. Communists were systematically eradicated and thieves were punished by amputating one of their hands or feet. Meanwhile, the Taliban managed to nearly eradicate the majority of the opium production by 2001.

Following the Taliban's harsh treatment of Afghanistan's Shia minority, Iran stepped up assistance to the Northern Alliance. Relations with the Taliban deteriorated further in 1998 after Taliban forces seized the Iranian consulate in Mazari Sharif and executed Iranian diplomats. Following this incident, Iran almost went to war with the Taliban regions of Afghanistan but intervention by the United Nations Security Council and the United States prevented an imminent Iranian invasion.

International Relations

Only Pakistan, Saudi Arabia, and the United Arab Emirates recognized the Taliban government. The state was not recognised in the UN. Turkmenistan, however, was known to have held official meetings and agreements with Taliban government ministers. One reason for lack of international recognition was the Taliban's disregard for international law as demonstrated by their actions on taking power. For example, one of the first acts of the Islamic Emirate was the murder of the former President of Afghanistan, Mohammad Najibullah. Before the Taliban had even taken control of Afghanistan's capital they sent out a squad to arrest, torture, mutilate and murder Najibullah, leaving his body hanging from a street lamp outside the presidential palace for two days. As Najibullah was staying in the United Nations compound in Kabul, this was a violation of international law. As a further example, the Taliban regime was also heavily criticised for the murder of Iranian diplomats in Afghanistan in 1998. The Taliban supported the Islamic militants operating in Chechnya, Kashmir and Xinjiang, thus antagonizing Russia, India and the People's Republic of China simultaneously.

Sanctions

In 1999, the UN Security Council established a sanctions regime to cover individuals and entities associated with Al-Qaida, Osama bin Laden and/or the Taliban. Since the US Invasion of Afghanistan in 2001, the sanctions were applied to individuals and organizations in all parts of the world, also targeting former members of the Taliban government. On January 27, 2010, a United Nations sanctions committee removed five former senior Taliban officials from this list, in a move favoured by Afghan President Karzai. The decision means the five will no longer be subject to an international travel ban, assets freeze and arms embargo. The five men, all high-ranking members of the Taliban government:

- Wakil Ahmad Muttawakil, former foreign minister.
- Fazal Mohammad, former deputy minister of commerce.
- Shams-us-Safa Aminzai, former Taliban foreign affairs press officer.
- Mohammad Musa Hottak, former deputy minister of planning.
- Abdul Hakim, former deputy minister of frontier affairs.

All had been added to the list in January or February 2001. Mohammed Omar continues to speak in the name of this Emirate.

FOREIGN INTERFERENCE AND WAR

After the fall of Najibullah's government in 1992, the Afghan political parties agreed on a peace and power-sharing agreement (the Peshawar Accords). The accords created the Islamic State of Afghanistan and appointed an interim government for a transitional period to be followed by general elections. According to Human Rights Watch:

The sovereignty of Afghanistan was vested formally in the Islamic State of Afghanistan, an entity created in April 1992, after the fall of the Soviet-backed Najibullah government. With the exception of Gulbuddin Hekmatyar's Hezb-e Islami, all of the parties were ostensibly unified under this government in April 1992.

Hekmatyar's Hezb-e Islami, for its part, refused to recognize the government for most of the period discussed in this report and launched attacks against government forces and Kabul generally. Shells and rockets fell everywhere.

Gulbuddin Hekmatyar received operational, financial and military support from Pakistan. Afghanistan expert Amin Saikal concludes in *Modern Afghanistan: A History of Struggle and Survival*:

Pakistan was keen to gear up for a breakthrough in Central Asia. Islamabad could not possibly expect the new Islamic government leaders to subordinate their own nationalist objectives in order to help Pakistan realize its regional ambitions. Had it not been for the ISI's logistic support and supply of a large number of rockets, Hekmatyar's forces would not have been able to target and destroy half of Kabul.

In addition, Saudi Arabia and Iran – as competitors for regional hegemony – supported Afghan militias hostile towards each other. According to Human Rights Watch, Iran was backing the Shia Hazara Hezb-i Wahdat forces of Abdul Ali Mazari to "maximize Wahdat's military power and influence". Saudi Arabia supported the Wahhabite Abdul Rasul Sayyaf and his Ittihad-i Islami faction. A publication by the George Washington University describes: utside forces saw instability in Afghanistan as an opportunity to press their own security and political agendas.

Conflict between the two militias soon escalated into a full-scale war. Due to the sudden initiation of the war, working government departments, police units or a system of justice and accountability for the newly created Islamic State of Afghanistan did not have time to form. Atrocities were committed by individuals of the different armed factions while Kabul descended into lawlessness and chaos as described in reports by Human Rights Watch and the Afghanistan Justice Project. Because of the chaos, some leaders increasingly had only nominal control over their (sub-)commanders. For civilians there was little security from murder, rape and extortion. An estimated 25,000 people died during the most intense period of bombardment by Hekmatyar's Hezb-i Islami and the Junbish-i Milli forces of Abdul Rashid Dostum, who had created an alliance with Hekmatyar in 1994. Half a million people fled Afghanistan. Human Rights Watch writes:

Rare ceasefires, usually negotiated by representatives of Ahmad Shah Massoud, Sibghatullah Mojaddedi or Burhanuddin Rabbani [the interim government], or officials from the International Committee of the Red Cross (ICRC), commonly collapsed within days.

Southern and eastern Afghanistan was under the control of local commanders such as Gul Agha Sherzai and others. In 1994, the Taliban (a movement originating from Jamiat Ulema-e-Islam-run religious schools for Afghan refugees in Pakistan) also developed in Afghanistan as a politico-religious force. When the Taliban took control of the city in 1994, they forced the surrender of dozens of local Pashtun leaders. In 1994, the Taliban took power in several provinces in southern and central Afghanistan.

In late 1994, most of the militia factions (Hezb-i Islami, Junbish-i Milli and Hezb-i Wahdat) which had been fighting in the battle for control of Kabul were defeated militarily by forces of the Islamic State's Minister of Defense Ahmad Shah Massoud. Bombardment of the capital came to a halt. The Islamic State government took steps to restore law and order. Courts started to work again. Massoud tried to initiate a nationwide political process with the goal of national consolidation and democratic elections, also inviting the Taliban to join the process but they refused as they did not believe in a democratic system. Key Documents and Institutional Frameworks

After 30 years of conflict, Afghanistan is now among the poorest and least developed countries in the world. In 2007 the country ranked 174th out of 178 on the United Nations Development Program (UNDP) human development index and had showed some deterioration in real terms in comparison with results for 2004. Such conditions entrench a cycle of underdevelopment, vulnerability and conflict, perpetuating Afghanistan's position as a source of concern for regional and international security. In an effort to break this cycle, the post-Taliban Afghan government has set a course for development and reconstruction. The frameworks that set out priorities and strategies for this effort are as follows.

Millennium Development Goals (MDGs)

Afghanistan came late, in 2004, to these UN-sanctioned targets to enable more of the world's population to enjoy the minimum requirements of human dignity by the year 2015. Special MDGs were developed to reflect local realities in Afghanistan; the baseline was set with data from 2002-2005, and the deadline was extended from 2015 to 2020. The key issues reflected in Afghanistan's MDG targets are: poverty and hunger; universal primary education; gender equality; child mortality; maternal health; HIV/AIDS, malaria and other diseases; environmental sustainability; a global partnership for development; and security.

Interim Afghanistan National Development Strategy (I-ANDS)

Informed by the Afghanistan MDGs, the 2006 I-ANDS lays out a five-year program of action in four areas: security; governance; rule of law and human rights; and economic and social development. Released by the Afghan government at the 2006 London Conference, it also addresses cross-cutting issues such as the narcotics trade, gender inequity and corruption. The I-ANDS will be replaced in mid-2008 by a more developed strategy that is expected to lead to a fully costed, prioritized and sequenced development strategy.

THE AFGHANISTAN COMPACT

Intrinsically linked to both the Afghanistan MDGs and the I-ANDS and signed at the 2006 London Conference, the Afghanistan Compact is a political agreement by which Afghanistan is committed to make progress in the I-ANDS and the international community has agreed to provide resources to support this endeavour and to improve the effectiveness and accountability of such assistance.

Coordination and Oversight

Adherence to the Afghanistan MDGs, the I-ANDs and the Afghanistan Compact is coordinated and overseen by three primary mechanisms:

- the Joint Coordination and Monitoring Board (JCMB), co-chaired by the Afghan government and the United Nations, which is primarily responsible for the implementation of the Afghanistan Compact;
- the Afghanistan Development Forum (ADF), which brings the Afghan government and the donor community together on an almost annual basis to review priorities and strategies; and
- the Agency Coordinating Body for Afghan Relief (ACBAR), which supplements the activities of the ADF by acting on

behalf of the international and national NGOs active in Afghanistan and is concerned with the civil-society dimension of the ANDS.

Donor Conferences

A prominent feature of Afghanistan's post-Taliban reconstruction and develop-ment is the international donor conference. The 2002 Tokyo International Conference on Reconstruction Assistance to Afghanistan resulted in pledges estimated at US$4-5 billion. The 2004 Berlin Conference on Afghanistan resulted in pledges of over US$8 billion, which were later surpassed by pledges from the 2006 London Conference of over US$10.5 billion.

Development and reconstruction funds are channelled primarily through two instruments: the Afghan budget, and the Afghanistan Reconstruction Trust Fund (ARTF). Established at the 2002 Tokyo conference, the ARTF is currently funded by pledged contributions from 27 countries amounting to US$2.27 billion, of which US$1.83 billion have been received and disbursed. It is administered by the World Bank, while decisions about the allocation of funds are carried out by the World Bank, the UNDP, the Asian Development Bank and the Islamic Development Bank, in cooperation with the government of Afghanistan and the Special Representative of the Secretary-General. Its primary function is to cover recurring costs from the Afghan budget, such as salaries for teachers, health care workers, and civilian staff in ministries and provinces.

Provincial Reconstruction Teams (PRTs)

Operating in 25 provinces, PRTs are hosted and assembled by individual countries, including Germany, the United Kingdom and the Netherlands. They comprise military units, civilian political advisors and development advisors working in an integrated fashion to provide humanitarian assistance and to support development activities. The priorities and configuration of each PRT are set out by the host country to reflect the conditions and needs in the particular province, but the overriding objective is to contribute to the stability, security and outreach of the central government's authority and to support local and provincial administrations. The primary mechanisms for achieving these objectives are regular interaction with the local authorities and the population, visibility, information-gathering with regard to security and stability, and support for the Afghan National Police. It is also important to note that, despite the internal integration of PRTs, their military components are part of NATO's International Security Assistance Force (ISAF) efforts.

PAKISTAN'S GAINS FROM REHABILITATED U.S. NOTICE

The United States had been moving away from the sanctions policy toward both India and Pakistan that it had imposed after each country's nuclear tests in May 1998 and used this opportunity to drop many of the provisions affecting financial and non-sensitive material assistance temporarily.

The United States also approved a financial aid package for Pakistan that permitted the rescheduling of its international indebtedness, lifting a cloud from its economy. But the most important gain for Pakistan was the sudden U.S. need for Pakistan's armed and intelligence support, a reflection of Pakistan's geopolitical importance in pursuing the initial stages of the war against terrorism in Afghanistan—giving Pakistan an unexpected opportunity to get back into the good graces of Washington.

During most of the 1990s, the Clinton administration had courted India assiduously, even before the ascent of the Bharatiya Janata Party (BJP) and the shock of the nuclear tests in early 1998, and continued to seek an improved relationship despite the nuclear shocks.

Pakistan's covert armed operations across the line of control (LOC) in Kashmir near Kargil in May 2001 precipitated a mini-war with India that could have escalated. President Clinton's use of his good offices to persuade Pakistani Prime Minister Nawaz Sharif to end this conflict and withdraw Pakistani paraarmed forces behind the LOC measurably improved Delhi's disposition toward the United States. Much the same trend toward a closer U.S.-India relationship continued in the Bush administration. The increasing tilt toward India and away from Pakistan was in sharp contrast to the special relationship Pakistan had had with Washington during the Cold War years. But the 9/11 crisis showed, at least momentarily, that India's armed and intelligence value to the United States in launching the war on terrorism in Afghanistan was less than that of Pakistan's, once it was clear that Pakistan's cooperation was readily available.

In calculation to reviving Pakistan's importance, the U.S. armed presence within Pakistan, albeit limited and restricted largely to southern Pakistan, could have been construed to have an implicit deterrent value against direct Indian aggression on Pakistan, at least while the tempo of operations in Afghanistan remained high and Pakistan's active cooperation in pursuit of al-Qaeda and Taliban elements who fled into Pakistan was needed.

This calculated judgment may have eased Pakistan's initial decisions to shift some armed capability away from the east, facing India, to seal the borders and provide a form of backstopping of U.S. and allied operations against al-Qaeda and Taliban forces, raising barriers to cross-border infiltration.

It became clear later, however, that this unspoken deterrence was not comprehensive or robust. It did not dissuade India from mounting a sustained conventional armed confrontation in December, and the United States moved rather slowly in 2002—staying far quieter about the risk of nuclear war in the subcontinent than its previous policies would have implied—before it began to press India to unwind the confrontation in June and July. Nevertheless, the operations in Afghanistan gave Pakistan opportunities to put its relationship with Washington on a more productive footing, and to compete for Washington's attention after years of losing ground.

If momentum is sustained in repairing this relationship, it could pay very significant dividends to Pakistan over time. It is too early to tell at this juncture whether this will be the case.

Judging by the reaction of its media and attentive public, Indians were greatly outraged by the attention Pakistan got from the United States after Musharraf signaled his support to Bush and U.S. armed operations in Afghanistan began. This belied the fact that U.S. efforts to build a broader relationship with India not only stayed in high gear but intensified, drawing satisfaction from India's strong rhetorical support of, and offer of its facilities for use in, the war against terrorism. India's disarmingly positive reception of Bush's decision to withdraw the United States from the Anti-Ballistic Missile (ABM) Treaty, coincidentally announced on December 13, 2001, was received by the Bush administration as an unexpected boon.

Thus, while the war against terrorism brought Pakistan back to the foreground, it did nothing to diminish India's growing influence in Washington, although this would not have been apparent to an outsider watching the intense indignation and recrimination portrayed in the Indian press and television.

HOW PROGRESSIVES GOT AFGHANISTAN WRONG

Against the sunny predictions of the cruise missile left, Afghanistan is in ruins. Western bombings in Herat, Farah, and Kunduz have led to mass civilian death, while nighttime house raids murder more intimately in Ghazi Khan and Khatabeh.

The casualty figures should shame the war's supporters. Bob Dreyfuss and Nick Turse of the *Nation* calculate that even by conservative counts, the deaths of 6,481 civilians were directly attributable to ISAF and the Afghan government with which it is allied. Thousands more have been killed by insurgents, fighting a war of the West's making.

Nor has this blood soaked path led to a promising post-Taliban future. Afghanistan has the worst rate of infant mortality in the world. Half of Afghan children suffer irreversible harm from malnutrition.

The UN's 2013 Human Development Index ranks Afghanistan 175 out of 186 countries. Thomas Ruttig of Afghanistan Analysis Network writes that "economic activity in general [is] falling," unemployment and crime are rising, and that 60 percent of children are malnourished. Just 27 percent of the population has access to safe drinking water.

The record of Hamid Karzai's government is blighted by torture, corruption, warlords, and a fraudulent 2009 election.

Nor has freedom and safety for Afghanistan's ever-instrumentalized women come about.

In March of 2013, the ISAF-backed Karzai endorsed a statement that refers to women as "secondary," bars violence against women only for "un-Islamic" reasons, and advocates gender segregation in schools, workplaces, and public spaces. In 2012 the burn unit of an Afghan hospital admitted a record number of women who tried to set themselves on fire. And Suraya Pakzad, who runs women's shelters in the country, has described cases of women being publicly stoned while ISAF-trained Afghan troops looked on.

Moreover, the war's hideous violence has benefited the ultra-misogynistic Taliban. A November 2013 study conducted by a team of scholars from Yale and Princeton finds that among Afghans "Harm inflicted by the International Security Assistance Force (ISAF) is met with reduced support for ISAF and increased support for the Taliban, but Taliban-inflicted harm does not translate into greater ISAF support."

All of these outcomes are perfectly predictable and were in fact anticipated by many. As the United States prepares to withdraw most of its forces from Afghanistan, it is worth looking back at the debates many had during the lead-up to and early phases of that war.

While it is easy to say in hindsight that such writers as Tariq Ali and Marjorie Cohn were correct to oppose the intervention and that others like Michael Bérubé, Michael Kazin, Todd Gitlin and Michael Walzer were wrong to endorse it, an examination of how the latter group got it wrong is necessary.

Clarifying the analytic errors made by the imperialist "left" at the time are important because some have since taken similar approaches to Iraq and more recently to Libya and Syria.

"Progressive" boosterism for the Afghan war had several calling cards. Chief among them was how authors touted their credentials in opposing past cases of US aggression, in some cases professed concern for the Palestinians, and bragged of a left-of-center track record on social and economic issues.

However, the left-imperialists believed that differences in the tactics and ideological orientation of the US' enemies in Afghanistan were major reasons that the Afghan war was legitimate whereas the ventures in Vietnam and Nicaragua were not. Cruise missile leftists ignored that while the context of US military action had changed, no moment of rupture had taken place within the American state that directs that military.

By contrast, leftists who opposed the war in Afghanistan did so because they understood that the character of US power and its allied states is such that wars against the smaller and poorer nations are exercises in accumulation and imperialism by their very nature.

The cruise-missile leftists also made sure to attack those who were not so eager to drop cluster bombs on Afghan villagers. For example, Chomsky accurately pointed to a September 16, 2001 report that the US government "demanded" that Pakistan end "truck convoys that provide much of the food and other supplies to Afghanistan's civilian population."

Chomsky used Burns' report to decisively show that the US was taking actions that it knew would harm Afghan civilians, and that it was therefore unreasonable to believe the war was going to liberate Afghans or even attempt to do so.

In response to this, Bérubé raged that Chomsky was exhibiting "a repellent mix of hysteria and hauteur," without even attempting to refute the argument.

Progressive warmongers frequently accused anti-imperialists of claiming in a simplistic way that the US is incapable of helping the world's oppressed. Yet in the same breath such cruise missile leftists would demand simplistic, unequivocal declarations of the US' moral superiority.

Gitlin wrote that the anti-imperialists were "Like jingoists who consider any effort to understand terrorists immoral, on the grounds that to understand is to endorse, [because these leftist] hard-liners disdain complexity."

For Gitlin, the problem is that anti-imperialism is a "cartoon view of the world [where] there is nothing worse than American power — not the woman-enslaving Taliban, not an unrepentant

Al Qaeda committed to killing civilians as they please." According to Gitlin's one-dimensional view, there was no room for considerations such as the degree to which bombing and occupying Afghanistan and propping up a warlord regime with its own rather patriarchal tendencies might have adverse effects on the people of that country, particularly Afghan women.

To Gitlin, it was necessary to overlook complications such as the fact that ISAF's (ultimately failed) "rescue" of Afghan women would inevitably mean killing, detaining or horribly wounding thousands of their fathers, grandfathers, brothers, community members, and friends—and quite a few Afghan women themselves.

Anti-imperialist arguments against war in Afghanistan can be roughly divided into three categories. The first category of anti-war argument was to point out, asChomsky and Cohn did, that the invasion of Afghanistan violated international law and was also fundamentally unjust.

The second involved identifying the US state as imperialist, and thus pre-occupied with the standard concerns of imperialism: militarized accumulationand geostrategic advantage — goals which tend to harm the peoples of the South.

Arguments of this variety were supported by the third approach, which showed that Western policy in Afghanistan belied the idea that ISAF's actions would better the lives of Afghans. For example, Chomsky pointed to the UN's Food and Agriculture Organization, who advised that the bombing of Afghanistan "had disrupted planting that provides 80 percent of the country's grain supplies."

And Arundhati Roy took the same approach when she noted, just before the war began, that "the UN estimates that there are eight million Afghan citizens who need emergency aid. As supplies run out – food and aid agencies have been asked to leave – the BBC reports that one of the worst humanitarian disasters of recent times has begun to unfold."

By contrast, much of the "progressive" defense of the war in Afghanistan, and the War on Terror more generally, was based on vacuous excoriations of the Left for its failure to "live up to its core values."

Similarly, then-*Dissent* editor Michael Walzer explained that he had "a modest agenda: put decency first." Bérubé dismissed "morally odious" the idea that "the bombing of Afghanistan was the moral equivalent of the 9/11 attacks."

Gitlin described Roy as "in the grip of a prejudice invulnerable to moral distinctions" because she compared the corruption and brutality of Bush to that of bin Laden. In place of engagement with details and complexities, what the progressive imperialists offered were arbitrary, content-free, ill-defined concepts being put forth by tut-tutting, finger-wagging white guys with tenure.

Little has changed. The pro-war progressives have made the same points amid the 2011 NATO bombing of Libya and leading up to the military campaign that the US nearly undertook in Syria in 2013 and may attempt again in the future.

For example, in the spring of 2012 Bérubé was denouncing anti-imperialists who opposed NATO's war in Libya.

He boasts that the intervention prevented a massacre — even though NATO and the forces whose victory they enabled actually carried out multiple massacres. In so doing, Bérubé resurrects Walzer's question of whether a "decent left" was possible, though Bérubé thinks the phrasing could be tweaked:

The question, rather, should have been whether there can be a rigorously internationalist left in the U.S., a left that will promote and support the freedom of speech, the freedom to worship, the freedom from want, and the freedom from fear—even on those rare and valuable occasions when doing so puts one in the position of supporting U.S. policies.

Set aside that in Libya NATO did no such thing. Bérubé blithely assumes, as pro-war progressives had in Afghanistan, that NATO states act in pursuit of the freedom of oppressed peoples. It is holding idealist beliefs such as these despite all evidence to the contrary that causes Bérubé to celebrate in Libya, as he had in Afghanistan, an empire shedding of the blood of dark-skinned people.

On Syria, *Dissent* editor Michael Kazin was upset by the tenor of Dreyfuss's opposition to Western intervention. Though Kazin is equivocal about the merits of bombing Syria, he thinks it reasonable "to want to punish the Syrian government for violating a ban on [sarin gas] the first weapon which nearly every nation agreed, back in the 1920s, never to use again."

As with Bérubé's misdiagnosis of the Libyan war, there's no need to dwell on Kazin's easy acceptance of the claim that it was Bashar al-Assad's government who used sarin gas in August 2013 despite significant evidence to the contrary.

Kazin's basic error is to principally focus on the nature of Assad's regime while ignoring the character of the institutions that determine policy within Western states and overlooking how that could undermine the chances that their bombing of Syria will create a just peace in that country.

Furthermore, Kazin took exception to leftists who he felt opposed bombing Syria in overly strident terms, on the grounds that this allegedly "dishonors the vision of a left which, at its best, has always adhered, in essence, to the motto of the late, great New York City daily PM: 'We are against people who push other people around, just for the fun of pushing, whether they flourish in this country or abroad.'"

Presumably the civilians who would die in a US-led bombing campaign, and in the likely escalation of the Syrian war, might feel "push[ed] around" by the cruise missiles falling on them but Kazin could not see that.

An opposition to those who "push other people around" is the vaguest of vague abstractions, belied most of all by its inattention to the biggest bully on the block: the American ruling class. Indeed, while it may be a fine principle on which to supervise recess, it completely overlooks the myriad complexities and contingencies that characterize any war and most certainly the one in Syria.

In the debates over the West's imperialist aggression against Afghanistan, the assessments made by the radical Left proved correct primarily because they derived from observable phenomena.

And among the most significant lessons to draw from progressive support for the war in Afghanistan is one that progressives had to no excuse not to know by 2001: while there is often a shortage of immediate results-yielding ways to support people in the Global South dealing with problems of inequality and human rights, one surefire way to not be of use is to rally support for imperial armies to invade, bomb, militarily occupy, jail en masse, torture, and kill the people in question.

TALIBAN'S TRAIL LEADS TO PAKISTAN

The Idea of creation of Taliban to use it to achieve Pakistan's strategic objective in Afghanistan was the brain wave of retired Major General Nasirullah Babar. The former director-general of Pakistan's Inter-Services Intelligence (ISI), Lieutenant-General Hamid Gul, nicknamed the "godfather of the Taliban", is believed to be behind moves to help the Taliban establish a base in Pakistan's autonomous Pashtun tribal belt, which borders eastern Afghanistan.

Already, many Pashtun Taliban are believed to have settled in the tribal areas following their hasty withdrawals from first Mazar-e-Sharif, Kabul and then Kandahar. It is believed that the Taliban split into a number of wings in order to establish political clout in the tribal area. One group, comprising diplomats and some lower-ranked ministers in the previous Afghanistan government, announced in a press conference as having split from the Taliban, but it refused to condemn either Taliban leader Mullah Omar or Osama bin Laden and his Al-Qaeda network.

Independent reports from Islamabad and Peshawar suggest that Osama Bin Laden, who suffers from renal deficiency, has been periodically undergoing dialysis in Peshawar military hospital with the knowledge and approval of the ISI.

Bibliography

Abdul Qadir : *Criminal Law of Islam*, Kitab Bhavan, New Delhi, 1999.

Ahmad, Ilyas : *Sovereignty, Islamic and Modern*, Allies Book Corporation, Karachi, 1965.

Amitabh Sikdar: *India and China : Strategic Energy Management and Security*, Manas, Delhi, 2009.

Arend, A.: *International Law and the Use of Force*, London, Routledge, 1993.

Bahedur, Kalim : *The Jamaat-i-Islami of Pakistan*, Progressive Books, Lahore, 1978.

Basrur, Rajesh M., and Hasan-Askari Rizvi, *Nuclear Terrorism and South Asia and Afghanistan*, Albuquerque, NM: Sandia National Laboratories, February 2003.

Debray, Regis. *Revolution in the Revolution*. New York: Grove Press, Inc., 1993.

Evelyn Goh, *Meeting the Afghanistan Challenge: The U.S. in Southeast Asian Regional Security Strategies*, DC: East-West Center, 2005.

Fatima, T. : *Islamic Law and Judiciary*, Deep & Deep Publications, New Delhi, 2001.

Giustozzi, Antonio: *Koran, Kalashnikov, and Laptop: The Neo-Taliban Insurgency in Afghanistan*, New York: Columbia University Press, 2008.

Hoffman, Bruce, *Inside Terrorism in Afghanistan*, New York: Columbia University Press, 1998.

Ikram, S.M. : *Muslim Civilization in India*, Oxford, New York, 1981.

Kalim, M. Siddiq : *Studies in Pakistan Culture : an International Perspective*, Manohar Publications, New Delhi, 1993.

Keane J.: *Democracy and Civil Liberty in Afghanistan*, London, Verso, 1988.

Kilcullen, David: *Counterinsurgency*, Oxford University Press, 2010.

Krepinevich, Andrew Jr.: *The Army and Vietnam,* Johns Hopkins University Press, 1988.

Laquer, Walter: *The New Terrorism: Fanaticism and the Arms of Mass Destruction,* Oxford: Oxford University Press, 1999.

Mohiuddin, Ahmad : *Saiyid Ahmad Shahid,* Modern Pub., Lucknow, 1975.

Nagl, John A.: *Learning to Eat Soup with a Knife: Counterinsurgency Lessons from Malaya to Vietnam,* University of Chicago Press, 2005.

Oudha, Abdul Qadir : *Criminal Law of Islam,* Kitab Bhavan, New Delhi, 1999.

Paget, J.: *Counter-insurgency Campaigning,* London: Faber & Faber, 1967.

Rosen, P.: *Societies and Military Power: India and its Armies,* Ithaca, Cornell University Press, 1996.

Shaun Narine, *Explaining ASEAN: Regionalism in Southeast Asia,* Boulder, CO: Lynne Rienner Publishers, 2002.

Smith, W. C. : *Modern Islam in India : a Social Analysis,* Manohar Publishers, New Delhi, 1985.

Zafeeruddin, M.M. : *System of Modesty and Chastity in Islam,* Idara Ishaat-e-Diniyat Pvt. Ltd, New Delhi, 1995.

Index

O

P

R

S

T

❑❑❑